# Foreword

This book, written toward the end of John Burr Williams' long and fruitful career, reflects a combination of practical experience, empirical knowledge, theoretical skill, and a gift for written expression possessed by few individuals in any field. An eager student of science, technology, business practice, and political history throughout his life, Williams launched his career as a security analyst in a prominent Boston financial firm. He soon established himself as an expert financial consultant while working continuously and successfully on his own account. From the beginning he brought to his work the intense curiosity that motivates any great scientist, in his case, focussed on understanding how business works, how it succeeds or fails in a market economy driven by free enterprise. He surveyed various industries and the financial sector: toured individual regions, conducted—in effect—in-depth interviews of representative managers and owners, collecting and analyzing their financial data.

He was not content only with accumulating facts, estimating the intrinsic value of securities, and describing the workings of individual business and financial enterprises. He wanted to understand how the economy worked *as a whole*, how its various sectors influenced one another, and how it interacted with other economies through international markets. This desire was motivated in part by his perception that the futures of individual investments depended on the entire system. To be the best possible security analyst, one had to become a student of general economics. He was motivated perhaps in even greater measure by an obsessive need to understand the world around him in terms of general principles, and so he became a student of economic theory. Williams associated himself with several of the most important theorists of the time: Joseph Schumpeter, Alvin Hansen, Wassily Leontief, and Nicholas Georgescu-Roegen. Scholarly work occupied much of his time and energy, depending on the demands for attention to his security analysis business. His first book, *The Theory Of Investment Value*, based on his Ph.D. thesis and first published by the Harvard University Press, has long been regarded as a classic in finance literature. His *Theory of Flexible Exchange Rates*, written some years later, appeared before exchange rates became flexible and before many economists realized their potential importance.

He published several seminal articles as well, but these published works only reveal the tip of an iceberg. A number of book-length manuscripts that he worked on intermittently through the years remain unpublished. Part of the reason for this was, no doubt, the fact that as a professional security analyst he lacked an academic base, so important for twentieth century researchers. His work habits were more like the independently wealthy, nineteenth century English scientists who worked in their home laboratories. He was consequently not immersed in University argot or in the intellectual fashion of academe. Moreover, he wrote not only for fellow intellectuals, as most of us do, but for lay people as well. For this reason, he chose an engaging literary style that emphasized the use of simplified examples of real life situations to drive home theoretical points. On the other hand, he was a theorist and a scientist, not a pop-scientist or pop-financial-wizard. And like many original thinkers, he could not resist overstating how his ideas differed from standard theories of the time. Publishers found it difficult to place his unique contributions in a standard test book niche.

Now, however, a break has occurred with the publication of this book, *Interest, Growth and Inflation*. In this work, Williams develops a macroeconomic theory of the market economy based on an empirical description and financial analysis at the microeconomic level. He describes the various classes of borrowers, lenders, and market mediators and the special characteristics of each that influence the demand and supply for loans. Observing that virtually all checking account money (demand deposits) originate in credit (and hence in debt), he shows how individuals, firms, and financial institutions adjust portfolios of short- and long-term securities, stocks, and idle balances in response to interest rates, how the accumulation of debt plays a dominant role in these adjustments, and how production, labor, productivity, banking reserves, government finance and regulation, interest rates, credit, employment, and capital investment interact over time.

The examples used to weave this complex story are drawn from the economy of the 1970s, but most of them are as pertinent today as they were thirty years ago, even if the particular numbers would now be very different. Moreover, to the extent that economic regulation and practice have changed (for example the current use of credit cards), the examples provide readers now with a basis for comparing current with previous situations and thus a means for evaluation the alternative approaches provided by history.

The reader will find a number of contentious comparisons of the author's theory with those of other theorists, economists may well be put off by these assaults on their mentors. The lay person may wonder what all the fuss is about. My own view is that Williams' ideas should be understood as a substantial elaboration of standard economic theory that incorporates especially important, empirically relevant characteristics of standard relationships.

For example, his micro descriptions of the various classes of economic institutions are aimed at the qualitative character of demand and supply. He still explains the determination of prices and interest in standard terms. In this sense, his theory is classical. Moreover, the novel parts of his analysis are closely related to ideas of his mentor Schumpeter, to the Keynes he often criticized, and, especially interestingly, to two contemporaries from his Harvard years, James Tobin and Hyman Minsky.

Thus, his emphasis on invention and innovation as a driving force, coupled with bank *created* credit, is the essence of Schumpeter's Theory of Economic Development, albeit worked out with consummate detail by Williams. Further, in relationship to Schumpeter, he did not see demand/supply equilibrium based on firm and household optimization as a theory of *behavior*, but only on a special situation which, if brought about at all, was brought about by an adjustment process by individuals who groped their way along by trial and error, adapting as well as possible but imperfectly to existing conditions.

The latter assumptions play an important role in Keynes' work as well, but like many business oriented economists, John Burr Williams felt uncomfortable with much of Keynes' own contentious arguments and sprinkled his writings with criticisms here and there. Carefully read, however, the reader will see a far more Keynesian view of the economy than Williams would ever have admitted. For example, he emphasized the interest sensitivity of certain key classes of real and financial markets in an empirically detailed manner that gives an explicit micro-foundation to monetary policy. Moreover, by focussing attention on the shift between long- and short-term loans, his "encroachment theory of interest" implicitly makes use of a Tobin-like portfolio model of the demand for money and yields a theory of the term structure of rates, something virtually absent in standard economic treatises. His emphasis on the over-riding influence of the current level of debt (= the *accumulation* of past borrowing) on the current demand and supply for loan reminds us of Hyman Minsky who could not have presented his own theory in more cogent terms that Williams does in this book on pages 225-232. Finally, his growth and discount theorem that equates the long-term interest rate with the growth rate of the economy is analogous to the von Neuman model of general equilibrium.

To summarize, for the theorist, Williams can be seen as a behavioral economist whose agents adapt to current information but are constrained by their stock of contractual obligations and government regulation. Like Friedman, Keynes, Tobin, and Minsky, he recognizes the powerful potential role—for good or bad effect—of government monetary and fiscal policy. Like most economic theorists of the nineteenth and the first three quarters of the twentieth century, he uses demand/supply equilibrium as a tool of analysis not as a literal description of the real world. In short, John Burr Williams brings a broad and detailed empirical realism to bear on the fundamental problem of understanding how our economic system really works. In this regard, he belongs in the class of economic theorists who demand that economic principle be drawn from and tested against practice with the ultimate goal of making the system work better.

The reader may notice a few small glitches in the text: a repeated paragraph, an occasional typographical or stenographic error. The publisher has wisely decided to publish the manuscript as Williams left it only a short while before his death. In any case, if you want to understand money, the role of credit and the influence of government on how the economy works, you will want to read this book. And you will enjoy the effort expended far more than that required to plow through most books about our dismal science.

John Burr Williams was one of the most unusual men I have been privileged to know. He was a businessman, a scholar, an inventor, a scientist, and intrepid traveler. He was a participant in the eastern financial establishment, yet a totally independent thinker. He was a sharp critic of the standard economics of his day and of its leading proponents; yet, he had been a devoted student and friend of several of them. He brought a unique perspective to economic analysis, developing it in a highly original manner, yet his work does not contradict but radically extends and amplifes the classic corpus of economic theory.

I met Williams early in my career. We recognized common interests and maintained an active interaction until he passed away. I was a guest a number of times in his home and came to know his wife Edith, daughter Nancy, and son John,Jr. One of these occasions occurred shortly before he died when my wife, Barbara, who had a keen interest in the stock market, and I visited the Williams' at their home in Wellesley Hills, Massachusetts. He spent several hours showing Barbara his records and explaining his methods. Edith accepted Barbara with equal warmth and affection. We enjoyed a wonderful stay, sharing ideas and reminiscences. I often think of these times in Wellesley Hills and continue to incorporate into my own work ideas stimulated by our conversations.

John Williams, Jr. carries on the security analysis business founded by his father. It is my privilege to introduce you to this example of his father's scholarly work. Hopefully, John Burr Williams, Sr.'s astute insights into the workings of our economy will help those charged with guiding it in private and in public institutions.

Richard H. Day
Professor of Economics
University of Southern California
October, 1998

# INTEREST, GROWTH, AND INFLATION
## or
## THE CONTRACTUAL SAVINGS THEORY OF INTEREST

By

John Burr Williams

Fraser Publishing Company

Published in 1998 by Fraser Publishing Company


Library of Congress Catalog Number: 98-74386

ISBN: 0-87034-131-6

To my Wife

Edith

# PREFACE

In the capital market today the biggest borrowers are homeowners, municipalities, public utilities, and the United States Treasury. Their new issues of bonds and mortgages far outweigh those offered by profit-seeking firms in business for themselves. Loans for housing, furniture, cars, roads, schools, armaments, welfare payments, and other purposes not ruled by the profit motive dominate the interest rate. Even public utility companies when they borrow cannot maximize their profits as businessmen always have been said to do. The law restrains them. Competitive firms, in contrast, though free to maximize, nevertheless rely so much on self-financing that loans to them are much reduced. Most of their reinvestment of earnings serves merely to keep the company competitive. Hence the time has come for us to shift the present emphasis of standard theory. we must talk less about profit-seeking firms, and more, much more, about other borrowers, including those who are the biggest borrowers of all. Only thus can we make our theory fit today's statistics.

Of overriding importance, moreover, are the rules laid down by insurance commissioners and bank examiners, rules about bond ratings, interest coverage, the debt-equity ratio, and collateral hypothecated, rules that define legal investments and restrict the largest lenders of all. These rules hold the volume of new issues in check, keeping bond prices up and interest rates down.

Traditional theory has much to say about time preference. It claims that interest paid to savers should make them postpone consumption from the present to the future. True, but inconsequential, because most saving is done for other motives. People use life insurance for protection against untimely death, they meet the instalments on their car loans as a way of buying transportation, and they make repayments on their mortgage loans to keep a roof over their heads. They borrow first, pay later with contractual savings. Time preference, therefore, should play only a minor role in modern interest theory.

Nor can liquidity preference serve instead, as I will take pains to prove. To show how the short-term interest rate is derived from the long-term, I offer the *Encroachment Theory*.

Critics and defenders of modern capitalism both need to know how the American system really works. They cannot hope to end its vices or keep its virtues unless they base their recommendations on sound knowledge. Mere good intentions are not enough. In particular, public officials seeking to control the business cycle, and investors trying to forecast the movement of interest rates, both need a new and broader theory of interest. To help them I offer the *Contractual Savings Theory of Interest.*

A few earlier writers have suggested that the rate of growth and the rate of interest are tied together in some loose way. I now seek to prove that a strong chain of cause and effect, a firm financial linkage, does indeed join one to the other. *The faster the growth, the higher the rate of interest will be.* Inflation, moreover, can make growth, measured in money, go on still faster. Hence I have entitled this book *Interest, Growth, and Inflation.*

J. B. W.

Wellesley Hills, Massachusetts

# FOREWORD

The present book is a companion to three others. One is entitled *The Current Assets Mechanism*. In that book I raise further doubts concerning accepted doctrine. I show that the Current Assets Mechanism upsets the old rule about selling price being equal to short-run marginal cost when free competition prevails. Instead the Mechanism causes price to equal full cost (or "average cost"). The new rule explains how it is possible for firms in a highly competitive industry to make both ends meet financially. This rule turns out to be very important, for it leads us to a wholly new theory of wages, and a wholly new theory of profits too.

In another book, entitled *The Economics of Major Industries*, I examine one industry after another, and show how the new findings govern the entire free enterprise system today.

In still another book, entitled *Money and Business Cycles*, written many years ago, I show how to fuse Algebra and Accounting into a new tool of analysis that I call Symbolic Accounting. Like Analytic Geometry, which is a fusion of Algebra and Geometry, this new tool is very useful in solving many elusive problems of theory.

The present book, called *Interest, Growth, and Inflation*, together with the other three, make a foursome that I call *The Free Enterprise System*.

In the beginning, it was scientific curiosity that led me to investigate all of these questions. I wanted to know the answer myself. Now I am glad to share my findings with all who care to listen.

I wish to express my sincere appreciation for comments pro and con from the following economists with whom I have talked about the Contractual Savings Theory of Interest. Beside each name I gave the date of our first conversation.

| | |
|---|---|
| March 17, 1965 | Gottfried Haberler |
| May 21, 1965 | Martin H. David |
| August 12, 1966 | Roger W. Valentine |
| September 23, 1966 | James A. O'Leary |
| September 23, 1966 | Robert H. Parks |
| September 23, 1966 | Martin L. Leibowitz |
| September 23, 1966 | Sidney Homer |
| March 29, 1967 | Elizabeth M. Gilboy |
| October 13, 1967 | F. Thomas Juster |
| December 28, 1967 | Nicolas Georgescu-Roegen |
| March 6, 1968 | A. C. Patton |
| March 29, 1968 | Ira Horowitz |
| March 29, 1968 | Ross M. Robertson |
| May 1, 1968 | John Culbertson |
| November 18, 1969 | Reno S. Knouse |
| November 19, 1969 | Morris A. Copeland |
| May 12, 1970 | David B. Crane |
| May 21, 1970 | William L. White |
| June 18, 1970 | Richard H. Day |
| June 18, 1970 | Donald D. Hester |
| June 18, 1970 | Kenneth R. Smith |
| June 22, 1970 | Sally S. Ronk |
| June 23, 1970 | E. E. Zajak |
| February 24, 1971 | Richard V. Clemence |
| March 1, 1971 | Rita Rodriguez |
| March 2, 1971 | Wassily W. Leontief |
| April 21, 1971 | William N. Keenan |
| April 21, 1971 | Robert J. Hawkins |
| April 21, 1971 | Edward I. Altman |
| June 3, 1971 | Dalip S. Swamey |
| August 2, 1972 | Z. Aubrey Silberston |
| September 11, 1972 | Simon N. Whitney |
| September 22, 1972 | Peter J. D. Wiles |
| January 26, 1973 | Peter Fortune |
| April 16, 1973 | Robert A. Gordon |
| April 18, 1973 | John M. Letiche |
| April 20, 1973 | Marvin May |
| April 20, 1973 | J. Fred Weston |
| April 23, 1973 | Ramon E. Johnson |
| May 30, 1973 | Shaw Livermore |
| June 7, 1973 | Hendrik S. Houthakker |
| December 28, 1973 | Edward J. Nell |
| December 28, 1973 | Neal Skowbo |
| April 12, 1974 | Frank C. Genovese |
| October 23, 1974 | John R. Meyer |
| October 23, 1974 | John Lintner |
| November 14, 1974 | Martin Bronfenbrenner |

I have also lectured on the subject on the following occasions:

Mar. 29, 1968 at Indiana University, at Bloomington
Nov. 18, 1969 at State University of New York, at Albany
June 18, 1970 at University of Wisconsin, at Madison
May 10, 1971 at New York University, at Trinity Place, N.Y.C.
Apr. 16, 1973 at University of California, at Berkeley
Apr. 20, 1973 at University of California, at Los Angeles
Apr. 23, 1973 at University of Utah, at Salt Lake City
Apr. 12, 1974 at Babson College, at Wellesley
Nov. 14, 1974 at Wellesley College, at Wellesley

# Contents

# CHAPTER I
## QUESTIONS AND ANSWERS

### 1. Questions

How are interest rates determined?

Who are the major borrowers and lenders? What are the needs of each? What rules control their dealings?

In setting the level of rates, are some borrowers more important than other borrowers? Do homeowners, for instance, with their elastic demand for loans, exert more effect on rates than corporations do, with their inelastic demand?

Furthermore, are some lenders more important than other lenders? Do insurance companies, pension funds, and savings banks dominate the market, overwhelming private investors? Or do these large institutions merely serve as agents for small savers, making no change in the final result?

Moreover, does contractual saving differ fundamentally from optional saving? Which is larger? Do insurance policyholders, pension fund contributors, and homeowners when repaying their mortgage loans, obey special rules of their own? Must these contractual savers ignore a change in the interest rate?

Are most lenders unwilling to lend as much as borrowers would like to borrow? Can firms seldom push their investment in plant and equipment as far as they see fit, and are they usually forced to stop well short of the point that would maximize their profits? To what extent do rules about interest coverage and the debt-equity ratio hold borrowing and lending in check?

How do savings by private persons compete with loans granted by commercial banks? Which are dominant? Does bank credit have an incremental cost of almost nothing to the lender?

How are long and short-term rates tied together?

Does inflation cause high interest rates? If so, how? Lenders, to be sure, seek rates high enough to offset inflation, but they lack the power to enforce their demands. Yet rates stay high. What is the mechanism that keeps them up?

Does inflation discourage people from saving for their old age?

Do labor unions cause inflation? Or is the federal deficit to blame? Or Federal Reserve policy? Or must all three work together?

If growth in the money supply were brought to a halt, would interest rates drop to zero eventually?

It is a curious fact that the rate of growth in the country's national dividend, measured in money, is about the same as its rate of interest on long-term bonds. We do not find one to be several times as large as the other. Is this a mere coincidence, or is there some link of cause and effect between the two, a link of vast importance to the whole science of economics?[1]

When we talk about growth in the national dividend, what kind of growth do we mean? Growth yesterday? Today? Or tomorrow? Since growth in times gone by is water over the dam by now, how could past growth control today's interest? At first blush this would seem impossible. But let us not jump to conclusions.

Finally, what causes growth? Can the Federal Reserve Board, through its control of the money supply, determine the rate of growth of the national dividend? If so, does the Board thereby unwittingly fix interest rates on bonds and mortgages, on notes and bills, on long and short-term loans, on debts of every kind?

The simple question we asked at first, namely how are interest rates determined, now proves to be a whole cluster of questions. Among all these questions let us try to pick the most promising to investigate, and select this one:

> Is the rate of growth in the national dividend a major factor in setting the rate of interest on loans of all kinds? If so, what is the mechanism? How does it work? Why are the two rates so nearly the same?

## 2. Critique of Traditional Theory

The traditional theory of interest is the work of many famous minds, ranging from Adam Smith, David Ricardo, Eugen von Böehm-Bawerk, and Irving Fisher to Joseph Schumpeter and Paul Samuelson. How can this theory, therefore, possibly be wrong?

Nothing, of course, is wrong with its logic. Its premises, however, are out of date. They do not fit today's statistics.

---

[1] See, for instance, Edmund S. Phelps' "The Golden Rule of Accumulation: A fable for Growthmen" in the *American Economic Review*, Sept. 1961, pp. 638-643, Phelps, however, asks a different question from ours. He asks what *ought* to be the rate of profit and growth, not what *is* this rate in fact.

The faults of the old theory lie in its hidden assumptions. Failure to state these assumptions explicitly is what has made it go astray. Yet so great is its repute that it is seldom attacked.

Nowadays, to be sure, many writers on investments and the money market ignore traditional theory completely; thus in effect they reject it. But we must not stop there ourselves. If the old theory won't suffice, then we must devise a better one. We must not let the problem go unsolved.

What, in fact, are the faulty premises of traditional theory?

On the supply side, when the theory says that interest is the price paid for the use of savings, it falsely goes on to imply that the higher the price for savings, the larger the supply will be. In truth, however, most saving is not optional at all, but strictly contractual, and so its volume remains unchanged regardless of whether interest rates move up or down. Furthermore the old theory overlooks the vital matter of credit ratings. Unless a company is a good risk, it cannot borrow at any price, no matter how high. If so, the available supply of savings flows elsewhere. Moreover loans made by commercial banks are a large source of funds to borrow, and these funds come, not from private savings, but from outright credit creation, a process not included in traditional theory. On the supply side, therefore, the old theory, with its payment of interest as a reward for thrift, fails to account for more than a tiny fraction of the whole sum loaned and borrowed.

On the demand side, when traditional theory talks about the flow of savings into plant and equipment used by private industry, it falsely implies that this flow is large enough all by itself to set the interest rate for the entire economy. This hidden premise of the old theory lets us think that everyone simply copies the rate that emerges from loans to private industry. This premise is false because it mistakes the part for the whole. Yet in truth private industry takes but a very small share of the total volume of savings. Public utilities, the federal government, numerous states and municipalities, and home mortgages take much more, many times more. It is a mistake, therefore, to talk as though the marginal productivity of new capital borrowed by strictly competitive firms could set the interest rate for the whole economy.

Looking at the industrial sector again, we find that reinvested earnings and reserves for depreciation, rather than new issues of stocks and bonds, provide most of the money spent on capital improvements.

Furthermore these outlays are usually made "to keep the company competitive", to help it stay in business. They protect the earning power of old assets, but they often fail to earn much of a profit themselves. Standard theory overemphasizes marginal productivity.

Statistics show that the old theory of interest, resting as it does on the earning power of plant and equipment, though entirely correct in its logic, is extremely narrow in its coverage. I do not seek to refute it, but just to deflate it.

### 3. Answers

By process of elimination we shall find that the interest rate is determined neither in the industrial sector nor the public utility sector, nor in the government bond market nor the commercial paper market—though all these contribute to total demand—but instead the rate is determined in the home loan and municipal bond market. The residential sector as a whole is the place where price and quantity interact, and where the interest rate is really set. From here the rate simply spreads to all the other sectors in ways I will explain in due course.

Food and clothing, being quickly consumed, must be paid for with ready cash, but shelter, being slowly used up, can be paid for with borrowed money. This is the clue that points to housing as the heart of the whole theory of interest.

Shelter, or the residential sector as a whole, includes private houses, furniture and appliances, apartments, schools, roads, water and gas mains, bridges, public parks, and private cars with which to gain access to housing and places of employment. These capital goods absorb a huge volume of savings. Yet they are not ruled by the profit motive, and so the old theory of interest does not apply to them. Instead we need a new theory, one that I will call the Home Loan Theory of Interest. This theory shows how the demand for shelter rules the rate of interest. The faster the growth of this demand, the higher the rate of interest will be.

### 4. Plan of the Book

The most important discovery set forth in this book is embodied in the Growth and Discount Theorem. This theorem states that the rate of interest on borrowed money is controlled by the rate of growth in the national dividend. This growth in turn results from the increase in the money supply provided by the central bank, whose duty it is to finance the country's rise in population and its improvement in productivity with as little inflation as possible.

The book considers a series of questions, one after another, thus:

      1) What are the limits on lending?
      2) Who lends and who borrows?
      3) Where is the rate of interest determined?
      4) How is this rate copied elsewhere?

# CHAPTER II
# THE SEARCH FOR SAFETY

## 1. The Two Parties to a Loan

It takes two to make a loan. One party is not enough. Borrower and lender must both agree.

This obvious premise has far-reaching consequences that have yet to be fully explored. It leads to great improvements in the theory of interest, and lets us see at last how the rate of interest is ruled by the rate of growth.

There are two possible limits to the size of any loan, either (1) the amount the borrower would like to borrow, or (2) the amount the lender is willing to lend. The lower of these two limits will be the one to rule in every case. To say that borrowers always push their borrowing out to the limit set by the marginal productivity of new capital is wrong. Lenders seldom are willing to go that far.

Of great importance is the credibility of the borrower's word. Can the lender believe the borrower's promise to make his payments on time and in full? It is not enough for the borrower to be honest. He must be *able* to repay, as well as *willing* to do so. To make sure of the borrower's ability to repay, the lender looks at the borrower's earning power, and restricts the size of the loan accordingly. And to make sure of the borrower's willingness to repay, the lender invokes legal sanctions like the right to dispossess the borrower of his home or other assets. The lender also restricts the size of the loan in relation to these assets, so as to make sure that, if worst comes to worst, he can realize enough money in a forced sale to repay the loan in full. The lender insists, in other words, that the borrower retain an ample equity in the property hypothecated as collateral for his loan. Only in this way can the credibility, the believability, of the contract be kept high. Borrower and lender both need it to be kept high, very high.

Borrowers cannot get all the money they want simply by paying a premium for risk. Legal restraints on commercial banks, insurance companies, savings banks, pension funds, and trust departments prevent these investors from making high risk loans. Private investors, for their part, are but a small factor in the capital market. Hence these legal and prudential restraints on fiduciaries can serve us as a good starting point for our fundamental revision of the whole theory of interest.

The typical trustee is a cautious investor. He is not aggressive. He is very anxious to avoid losses, but strives much less to garner profits. Because savings banks and insurance companies don't want to see their A bonds fall to a B rating if things take a turn for the worse, they buy mostly triple-A bonds to begin with. They hope such bonds are so good they can never go bad. The men who sit on the investment committees seek in this way to escape all criticism forever after.

This policy, however, produces a lopsided demand. When most lenders insist on nothing but the best, who will buy anything else? And if weak bonds cannot be sold, will they ever be issued in the first place? Clearly no. As a result, money cannot be raised for uses that promise no more than a modest return. Capital outlays that lie close to the margin must almost always be foregone.

A would-be borrower, in order to make his bonds attractive investments for savings banks and insurance companies, must report good interest coverage and a moderate debt-equity ratio. Otherwise Moody will not rate the bonds Aaa, or even Aa, or merely A. Likewise Standard and Poor's will not rate them high enough to make them legal for trustees to buy under the "prudent man" rule. And even if interest coverage is ample, a new issue cannot win an Aaa rating if the trend of earnings is down, or the record of dividends erratic and the current ratio weak.

Moreover, unless an issue can meet legal requirements, the major investment banking syndicates will seldom underwrite the bonds and sell them to their clients. No, not at any price. These bankers have all the business they can handle, and do not want to tie their capital up in slow-moving B or C bonds.[1] The result is to slam the door on companies who try to borrow too much.

In a great emergency, to be sure, investment bankers may help to rescue a company from receivership by floating a risky issue for it. Halsey Stuart and Salomon Brothers did just this for the Baltimore and Ohio R.R. in July 1970 when they arranged a refunding of its 3⅞s due Aug. 1, 1970, and sold 11% bonds[2] rated A to replace the maturing

---

[1] Most of the bonds that now have poor ratings were good bonds when first issued, but have now fallen from grace.

[2] Secured by pledge of Chesapeake and Ohio R.R. 11% bonds.

bonds. But such rescues are rare. No bankers were willing to risk a Penn Central issue in June 1970. If the Baltimore and Ohio bonds had not been a refunding issue, even these bonds would doubtless have been turned down by the bankers. Hence it remains true that a company already deeply in debt can seldom sell still more bonds, no matter how well it hopes to use the extra money. Venture capital, to be sure, will go into the common stocks of new companies, but not into the B bonds of old companies. Speculative bonds find very few buyers.

Undistributed profits, as contrasted with borrowed money, may sometimes go into marginal outlets, but these funds come out of the pockets of stockholders, not bondholders. In practice, stockholders exercise no veto on this use of their money. Assets with low earning power, however, cannot qualify afterwards as security for a safe loan. But in any event, since reinvested profits circumvent the bond market, they exert no effect on the level of interest rates in general.

An analogy with the Pure Food and Drug Act will drive the point home. In the case of meat and poultry, federal inspectors working in the packing houses forbid the sale of impure food. In the case of bonds, state examiners auditing the banks and insurance companies forbid the purchase of unsafe bonds. Thus in neither case does the quality of the product escape the regulation of the government. This regulation of quality affects quantity at the same time. In the case of bonds, it makes the volume of new issues become much less than would be justified by calculations of marginal productivity alone. The Legal List puts a limit on the volume of lending. It overrides all other considerations.

## 2. The So-Called Premium for Risk

Inclusion of a "premium for risk" in the rate of interest paid on hazardous loans is not a satisfactory protection for most lenders.

For small investors in particular this device will not work. They do not hold a sufficient variety of issues to give them proper diversification. If one issue goes bad, they lose so much they cannot make it up on others.

Even large investors cannot get genuine diversification. The difficulty is that losses come in bunches. If one railroad bond goes bad, a dozen others often do so too. And likewise for airline bonds or even municipal bonds. What hurts one bond hurts others too. Consequently the only good protection a lender can obtain is to restrict the size of his loans severely. By refusing to let borrowers take on too much debt, he can get rid of the risk in large measure.

Lending money is like writing windstorm insurance. When hurricane losses come, they hit all in the same year, all in the same locality. In this way windstorm insurance differs from fire insurance. Fire losses are spread out evenly from year to year and place to place. While it would be safe enough for a small insurance company to confine its underwriting of fire policies to a single state like Florida, such a company should never allow its exposure on windstorm policies to be concentrated within a restricted area, no matter how high the premium rate. The same argument applies to flood insurance, crop insurance, and earthquake insurance.

Likewise subject to losses that come in bunches are business loans of all kinds, whether short-term paper or long-term bonds. The risk on these loans, therefore, should be held down by a safe debt-equity ratio.[3] No oversize premium for risk can possibly offset the hazard on loans too large to begin with. Yet lenders sometimes overlook this fact.

Many lenders are obliged to buy nothing but prime-rated names. Large banks supply such paper to their customers and correspondents through their money desk. Credit ratings on commercial paper and finance paper are supplied by Dun and Bradstreet, while credit ratings on bonds are supplied by Moody, Standard and Poor's, and Fitch.

### 3. Interest Coverage and the Debt-Equity Ratio

A bookkeeping quirk ties interest coverage and the debt-equity ratio together. When one is good the other is good, but when one is bad the other is bad. They work together, as shown in the accounts below:

|  | Good | Bad |
|---|---|---|
| Bonds | $100,000,000 | $200,000,000 |
| Capital and surplus | 200,000,000 | 100,000,000 |
| Total | $300,000,000 | $300,000,000 |
| Debt-equity ratio | 1 for 2 | 2 for 1 |
| Operating profit @10% of assets | $ 30,000,000 | $ 30,000,000 |
| Interest expense @6% of debt | - 6,000,000 | -12,000,000 |
| Taxable earnings on equity | $ 24,000,000 | $ 18,000,000 |
| Income tax @50% of earnings | -12,000,000 | - 9,000,000 |
| Net income | $ 12,000,000 | $ 9,000,000 |
| Interest coverage pretax | 5 times | 2½ times |
| Interest coverage after tax | twice | three-quarters |

---

[3] Cf. *The Wall Street Journal*, Feb. 7, 1972, p.1 "Shell Oil's credit rating was downgraded to double-A by Moody's Investors Service, which cited the petroleum company's debt having 'more than doubled in the past five years'. The change from triple-A could cost Shell as much as $4.5 million additional interest over the life of its 30-year debentures that are to be offered Thursday, some market analysts said." (More details are given on p. 16 of the *Journal*.)

In order for an overextended company to push its debt-equity ratio up to 2 for 1, as shown above, it would need to finance partly with first mortgage bonds paying 5%, let us say, and afterward with second mortgage bonds paying 7%. A conservative enterprise, in contrast, with smaller debt, could probably borrow at only 5% to begin with, or well under the 6% shown above. This would let it report an interest coverage of 6 to 1 pretax. Clearly large interest coverage and a small debt-equity ratio go hand in hand.

Those fortunate companies who make a very high return on their investment can always show good interest coverage on their present debt, and can qualify for new loans if they wish. Likewise, when interest rates are very low, it is easy to show good coverage, but at such a time rules about the debt-equity limit may come into play, and hold borrowing in check in that way.

Some companies, to be sure, can find no good use for extra plant and equipment. Or, as a matter of policy, they may finance all their growth out of earnings, and may refuse to carry any debt at all. If so, they are not held in check by the usual rules about interest coverage and the debt-equity ratio.[4]

To help investors appraise their bonds, some public utility companies include a table in their annual reports showing interest coverage before and after income taxes, and also interest and preferred dividend coverage after taxes.[5] Railroads often show the ratio of fixed charges to total revenue.[6]

Safety requirements on bonds vary from industry to industry.[7] Manufacturing companies, for instance, are more exposed to the risks of the business cycle than public utilities are. Their sales and their profits undergo much wider swings. It is not safe for them to carry a heavy debt, therefore, and they need a stronger debt-equity ratio. Although they would like to borrow enough money, and build enough plant, to maximize their profits, manufacturing companies dare not do so, even if their bankers would let them.

---

[4] In Chapter XIII, §6, entitled *Marginal Productivity*, this whole question is considered in detail.

[5] See, for instance, the Annual Report of The Niagara Mohawk Power Corporation for 1971, p. 21.

[6] See the Annual Report of the Norfolk and Western Railway Company for 1970, p. 29.

[7] See Benjamin Graham and David L. Dodd, *Security Analysis* (New York: McGraw-Hill Book Co., 1951) 3rd ed., Chs. 23 & 24.

## 4. Borrowing Short, Long or Either Way

To get a loan, a borrower needs good collateral. He borrows short-term or long-term, depending on the kind of collateral he offers as security for his loan. Collateral like merchandise or an automobile that loses value quickly can only be pledged against a short-term loan, while collateral like a factory or a house that enjoys a long life can be pledged against a long-term loan. If a borrower can furnish collateral of either kind—either current assets or fixed assets—then he can borrow either way.

Lenders at short-term want their loans protected by current assets, not fixed assets, because current assets turn into cash quickly as current output is sold and receivables are collected. If all goes well, the turnover of current assets assures the repayment of short-term loans on time and in full, with an ample margin of safety.

Lenders at long term, in contrast, want their loans protected by fixed assets, not current assets, because fixed assets remain on hand long after current assets have all been lost on the way to bankruptcy. In that event, fixed assets can then be seized by the bondholders under the mortgage contract.

Any borrower who cannot offer both kinds of collateral must perforce borrow in only one kind of market, and cannot take advantage of a lower interest rate that may prevail in the other. Nevertheless there remain many borrowers who can choose between the two markets. When these latter borrowers shift from one market to the other they help to bring short-term and long-term rates into line with each other. Provided that borrowers can so shift, it is not necessary for lenders to be able to do so too. Borrowers alone can equalize rates.

Among those borrowers who can furnish either kind of collateral are business firms. These firms can borrow against their current assets, or their fixed assets, or both at once. In either case, however, a limit exists. Loans against current assets must not reduce the current ratio below two to one, and loans against fixed assets must not exceed 50% or so of the fair value of these assets. Commercial bankers, in granting short-term loans, observe the first rule, and investment bankers, in selling long-term bonds, observe the second. A corporation that has borrowed up to the hilt will then show a balance sheet like:

Balance Sheet After Borrowing to the Limit

| Current assets | $10,000,000 | Notes payable | $ 5,000,000 |
|---|---|---|---|
| | | Equity in current assets | 5,000,000 |
| Fixed assets | 10,000,000 | Mortgage bonds | 5,000,000 |
| | | Equity in fixed assets | 5,000,000 |
| | $20,000,000 | | $20,000,000 |

Usually the two items "Equity in Current Assets, $5,000,000" and "Equity in Fixed Assets, $5,000,000", are lumped together under the single heading "Capital and Surplus, $10,000,000", with the result that important details are covered up.

If a company has no debts to begin with, however, its balance sheet will look as shown in the first example below. Then it can borrow either long or short, and use the proceeds either way. If the company now borrows against current assets for investment in fixed assets, its new balance sheet will then look as shown in the second example below. But if it borrows and invests the other way, its new balance sheet will look as shown in the third example below.

Balance Sheet Before Any Borrowing

| Current assets | $ 5,000,000 | Equity in current assets | $ 5,000,000 |
|---|---|---|---|
| Fixed assets | 5,000,000 | Equity in fixed assets | 5,000,000 |
| | $10,000,000 | | $10,000,000 |

Balance Sheet After Borrowing Against Current Assets

| Current assets | $ 5,000,000 | Notes payable | $ 2,500,000 |
|---|---|---|---|
| | | Equity in current assets | 2,500,000 |
| Fixed assets | 7,500,000 | Equity in fixed assets | 7,500,000 |
| | $12,500,000 | | $12,500,000 |

Balance Sheet After Borrowing Against Fixed Assets

| Current assets | $ 7,500,000 | Equity in current assets | $ 7,500,000 |
|---|---|---|---|
| Fixed assets | 5,000,000 | Mortgage bonds | 2,500,000 |
| | | Equity in fixed assets | 2,500,000 |
| | $12,500,000 | | $12,500,000 |

Evidently a company that borrows against assets of one kind, and puts the money into assets of the other kind, faces a close limit on how much it can borrow. But if it puts the money into assets of the same kind as its liabilities, it faces a limit much larger. Thus with current assets of $5,000,000 to start with, it can borrow $5,000,000 more, provided all of the proceeds of short-term loans go into current assets. Likewise the limit is larger if all of the proceeds of long-term bonds go into fixed assets.

When lenders make short-term loans and the proceeds go into current assets, the lenders look mainly at the borrower's current ratio in weighing the risk. But when lenders make long-term loans and the proceeds go into fixed assets, the lenders look mainly at the borrower's interest coverage. Since a rise in the interest rate on a short-term loan does not hurt the current ratio, such a rise does not impede short-term borrowing. But a rise in the interest rate on a long-term loan does indeed hurt the interest coverage on it, and so such a rise does indeed reduce long-term borrowing. As a result, the demand curve for short-term loans is quite inelastic, while that for long-term loans is just the opposite,with respect to the interest rate. The short-term curve is almost vertical, the long-term quite sloping. Thus the curves are quite unlike in slope.

When firms use short-term bank loans to finance long-term fixed assets, obtaining the money by borrowing against their current assets, they often meet resistance from their bankers. Banks consider it bad practice to advance permanent capital to any firm. Consequently they often require their customers to pay off one loan before seeking another.

# CHAPTER III
## MAJOR BORROWERS AND LENDERS

### 1. Classes of Borrowers and Lenders

In the market for loans some borrowers can write only short-term paper, others only long-term, while a few can write either kind. Likewise some lenders need mainly short-term paper and others mainly long-term, while a few can use either kind. Consequently the important borrowers and lenders can be classified as shown below:

| Borrowers | Lenders |
|---|---|
| **Short-Term Borrowers and Lenders** | |
| Merchants | Commercial Banks |
| Automobile Owners | Finance Companies |
| Stock Speculators | Stock Brokers |
| **Borrowers and Lenders Either Way** | |
| U. S. Treasury | Balanced Mutual Funds |
| Municipalities | Fire and Casualty |
| Industrial Firms | Insurance Companies |
| **Long-Term Borrowers and Lenders** | |
| Homeowners | Savings Banks |
| Landlords | Life Insurance Companies |
| Public Utilities | Pension Funds |
| | Private Investors |

Purposely omitted from this list of lenders are foundations and endowment funds. Although the investment holdings of the Ford Foundation, the Rockefeller Foundation, Harvard, Yale, and other educational, philanthropic, scientific, and religious institutions add up to a huge total, nevertheless these organizations are not a source of new capital for industry. They do not save and reinvest their income. They spend it. When college endowments grow, it is because their common stocks rise in market price, or because they receive new gifts from alumni. The alumni in the beginning, to be sure, made and saved the money themselves, but the colleges did not. Endowment funds as such add nothing extra to the supply of money put out on loan. Consequently they provide no support for the rate of interest.

Also omitted from this list of lenders are persons who trade in the stock market on a cash account rather than a margin account, and so use no borrowed money. When one man buys shares of stock from another, the money that passes in payment goes from buyer to seller, and is never received by the corporation whose stock is being traded.

The payment is neither a loan nor a substitute for one. Hence it has no effect on the interest rate, and so these investors are omitted from the table above.

Since open-end mutual funds ordinarily use their cash receipts to buy common stock from some existing stockholder who wants to sell, the investments these funds make in shares already issued result in no capital formation. The money that passes through their hands does not help to satisfy the demand for loans from various kinds of borrowers. As a result their activities do not affect the interest rate, and so these funds are likewise omitted from the list of lenders in the table above.

Even when companies offer new stock, giving their stockholders the right to subscribe for new shares at less than the current market price, this procedure is not the same as the flotation of loans by these companies. The stockholders are assessed for the money; they are not permitted to bargain at arm's length about the rate of return they will receive. Rights are simply a negative dividend. The new stock merely offsets the excessive cash dividends already paid on old stock. All it does is make up for the previous shortage of reinvested earnings. It is not a loan.[1]

## 2. Self-Financing

All companies are self-financing in part. In order to borrow money to support their growth, they must supply additional money themselves by reinvesting part of their earnings. Otherwise their debt-equity ratio would fall too low.

The public utilities have little choice in the matter. They must reinvest enough to satisfy their bankers, and they must borrow enough to satisfy their regulators, because borrowed money costs less than equity money.[2] Public utilities, incidentally, are the largest borrowers in the corporate bond market.

The industrials, in contrast, often enjoy some discretion. They sell a small amount of bonds to pay for new plant and equipment, and finance the rest out of depreciation and earnings. If they were to sell no bonds at all, they would be obliged to pay less in common dividends, so as to have more left for reinvestment. In the 1960's many companies in the electronics industry did just this. Such firms, however, are too

---

[1] See my *Theory of Investment Value* (Cambridge, Harvard University Press, 1938; reprinted in Amsterdam by the North Holland Publishing Co., 1964), pp. 61-65
[2] See Chapter XII, §8

small a factor in the economy as a whole to have much effect on interest rates in general. For the typical firm, whether industrial[3] or public utility, reinvestment claims 40% or 50% of net income, and dividends claim 60% or 50%. Further research is needed to show just why this ratio is so common, at least while a company is prosperous and growing steadily.

### 3. Diagram of Loans and Lenders

Borrowers and lenders deal with each other by means of loans, or IOUs written on pieces of paper. These loans go by such names as "Treasury bills" or "home mortgages." The names thus reveal who the borrowers are, but not who the lenders are. Hence a special diagram is needed to portray both sides of the market at once, as shown in Diagram I.

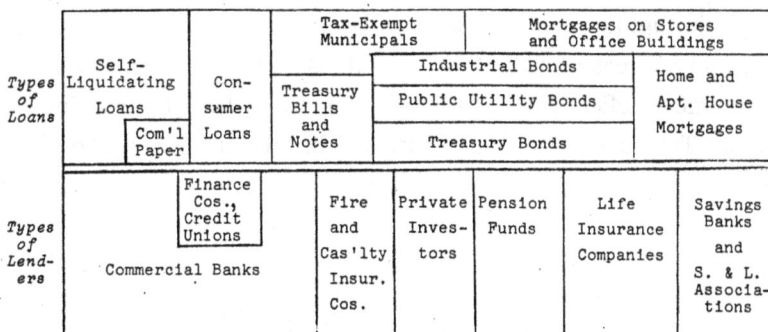

| Types of Loans | Self-Liquidating Loans (Com'l Paper) | Con-sumer Loans | Treasury Bills and Notes | Tax-Exempt Municipals / Industrial Bonds / Public Utility Bonds / Treasury Bonds | Mortgages on Stores and Office Buildings / Home and Apt. House Mortgages |
|---|---|---|---|---|---|
| Types of Lenders | Commercial Banks | Finance Cos., Credit Unions | Fire and Cas'lty Insur. Cos. | Private Investors / Pension Funds | Life Insurance Companies / Savings Banks and S. & L. Associations |

*Diagram I: Types of Loans and Lenders*

The upper half of the diagram depicts the components of the demand for money to borrow, while the lower half depicts the components of the supply of money to lend.

In Diagram I the various types of loans are shown above the double line, the various types of lenders below this line. The diagram implies that each lender usually makes the kind of loan that lies above his own space in the diagram. Thus savings banks make mortgage loans, and commercial banks make self-liquidating loans, whenever possible. Sometimes, however, they may deal with borrowers in other parts of the market. These various buyers of IOUs supply money to the particular borrowers who offer the proper terms in their loans.

---

[3] Retailers usually rent their buildings; they do not own them. Their leases, however, are analogous to the bonded debt of a manufacturing company

In this diagram short-term loans and lenders are grouped at the left, while long-term loans and lenders are grouped at the right. Loans to borrowers-either-way are put in the middle, and likewise for lenders-either-way.

The various rectangles fit together like boards on a wall. In each year the total area for demand is equal to the total area for supply.

What the diagram shows in each block is the *increase* in loans made during the year, not the total outstanding at the end of the year, but the increase during the year. Loans that are merely renewed from time to time make no demands on the supply of new savings. When an old issue of notes or bonds is refunded with a new issue of the same size, the refunding has no more effect on the rate of interest than if it had never occurred in the first place.[4]

The U.S. Treasury, because of the legal ceiling of 4¼% on its bonds, brought out no new issues of long-term debt for many years. Instead the Treasury used short-term bills and notes to finance the government deficit. Nevertheless the diagram still contains a place for new Treasury bonds because the law has recently been relaxed somewhat.

Traditional theory emphasizes the preference that individual savers show for present goods over future goods. It goes on to say that their savings are then loaned to firms in competitive industries who try to maximize their profits, and must estimate the marginal productivity of new plant and equipment when they borrow money for expansion. Traditional theory, in other words, talks mainly about loans from private investors to industrial firms. It neglects all other loans. As Diagram I reveals, the transactions between these two particular parties constitute but a small fraction, a very small fraction, of the total for the investment market as a whole.

## 4. Statistics on Loans and Lenders

A convenient source of the statistics needed for Diagram I on *Types of Loans and Lenders* is a survey compiled by the Bankers Trust Co. each year[5]. The latest is entitled *The Investment Outlook for 1972*.

---

[4] See Chapter VIII, §5.
[5] The surveys for 1969 and earlier were compiled by Mrs. Sally S. Ronk. Her doctoral dissertation is entitled *"The Sources and Uses of Funds Approach to Analysis of Interest Rate Development"*.

*Table I.   Uses of Funds, or Types of Loans, in 1972, Projected*

| Table Number | | Figures in billions of dollars |
|---|---|---|
| 1 and 2 | Investment funds | 93.3 |
| 10 | Gross new issues | |
| 10 | Manufacturing & mining bonds | 7.5 |
| 10 | Public utility  bonds | 13.0 |
| 10 | Real estate & commercial mortgages | 6.7 |
| 10 | Less retirements | -8.5 |
| 2 and 11 | Corporate stock, mainly for public utilities | 11.0 |
| 2 | Net new issues | 29.7 |
| | | |
| 2 and 12 | Municipal bonds | 17.5 |
| 8 | Home loans,            net increase | 26.5 |
| 9 | Apartment house loans,    "        " | 9.5 |
| 9 | Commercial buildings     "        " | 9.0 |
| 7 | Farm loans           "        " | 2.1 |
| 2 and 30 | Foreign securities | 0.5 |
| 2 and 25 | Term loans | 3.0 |
| | | |
| 1 | Government | 21.6 |
| 4 | U. S. Treasury | 21.6 |
| 4 | | |
| | | |
| 1 | Short-term funds | 41.2 |
| 3 and 25 | Bank loans to business | 8.6 |
| 3 and 13 | Open market paper | 2.0 |
| 3 and 13 | Nonbudgets agencies | 2.2 |
| 3 and 28 | Finance paper | 2.5 |
| 3 and 25 and 29 | Security credit | 1.0 |
| 3 and 27 | Trade credit | 8.5 |
| 3 and 14 | Consumer credit | 12.5 |
| 3 and 15 | Policy loans | 1.5 |
| 3 and 25 | Other bank loans | 2.4 |
| | | 156.1   156.1 |

*Table II.   Sources of Funds, or Types of Lenders, in 1972, Projected*

| Table Numbers | | Figures in billions of dollars |
|---|---|---|
| 1 | Savings institutions | 65.4 |
| 1 and 15 | Life insurance companies | 11.6 |
| 1 and 16 | Private noninsured pension funds | 7.5 |
| 1 and 17 | State & local gov't retirement funds | 8.6 |
| 1 and 18 | Fire & casualty insurance companies | 4.5 |
| 1 and 19 | Savings & loan associations | 21.7 |
| 1 and 20 | Mutual savings banks | 7.2 |
| 1 and 21 | Credit unions | 2.5 |
| 1 and 22 | Mutual funds | 1.8 |
| | | |
| 1 and 25 | Commercial banks | 59.6 |
| 1 and 25 | Bond & mortgage departments | 21.0 |
| 1 and 25 | Short-term loan departments | 38.6 |
| | | |
| 1 | Business corporations | 22.6 |
| 1 and 27 | Nonfinancial | 16.9 |
| 1 and 28 | Financial | 5.7 |
| | | |
| | Other investor groups | 12.7 |
| 1 and 29 | Federal agencies | 8.5 |
| 1 and 17 | State & local governments | 3.5 |
| 1 and 17, 23, 29 | Others | 0.7 |
| | | |
| | Miscellaneous | -4.2 |
| 1 and 31 | Individuals and others | 12.0 |
| 1 and 30 | Foreign investors | -1.5 |
| 1 and 14 | Noncorporate business | 0.6 |
| 1 and 2, 3, 4, 6, | Less funds raised by intermediaries | -15.3 |
| | | 156.1  156.1 |

These tables give uses and sources of funds, and provide the figures for my diagram. Tables I and II below are derived from this survey.

These tables show that nearly all of the nation's saving is funneled through financial intermediaries, and hardly any is placed directly by private persons. In 1972 individuals are expected to lend only $12.0 billion out of a total of $156.1 billion. In earlier years they lent even less.

### 5. Comparison of Residential with Industrial Sector

The Bankers Trust Co. tables list two kinds of loans for which the demand is elastic. One kind consists of loans to the residential sector, the other of loans to the industrial sector, as shown in Table III below. These figures show that the residential sector is four or five times as important as the industrial sector in setting the rate of interest.

*Table III. Residential and Industrial Lending in 1972, Projected*

| Table No. | | |
|---|---|---|
| | Residential sector, *net* lending | |
| 8 | Home loans | $26.5 billion |
| 9 | Apartment house loans | 9.5 " |
| 12 | Municipal bonds | 17.5 " |
| 14 | Consumer loans on cars, etc. | 12.5 " |
| | | $66.0 " |
| | Industrial sector, *gross* lending | |
| 10 | Manufacturing and mining bonds | $ 7.5 " |
| 11 | Manufacturing and mining stocks | 2.9 " |
| 10 | Finance and real estate bonds | 5.2 " |
| 11 | Finance and real estate stocks | 1.8 " |
| 10 | Commercial and other bonds | 1.2 " |
| 11 | Commercial and other stocks | 1.2 " |
| 10 | Less bonds retired (my estimate) | -4.0 " |
| 11 | Less stocks retired (my estimate) | -0.8 " |
| | | $14.8 " |

Home loans made by savings banks play a very large role in the theory of interest. Because these loans are usually repaid in small instalments spread over many years, the show with great clarity how the long-term rate of interest is tied to the gradual growth of the national dividend. The process will be described in detail later in two chapters entitled *Loans to Homeowners* and *The Cash Flow of a Savings Bank*. Impatient readers, eager to savor the meat of my argument, can turn to these two chapters at once. There they will see the reasons why interest and growth always go hand in hand.

Public utility bonds are omitted from Table III for a special reason, a reason about which more will be said in a later chapter. Suffice it to state here that the volume of borrowing by public utilities is not held in check by the level of interest rates. The regulatory commissions set the price of electricity high enough to let the companies borrow all the money they require. As a result, the interest rate on utility bonds is a rate copied, merely copied, from the rate set elsewhere. This makes the demand for loans by the utilities very inelastic.

Likewise for industrial firms, money reinvested in plant and equipment, but obtained from undistributed earnings rather than new bond issues, is omitted from this table. When firms avoid the bond market, they put no pressure on bond prices[6].

Evidently Table III is quite correct in claiming that the residential sector of the economy is of major importance in setting the rate of interest.

Only half of the demand for money to borrow enjoys an elastic demand. The other half, as we shall see, suffers from extreme inelasticity. It refuses to abate when interest rates rise. Consequently *half* of the demand—the elastic half, mainly residential—is forced to absorb *all* of the change in volume when rates rise or fall. No wonder that home building undergoes such wide savings during the business cycle!

## 6. Institutional Investors

Institutional investors, unlike private investors, are always under pressure to put their money to work. New money flows in every day. To let it pile up week after week, earning no interest, would be wasteful indeed. Even to speculate with it, and shift it back and forth between short and long-term investments, would be dangerous. Consequently it comes to pass that the treasurers of insurance companies, pension funds, and savings banks usually adhere to a standard policy. They invest their cash income almost daily, just as fast as it flows in, regardless of changes in interest rates from time to time. They seem to be afraid of idle money.

---

[6] See §2 above, on *Self-Financing*. Also see Chapter XIII, §7, *Dividend Policies*, infra.

# CHAPTER IV
# FINANCIAL INSTITUTIONS

## 1. The Primary Business of Various Lenders

Various lenders such as commercial banks, savings banks, insurance companies, pension funds, and so forth all have a primary business of their own that determines what kind of investments they can make. Moreover, rigid laws restrict their choice.

The primary business of commercial banks is to make short-term self-liquidating loans. If these banks cannot find enough short-term loans, they use up the rest of their lending power by making intermediate "term loans" due in three to five years. They also buy Treasury, municipal, and corporate bonds of near maturity.

The primary business of savings banks is to make long-term mortgage loans on private homes, apartment houses, and other real estate. The law, however, forbids these banks to invest every last dollar of their funds in mortgages, and so they use some of their lending power to buy long-term bonds as well. Hence savings banks encroach somewhat on the preserves of other lenders.

The primary business of life insurance companies is to accumulate reserves for the payment of death benefits when their policyholders die. Because these reserves are a long-term liability, life insurance companies invest their premium income in long-term securities like corporate bonds and real estate mortgages. These companies have no need for short-term paper too, since they enjoy a steady cash flow from premium income.

The primary business of fire and casualty insurance companies is to hold unearned premium reserves against possible losses that may befall their policyholders in the future. These companies are mature, and their assets grow at about the same rate as the national dividend grows. Because these assets must be protected against temporary shrinkage in market value, such as occurs when rates of interest rise, fire and casualty companies should keep most of their money invested in bonds of near maturity. But these companies, unlike commercial banks, do not need to make large payments against demand deposits; hence they can safely use somewhat longer maturities than commercial banks can. Consequently they often buy issues with a maturity of eight or ten years if these look cheaper than short-term issues.

The primary business of pension funds is to accumulate reserves for the payment of pensions to persons who retire after contributing to the fund for many years. Since these reserves, like those of life insurance companies, are long-term liabilities, pension funds also invest mainly in long-term bonds, real estate mortgages, and common stocks.

The primary business of endowment funds is to pay current income to universities, churches, foundations, and so forth at a steady rate. This being a long-term obligation easily upset by extreme changes in short-term interest rates, endowment funds must buy only long-term issues. In contrast to life insurance companies, they cannot let their assets grow at compound interest. Instead they must disburse their income as fast as received. When old bonds mature, they use the proceeds to buy new bonds as a replacement, but this does not put any new money into the loan market.

The primary purpose of personal investments is to pay the private individual a steady income to supplement or replace his earnings from wages, salaries, fees, or commissions. Since this purpose is a long-term obligation, one that could easily be upset by wide swings in short-term interest rates, the individual prefers to put his money into long-term issues. He may buy directly for himself, or indirectly through his savings bank. Sometimes he reinvests part of his investment income at compound interest to provide for his old age, but seldom does he reinvest the whole of it. Thus he does not proceed as a life insurance company or a pension fund does while it is waiting for its long-term liabilities to fall due.

Although universities and charitable foundations do not need to be paid "wages of abstinence" to keep them from consuming their capital, nevertheless these large investors are very sensitive to the rate of interest in another way. If Harvard University, for instance, after seeing the interest rate rise for many years, finally becomes accustomed to a return of 6% on its endowment, it may plan its budget accordingly. If so, it will commit itself to a salary scale for its faculty that is predicated on this 6% return. Were the rate now to drop back to 4%, where it lay in the 1950s, the university would inevitably suffer a bad deficit. Unable to cut its expenses quickly, it would be forced to dip into capital, perhaps for many years in a row. What Harvard was doing, other large investors would be doing too.

The process might be obscured by the rise in bond prices that would result from the drop in interest rates As old 6% bonds were refunded with new 4% issues, prices would rise a lot on bonds with ten or fifteen years still to run before maturity. The university might sell some of these for a capital gain, but the gain would be illusory. What good does it do to sell a 6% bond at 130, spend the non-recurrent gain of 30 points, and reinvest the balance of 100 at 4% for 25 years? Taking capital gains in this way is the road to ruin. If interest rates should drop only 2% during the next decade, many university, endowment, and pension funds, having already committed themselves to heavy expenses in the future, could find themselves deep in the red.

Fundamentally the danger springs from the fact that interest rates change much more than wage rates do. Within a single decade, rates on new AAA bonds have risen from 4% to 8%, and perhaps may decline as much some time in the future. Wage rates, in contrast, do not jump around like this. Any investor who makes long-term commitments to pay someone else's wages out of his own interest income is riding for trouble. It is like going short of the market in common stocks or staple commodities. Unfortunately in the bond market this danger is not well understood.

## 2. Lending Short or Long

Short-term loans are often self-liquidating, but long-term loans are seldom so. Money borrowed at short term usually goes into work in process or stock-in-trade, and is recovered when the goods are sold. It is thus available to repay the loan when due, whether or not the borrower makes a profit himself in the end.

Money borrowed at long term, however, usually goes into plant and equipment or houses and apartments, and can only be recovered if the borrower earns enough to pay interest and sinking fund year after year. If earnings are insufficient, the loan cannot be repaid—unless some other source of cash can be found. Hence long-term loans are inherently more risky than short-term.

Safe short-term and safe long-term loans are both hard for the small investor to make by himself. Both require a credit investigation to find out if the borrower's earning power is large enough. Commercial banks are expert at this with short-term loans, savings banks with long-term loans. Both types of banks, therefore, serve as financial intermediaries for small savers. Both accept deposits, both invest the funds, and both protect them from loss.

Commercial banks pay no interest on demand deposits, but savings banks do so on time deposits. Commercial banks, to make up for their lack of interest payments, render certain services, like letting depositors draw checks on their accounts. In both cases banks offer inducements of one kind or another to obtain deposits

One of the main functions of savings banks is to augment the supply of funds to lend at long-term by securing this money from a multitude of persons who really lend at short-term—or on call, to be exact. While the procedure of lending long and borrowing short is inherently dangerous, savings banks reduce this risk by resorting to a very large number of suppliers of funds deposited on call. Experience shows that very few of these lenders ever want to get their money back all at the same time. It takes a real panic to cause wholesale withdrawals.

In contrast to depositors in savings banks, a few private commercial firms really do need to get their money back just as soon as their short-term loans run out. Lenders whose regular business is seasonal want to use the money themselves when their own industry picks up. Fortunately different lenders of this kind have money idle at different times of the year, and so the total supply of private short-term money out on loan does not vary much from one season of the year to the next.

Short-term funds are often invested in Treasury bills or commercial paper. When commercial paper is used, bill brokers usually perform the function of tunneling the money from lender to borrower.

## 3. Commercial Banks

Commercial banks have special needs of their own. They must buy short-term paper only. They cannot safely make long-term loans.

Since the deposits of commercial banks are payable on demand, these deposits should never be invested in long-term bonds, whose market price might shrink temporarily as a result of a rise in interest rates in general. It is not enough for the bonds to be sure of payment at maturity. If they still have twenty years more to run, let us say, and pay only 3%, when the long-term rate is up to 7%, they will sell at only 62. Had a bank bought those bonds at par when they were first issued many years ago, the bank would now show a huge paper loss on them. Yet the bank might be forced to sell them suddenly in order to raise money to meet checks drawn on its demand deposits. Consequently long-term bonds, no matter how sure of payment at maturity, are not a safe investment for commercial banks. Only short-term paper can meet the needs of such a bank.

## 4. Finance Companies

Finance companies borrow short-term money by selling their own notes (often to banks) at one rate of interest, and they relend it by buying the notes of the ultimate user of the money (the purchaser of an automobile, for instance) at a higher rate of interest. Since finance companies are willing to repurchase their own notes before maturity, reselling them to other lenders, they make it easy for persons to put idle money to work for very short periods of time like ten days or two weeks. They relend their money themselves for a longer time, often to buyers of automobiles who borrow on 30-month instalment loans. The finance companies are thus a striking example of borrowing short and lending long.

Bill brokers, who buy and sell commercial paper, also funnel short-term money from lender to borrower. These brokers make a practice of repurchasing any notes that the lender may want to sell before maturity. The lender can thus put his money to work for 22 days, let us say, by investing in 90-day paper for a small part of the time this paper is outstanding.

Government bond dealers buy and sell Treasury bills in the same way.

## 5. Savings Banks

When interest rates go very high, savings banks are tempted to divert their cash flow from mortgage loans to long-term bonds instead. On these bonds they can hope to make a quick capital gain if interest rates should fall within the next few years. But no such gain can be made on mortgage loans. Bonds, moreover, enjoy better marketability, a factor much in their favor should depositors want to withdraw their money in order to buy bonds for themselves.

One thing that often makes interest rates rise in the first place is heavy long-term borrowing by municipalities and corporations whenever short-term borrowing is restricted by a squeeze on bank reserves. These borrowers outbid homeowners for the cash flow of insurance companies and savings banks. They are very insistent. Bonds then achieve a higher return than mortgages and homeowners are forced to defer to other borrowers.

Since many would-be home buyers can contrive to postpone their purchase of a new house for two or three years, the short-run elasticity of demand for mortgage loans is great. As a result, savings banks find it possible to divert some of their cash flow into bonds. High interest rates thus produce a severe shrinkage in residential building.

Commercial banks with savings departments are like mutual savings banks in their willingness to buy bonds when prices are low. Savings and loan associations, in contrast, do not buy many bonds, but they still buy mortgages in competition with other investors, and so they are tied to the rest of the money market in this way.

When bond prices are down, most lending institutions, to be sure, dislike to switch out of one bond into another. These lenders have a paper loss on their present holdings, but they need not reveal this loss so long as they do not sell their bonds, and so long as the bonds remain free of default. The result is to make the market inactive for old issues when bond prices go down a lot.

## 6. Life Insurance Companies

Life insurance companies, like savings banks, must adjust their lending policies to the needs of those to whom they lend. As a matter of fact, the adjustment is mutual, because insurance companies seek out the particular borrowers who can use them best.

Since life insurance companies have long-term liabilities to meet, they need to lend their money at long term too. Consequently they buy bonds and mortgages rather than notes and bills. This is indeed fortunate for the economy as a whole, because a great deal of durable plant and equipment is erected every year, and investment of this sort should always be financed with long-term securities.

Life insurance companies lend money not only to industrial companies and public utilities but also to landlords and homeowners. The companies choose whatever investments offer the highest return, net of the cost of supervision. In so doing the companies help to equalize the interest rates on various kinds of securities.

The amount of money that a life insurance company can lend is limited by its cash flow. Money comes into the company when it receives interest on its investments, or when some of its bonds are called for sinking funds, or when its mortgage loans are amortized month after month. Money also comes in when policyholders pay their premiums. On the other hand, money flows out when death benefits are paid to survivors, or when policy loans are made, or when commissions are paid to agents, or home office expenses are paid to clerks and suppliers. Money also flows out when premium taxes are paid. Nevertheless a large net inflow remains. This new money must be invested in bonds and mortgages as fast as it comes in. Both inflow and outflow are determined by contracts all made in previous years with borrowers or policyholders. As a result, the sum available for investment in the present year remains quite independent of the rate of interest at which new loans are currently being written.

It so happens that the external factors acting upon life insurance companies are largely offsetting, as shown in Table IV below:

Table IV.   Life Insurance Dollar in 1970

| | |
|---|---:|
| Premium income | 78.4¢ |
| Less death benefits, etc. | −55.8 |
|   " commissions to agents | − 7.1 |
|   " home and field office expenses | −10.2 |
|   " taxes | − 4.4 |
|   " dividends to stockholders | − 1.0 |
| Balance, net outflow | − 0.1 |
| Investment earnings and other income | +21.6 |
| Additions to policy reserves and surplus | 21.5 |

See *1971 Life Insurance Fact Book*, p. 60, published by the Institute of Life Insurance in New York.

This table shows that investment income of 21.6¢ out of each dollar of receipts accounted for all the annual growth of assets (and a trifle more) in 1970. These investment earnings of 21.6¢ came to 5.30% of invested assets.[1] In other words, the loan fund held by the life insurance companies grew over 5% in 1970 because of interest earned, but not at all because of other activities.

These other activities went on independently of the rate of interest earned on invested assets. They were ruled by forces wholly outside the money market. These activities would have had the same net result whether the interest rate had been higher or lower.

Evidently life insurance companies are largely self-financing. Their rate of growth is about equal to the rate of interest they earn. Assets

---

[1] See *1971 Life Insurance Fact Book*, p. 63, published by the Institute of Life Insurance in New York.

pile up at 5% per annum if the return on them is 5%. What a striking coincidence!

The assets of the life insurance companies constitute a fund that exists to protect their policyholders. Yet almost never is it drawn upon. The companies manage to pay all their bills by using their other receipts. Investment earnings, therefore, can be wholly reinvested. We shall find the same to be true of savings banks.

The savings that pour into life insurance companies and savings banks, though voluntary, are nevertheless contractual. The insurance companies have contracts with their policyholders, the savings banks with their mortgagors. Persons who fall to pay on time are penalized. Hence the inflow of cash is steady and reliable, not hit-or-miss and unpredictable.

It might be thought that a rise in interest rates would help the sale of insurance policies. Higher rates would make the assets of the companies grow faster at compound interest. Lower premiums, therefore, would suffice, because the money to pay death benefits would pile up faster. The insurance dollar would buy more in the end. Hence the public might be expected to take out larger policies. But things do not work out this way, at least to begin with. When interest rates rise, bond prices fall. Market value then becomes less than original cost. This impels the companies to set up a Valuation Reserve to mark their bonds down. Any interest they earn in excess of the standard rate is now credited to this reserve. None is used to cut the price of new policies. Nor is any increase made in the dividends, or refunds, paid to old policyholders. Instead the companies keep for themselves all the extra income they receive on new bonds bought at the new and higher level of interest rates. Sales of insurance, therefore, do not increase promptly when interest rates rise. It takes a great many years for higher rates to change the net premiums on new policies. No force is at work, therefore, to make buyers of life insurance start to save faster just as soon as interest rates rise higher, as would be required by the traditional theory of interest.

## 7. Pension Funds

Pension funds are like life insurance companies in that they have long-term liabilities to meet, and so they should invest their cash flow mainly in long-term bonds and mortgages. Pension funds are also like life insurance companies in that the flow of payments they receive from their contributors is very steady. Moreover, the flow of money from interest and sinking funds is also very steady. Most of these receipts involve contractual saving on a huge scale by their members and creditors, to the great benefit of the economy as a whole.

Although pension funds rely on contractual payments, nevertheless important changes may occur from time to time. If, at the start, an actuary assumes an interest rate of 5% for the future, but if later he assumes a rate of 7%, he can reduce the contributions required. The higher the rate, the faster the fund will grow at compound interest, and the smaller will be the need for future contributions. The result, therefore, is to make saving *decrease* as interest rates *increase*, just the opposite of what standard theory assumes.

The United States Social Security Pension Fund is unique in that this fund is invested exclusively in government bonds. When the Fund buys these bonds, and pays the Treasury for them, the money is not used for the construction of useful plant and equipment. No capital formation occurs. The money simply goes to pay the current expenses of the government. Consequently Social Security taxes are simply personal income taxes under another name. They are not a true example of capital formation financed by thrifty savers.

Before the days of Social Security and company pension funds, individuals were obliged to provide for their old age themselves. Likewise, before the days of Medicare they were obliged to pay their own medical bills all by themselves. Hence, years ago, money in the bank, and plenty of it, was needed much more than now. Life insurance was also more necessary years ago. Nowadays, however, Social Security taxes and other obligatory payroll deductions largely take the place of optional personal saving for many people.

Employer contributions to pension funds are a fringe benefit that many companies pay to their workers. These payments add to the employer's cost of hiring a man, and reduce the sum that he could otherwise pay the workman directly as wages. They are, in effect, a form of forced saving imposed upon the worker.

Sometimes the payments into the pension fund are made by the labor union to which the man belongs, part of his union dues being diverted to this use. In this case too, the contribution to the pension fund is a form of forced saving.

When chronic inflation is underway, contributors fear that their payments will shrink in purchasing power before the pensions become due. If the rate of shrinkage exceeds the money rate of interest earned by the fund, saving will be taking place at a negative real rate of interest. Yet the saving will continue, and the contributors will reluctantly accept the shrinkage. They will say that it is better to shave a slice off the top of high earnings now, and have a meager pension in one's old age, than to spend the extra money now, and be destitute later. They recognize that the marginal utility of a large income today is much less than that of a small income tomorrow. Consequently they do not need to be paid wages of abstinence to make them shift a slice of their income from age 40 to age 70. As far as pension funds go, therefore, traditional theory, with its insistence on savers' preference for present goods over future goods, does not apply.

Pension funds are now growing very rapidly, and have reached a huge size. In due course, however, they will cease to grow so fast, because more and more of their members will have reached retirement age. If the country were not growing at all, outgo for pensions paid would soon come into balance with income from contributions made. When old people are supported by young people in this way, no net saving occurs, and no new funds come into the loan market.

If population is growing, however, the membership of the pension funds will grow too, and at the same rate. Contributions received will then exceed pensions paid, even for a mature fund. The excess will be available for investment. In fact, the fund will be required by law to put the extra money to work in order to provide for its future liabilities as computed by its actuaries. The money will be spent for whatever IOUs are available—but there are plenty being put on sale every day. The money will force the price of these pieces of paper up; in other words, it will force the rate of interest down. The larger the excess cash flow of the funds, the lower the rate will become.

Many funds, unfortunately have never received contributions adequate to cover their actuarial liabilities. These liabilities meanwhile have been increased in midstream by agreements made with labor unions to pay higher pensions to workers on retirement.[2] Some of the money put into the funds, moreover, has been used to buy common

---

[2] Cf. Julian Gumperz, "Pension Funds in an Age of Discountinuity" in *The Financial Analysts Journal*, Nov.-Dec. 1970, vol. 26 No. 6.

stocks, especially "growth stocks" as a hedge against inflation. If these stocks should ever suffer a bad shrinkage in price, employers would need to make heavy supplementary contributions. This expense would hurt their reported earnings, and would make their stocks fall in price still more. Since the various companies invest in each others' stocks, a general bear market would force every company to increase its contribution to its own fund. The more the extra money that was put in, the more that earnings would be hurt, and the worse the fall would become. It is truly a vicious circle.

## 8. Fire and Casualty Insurance Companies

Fire and casualty insurance companies (which we shall henceforth call "fire companies" for short) do not enjoy a contractual flow of premium income from policyholders that would tend to make them grow rapidly, as life insurance companies do. Instead, fire companies grow only as fast as the country itself grows. The premiums these companies receive merely suffice to pay the losses they sustain and the expenses they undergo day by day, with but little to spare.

Even though their inflow and outflow of cash may remain in balance so long as the fire companies keep selling new policies to replace those that expire, nevertheless these companies must always be prepared to face outright liquidation, or a catastrophe like a great conflagration or hurricane. They must always keep on hand a very large sum of money to cover such losses on policies already sold. This money is put on deposit, as it were, with the companies by their policyholders. In this respect a fire company resembles a savings bank

During the interval while the policyholders' money is held in trust, the fire company can invest it in stocks and bonds. Whatever interest and dividends it earns on this money then belongs to the insurance company, not the policyholders. A fire company, therefore, may be called a device for obtaining money from outsiders to invest for the benefit of the company itself.

Competition to obtain money for investment in this way has become so keen nowadays that most fire companies fail to make any underwriting profit at all on the policies they sell. They do not succeed in keeping premium income higher than fire losses plus expenses. Sometimes they even show an underwriting loss. For all that, the business remains worth while because the interest earned on the money held in trust is so important. Since total assets are several times larger than stockholders' capital, and since all of these assets are invested for the benefit of the stockholders alone, a return of 5% on total assets can easily mean a return of 25% or more on stockholders' capital. Such a return will more than offset a slight underwriting loss.

While the money is being held in trust by the fire companies, interest and sinking fund payments provide a steady inflow of new money that must seek an outlet somewhere. The fire companies use this cash to buy various new or refunding issues of bonds currently being offered by municipalities, public utilities, and industrial corporations. The size of this cash flow is limited by prior contracts with the original debtors whose bonds are still held for investment. Consequently this cash flow—the supply of money to lend—does not respond to current changes in the interest rate

Inasmuch as the fire companies always set aside reserves for unearned premiums that tend to grow at the same rate as the country as a whole, these companies thereby function as net suppliers of money to lend. In this way they support the bond market, and keep the interest rate down.

The fire and casualty insurance companies are usually owned by their stockholders. Seldom are they mutual enterprises like most life insurance companies. Lacking the tax exemption that the mutuals enjoy on their investment income, the stock companies find it helps taxwise to invest part of their funds in municipal bonds. Since their liabilities are not payable on demand, they can safely buy tax-exempt issues of longer maturity than commercial banks can buy.

## 9. Mutual and Stock Companies

Most long-term lenders differ from long-term borrowers in a way not often discussed. Lenders are usually nonprofit associations, while borrowers are usually individuals or corporations. Mutual insurance companies, mutual savings banks, mutual investment trusts, charitable foundations, universities, hospitals, churches, and other nonprofit institutions are the largest buyers of bonds and mortgages. From an economic point of view, all of these organizations are not firms, but clubs or cooperative societies. Is it not surprising that, in a capitalistic economy, lending should lie so largely in the hands of quasi-socialistic institutions?

And why is it that, if lending is done in this way, borrowing is not done in the same way too?

The answer would seem to be that borrowers need equity capital to protect their side of the deal, while lenders do not. Borrowers agree to repay in the future, while lenders pay in the present. Borrowers might fail to complete their part of the contract, but lenders cannot fail to do so, because they pay their part when a loan is first made.

Since individuals and corporations possess equity capital, they alone can qualify as borrowers. Clubs and mutual organizations, in contrast, possess little or no such capital; hence they cannot qualify as borrowers. If a church, for instance wants to borrow money from a bank, it usually must get some private person to endorse its promissory note. A club, moreover, is seldom organized in a way that would let its creditors get their hands on its assets in case of default. Consequently a club cannot indulge in heavy long-term borrowing in the way a private person or a public corporation can do.

Not all lending, to be sure, is done by nonprofit institutions. Some is done by corporations. Yet incorporated life insurance companies like the Aetna, the Travelers, and the Connecticut General are nowhere near as large as mutuals like the Prudential, the Metropolitan, and the Equitable. Even in the fire and casualty field, stock companies like the Home and the North American confront large rivals like Liberty Mutual and others. All told, mutual banks and mutual insurance companies do far more long-term lending than stock companies do.

Short-term lending, in contrast to long-term, is seldom done by mutual companies. Commercial banks dominate this field, because the money they lend does not come from a host of small savers. Instead, this money is created afresh, by a stroke of the pen, when a bank buys a customer's note and credits his checking account. Thereafter, to be sure, the money may flow out of one bank to other banks, but meantime money will also flow from these other banks back to the first bank. The two flows cancel. In modern banking, the demand deposits of commercial banks, unlike the time deposits of savings banks, do not originate from the savings of the depositors themselves. Because demand deposits originate in a different way from savings deposits, and because demand depositors have the right to withdraw their money on a moment's notice, the law requires commercial banks to provide equity capital of their own to protect their deposits. Consequently most short-term lending remains outside the field of mutual institutions. Credit unions are a minor exception.

To the rule that mutual institutions are never large borrowers there may be one exception. If a city or town is deemed to be a club and not a firm, then its borrowings in the form of municipal bonds may be called the debt of a mutual organization. While the city itself shows no Capital and Surplus on its books, and thus differs from a corporation, nevertheless the property of its citizens is subject to attachment by its creditors if it defaults on its debts. In that sense it is much like a firm that borrows on its equity. Therefore, to call it nothing but a club, like a hospital or a mutual savings bank, is farfetched.

As for mutual investment funds, they are unlike mutual insurance companies in two important ways. In the first place, these funds seldom hire special salesmen of their own to sign up new members in the way that life insurance companies hire their own salesmen to sign up new policyholders. Instead mutual funds rely on some outside agency to sell their shares, and this agency retains the profit on the sales it makes. In the case of an insurance company, on the other hand, the selling profit goes to the company itself, and reverts to its policyholders.

In the second place, mutual funds differ from insurance companies in that the funds do not hire their own investment advisers in the way that life insurance companies hire their own actuaries. Instead, mutual funds are managed by an outside agency which charges a fee and retains any profit it can make thereon. These two outside agencies hold the funds in their grip, and make large profits from their contracts with the funds. As a result, mutual funds so-called turn out to be less than 100% mutual organizations.

For all that, it remains true that, even in the capitalistic United States, long-term lending is usually done by nonprofit mutual institutions, while borrowing is usually done by individuals and profit-seeking corporations.

## 10. Private Individuals

Private individuals usually make use of financial intermediaries when they lend money. They buy very few bonds and mortgages themselves. They supplied directly only $4.2 billion out of a total of $100.3 of new capital raised in 1970.

Investment bankers nowadays work with such a close markup on new bonds— $10 or less for a $1,000 bond—that they do not welcome orders from small savers. Furthermore the resale market on odd lots of less than ten bonds suffers from a wide spread between bid and asked prices. No wonder that small investors steer clear of the bond market!

Mortgages likewise are out of reach for small investors. It takes at least $15,000 or $20,000 to make a mortgage loan. Legal complications, like searching the title and recording the mortgage, are also involved. Hence small investors steer clear of mortgages too, and use savings banks or U.S. savings bonds instead.

Private individuals of large means, to be sure, can buy bonds and mortgages if they wish, but they usually prefer common stocks, which they buy in hopes of making a capital gain. For this reason they too are but a small factor in the bond and mortgage market. Insurance companies, pension funds, and savings banks are vastly more important.

When small investors entrust their savings to insurance companies, their main motive is to buy protection against untimely death. Whatever saving they perform along the way is purely incidental. When they buy insurance, they do not think of themselves as putting money out on loan in order to earn wages of abstinence. Likewise, when they place their money in savings banks, interest is not the inducement. Instead, their usual motive is to accumulate a down payment on a house or a car. Or they may be setting aside a fund for a rainy day. Here too they are not seeking wages of abstinence.

It takes a rate much higher than 4% or 5% to persuade most people to revise the family budget, and pour a sizable fraction of their income into an investment outlet. The hope of making 50% or more a year in the stock market, to be sure, will make people scrimp and save, but a mere 4% or 5% in the savings bank is not worth much self-denial. What money they do deposit in the bank, they put there for some better reason than the meager rate of interest it returns.

If 4% or 5% were really enough to entice potential savers, we would find homeowners economizing in every possible way in order to pay off their 6% and 7% mortgages in a very few years. Hardly any houses would remain encumbered for long. But the facts are otherwise. Few indeed are the families who carry no mortgage debt.

In a mild depression, savings deposits often rise, because men who keep their jobs are nevertheless afraid to withdraw money from the bank for use as down payments on houses and cars. Meanwhile they continue to make their weekly deposits of new savings as fast as ever. Fear promotes thrift, interest does not.

When people seek to provide for their old age, they usually put their savings into a pension fund handled by their employer. These pension plans are usually "contributory", with the employer paying 50% or 75% of the annual premium. The employees themselves then think they are getting something for nothing. They do not realize that their employer's contribution is like a tax on wages, with its entire incidence being on the wage earner himself. Instead, they believe the contribution comes out of the employer's profits. Yet this is not so. In hiring a man, a firm must reckon on his pension cost as well as his wage cost. What the firm pays out in one way, it cannot pay out in the other. It must always make both ends meet, year after year.

When we consider the motives of individual savers, therefore, and ask how these savers act when they put their money into savings banks, insurance companies, and pension funds, we see that high or low interest rates, within the range of 3% to 6%, do not move most people to action. Yet standard theory asserts that the current rate of interest is of crucial importance to the individual saver. It says that the higher the rate, the more he will save. Furthermore, the theory overlooks the fact that the private investor is a very small factor in the money market. It fails to see that his psychology does not matter anyway. What really counts is the behavior of large institutional investors.

Private individuals participate directly in the stock market much more than they do in the bond market and the mortgage market. In fact, nearly half of the trading in stocks is still done by individuals. A decade or more ago, before mutual funds and trust funds became so large, individuals did 80% of the trading, and institutions only 20%. Nevertheless these ratios do not matter even here, because the stock market itself is not a large collector of new capital, as we shall see in Chapter XIV. In fact, as a supplier of funds for industry, the stock market provided less than nothing[3] in 1968. Clearly the stock market

[3] See Bankers Trust Table 2, line 3 edition of 1969. This negative quantity may have been caused by the replacement of outstanding preferred stock by new issues of debenture bonds. Since dividends paid on preferred stock come out of net income, while interest paid on bonds comes out of pretax earnings, it is advantageous for corporations to replace stock with bonds.

Several years later, after heavy sales of bonds had impaired the debt-equity ratio, American Telephone and other public utilities issued preferred stock despite the tax load upon themselves. Fire and casualty insurance companies were among the large

is not the place where the interest rate is crystalized. Nor are individuals of much importance elsewhere. It is institutions who really dominate the capital market as a whole.

Although private persons fear inflation, financial intermediaries do not. Private persons try to protect themselves by demanding a rate of interest high enough to offset inflation, but financial intermediaries "have no soul"; they simply lend all their cash receipts at whatever rate they can get. Savings banks and life insurance companies do not sit back and compute the shrinkage in future purchasing power they will suffer if the cost of living continues to rise. Consequently their fears regarding inflation do not force the rate of interest up. Yet these institutions are by far the largest lenders. The present widespread fear of inflation, therefore, cannot possibly account for the present high level of interest rates. Some other cause must be at work, as we shall see.

## 11. Summary

Fortunately the needs of various borrowers, and the needs of various lenders too, overlap in many places. Most borrowers and most lenders enjoy a choice of partners. If they did not do so, the money market would lose its unity. It would be broken up into many separate submarkets, each with its own independent interest rate. But such is not the case. The overlapping needs of all parties tend to make a single rate emerge for the market as a whole.

Traditional theory, as we have now seen, has certain shortcomings. It needs to take account of the following facts:

> 1. Optional saving, induced by interest rates no higher than 3% to 6%, is small. It is overwhelmed by contractual saving, induced by other motives.
>
> 2. Profit-maximizing firms, with their eyes on marginal productivity, account for but a minor part of the total demand for savings. They are overwhelmed by other borrowers with other motives.
>
> 3. Legal rules about interest coverage and the debt-equity ratio prevent most borrowers from obtaining loans as large as they would like to secure.

Accordingly we must search carefully for ways to improve upon traditional theory.

---

buyers, because intercorporate dividends are taxed at only 15%, while bond interest is taxed at 50% or thereabouts.

# CHAPTER V
# LOANS TO HOMEOWNERS

## 1. The Mortgage Contract

Nowadays most mortgage loans on private homes are serviced by quarterly or monthly payments. A typical payment comes to 25% of the homeowner's aftertax income. Each payment covers three separate charges. The first is interest, the second is amortization, and the third is real estate taxes.

In the early years of the loan the interest payment is large and the amortization small, but as time goes on and the unpaid balance of the loan is reduced by amortization, the interest itself becomes small, while the balance left for amortization becomes large.

The real estate tax varies according to the tax rate prevailing in the municipality each year.

The different payments range in importance about as follows in a typical year: interest 6%, amortization 4%, and real estate taxes 4% of the loan. When interest rates are lower, the total monthly payment is lower too. This makes it possible for home buyers to afford a bigger loan and a larger house.

A larger house does not mean a larger tax, however, even though a larger house carries a larger assessment. When assessed values go up, tax rates go down, because the cost of running the town remains the same. Consequently the typical tax bill need not rise step by step with the mortgage loan when homeowners in general buy more expensive houses at lower interest rates.

## 2. Limits on Mortgage Loans

To every new loan there are two limits, either what the borrower would like to borrow, or what the lender is willing to lend. The borrower is lured on by hope of gain, the lender is held back by fear of loss. Usually the borrower asks more than the lender will grant. Thus the prospective borrower may want a loan of $30,000, but the lending bank may stop at $20,000.

In reaching a decision, a savings bank will be guided mainly by the aftertax income of the borrower. The usual limit on monthly payments is one week's take-home pay. If the loan offered to the borrower is not enough to buy the house he wants, he will have to make up the difference out of his own pocket. Otherwise he will have to settle for a cheaper house.

When banks make home loans, they look not only at the earning power of the borrower, but also at the equity money he puts behind his loan. On "conventional loans" this initial equity must be at least 20%, and is often 30%. In the end, however, the safety of the loan really depends upon the resale value of the house. This value depends in turn on the earning power of some new buyer. If the economy of the neighborhood is going downhill, then new buyers with earning power enough to service the old debt can seldom be found, once the original owner becomes unable to pay himself. Thus there is no getting around the fact that the earning power of homeowners in general is the ultimate safeguard for mortgage loans everywhere.

### 3. Borrowing up to the Hilt

The upper limit on mortgage loans often acts as the lower limit too. When a husband and wife agree to place a mortgage lien on their house, they usually try to get as large a loan as they can—unless the interest rate goes up a lot when the equity is too small. The mortgage, whether it be large or small, puts the house in jeopardy anyway, and so the couple are wise to secure as large a mortgage as they can in exchange for this concession. In other words, they might as well be hanged for a horse as a hen. If they do not need all of their savings as equity for the purchase of their house, they can leave the excess in the bank as insurance against a rainy day, getting interest on it meanwhile. Or they can use the money to pay cash for their next car rather than buy it on time. Since the interest rate on home mortgages is lower than on car loans, it is good business to raise the money for the purchase of their car by using the kind of loan that carries the lower rate of interest. If a family seeking a mortgage loan reasons in this way, the result is to make their loan directly proportional to the size of their aftertax income. No considerations of marginal utility alter the outcome in any way.

In the more complicated case where the savings bank charges a higher rate of interest on a large loan than a small one, the size of the loan is still determined by the aftertax income of the borrower. Families who have too little spare cash to make a large down payment pay the high rate. Their total loan, however, is still limited by the husband's take-home pay.

When savings banks make mortgage loans, they often charge a higher rate of interest on the whole loan if the borrower's equity in the house is small than if it is large. Today a bank may charge interest at the rate of 7¼% if the loan comes to 70% and the equity to 30%, but it may charge 7¾% if the loan comes to 80% and the equity to only 20%. In other words, in order for a family to increase its loan from 70% to 80%, it may be obliged to pay ½% more on the entire loan. This extra charge amounts to 11¼% on the final increment. The same result would have been reached if the family had obtained a large first mortgage at 7¼% and a small second mortgage at 11¼%. The table below, applicable to a total loan of $16,000 on a house worth $20,000, bring this point out clearly:

| Loan | | Rate | | Yearly Interest | | |
|------|----|------|----|------|----|------|
| $14,000 | at | 7¼% | = | $1,015 | = | basic cost |
| + 2,000 | at | 11¼% | = | + 225 | = | implied extra cost |
| $16,000 | at | 7¾% | = | $1,240 | = | total cost |

When a man seeks a mortgage loan, his bank asks him what other loans he already has outstanding. In a typical case the borrower will be making payments on his car equal to 5% of his aftertax income. When this is combined with payments on his house equal to 25% of his income, the total comes to 30%.

Payments on a car and payments on a house are really charges to the same account in the family budget. Any man who buys a house is sure to need a car. If a family lives in a neighborhood of single houses, it is not feasible to walk to work and walk to the stores. Only people in apartment houses can do this. These latter families, to be sure, walk only part of the way; the rest of the way they go by bus. For them, carfare is a substitute for automobile ownership. And the more they must pay for carfare, the less they can pay for rent. The two charges are tied together. They all belong in the same account in the family budget.

## 4. Housing as a Status Symbol

Everybody wants status symbols. We deplore this, we laugh at it, but we insist on it. And so we spend money, lots of money, on status symbols.

Housing is one of the best status symbols you can buy. It is far better than food, because nobody knows whether you had cabbage or caviar, liver or lobster, for luncheon. Nowadays housing is also better than clothing, because clothing is so cheap that even women with the lowest wages can still keep up with the latest fashions. They often wear castoffs, good castoffs. No one but a hippie need go round in rags. Housing thus remains the best way for successful people to flaunt their success, and show the rest of the world they stand at the head of the peck order.

The desire to flaunt one's success is not a lovable characteristic, to be sure, but it is deeply ingrained in human nature. Even if the Communists should take over the country, housing would still remain a status symbol. The big shots in the party would demand the best housing in order to show the rest of us who's boss.

Since housing is always wanted as a status symbol, it will remain in great demand long after overcrowding as such comes to an end. And as long as housing construction continues, mortgage money too will be in strong demand and interest will persist as an economic phenomenon.

In grandfather's day, to be sure, if a man borrowed money to buy a status symbol that he could not afford to pay cash for, the purchase would prove a failure. No one would be impressed by a big house that carried a mortgage, or a big car bought on time. Nowadays, however, when so many successful people get large salaries but amass no savings, a great many persons "use their credit" to buy status symbols, and manage to overawe their fellow citizens in this way.

It is not for us to praise or censure them. To do so would be to miss the point of the argument entirely. All that concerns us is the sociological observation that the love of status symbols helps support the rate of interest.

Incidently, status symbols are not a tool of production. They do not take part in any "roundabout method of production", to use the phrase introduced by Böehm-Bawerk in his *Positive Theory of Capital*.[1] Hence any theory of interest that makes extensive use of status symbols is a far cry from Austrian doctrine, excellent though that was in its own day.

Because housing as a status symbol is forever in demand, it always provides an outlet for the nation's savings. Continuous prosperity, therefore, is never at the mercy of recurring new inventions like the

[1] Cf. Eugen V. Böehm-Bawerk, *The Positive Theory of Capital* (New York: G.E. Stechert and Co., Reprint 1923), ch. II. The original German edition was printed in Innsbruck in 1888.

railroad, the automobile, and modern armaments. No failure of new industries to emerge need lead to another long depression, as alleged by Keynes. Better explanations can be found to account for the frightful slump of the 1930s.

## 5. Marginal Utility and Constraints on Demand

Although prices for most consumers goods are governed by marginal utility, this rule does not apply to housing. To be sure, when a family buys food and clothing rather than housing, it gets the same satisfaction from the last dollar spent on food as on clothing. In the case of housing, however, a special constraint intervenes. Housing is bought on credit, while food and clothing are bought with cash. In the case of housing, the creditor usually refuses to lend as much as the borrower would like to borrow. The lender is concerned only with the safety of his loan. He disregards the wishes of the borrower. Many a family would like to spend as much as 30% of their income on housing, but banks usually refuse to lend more than 25%. An unsatisfied demand is thereby created and perpetuated.

The credit policies of the savings banks thus produce a distortion of family budgets throughout the entire country. People spend for housing only what they are allowed to spend, not what they would like to spend. As a result, marginal utility does not determine the rate of interest.

For our purposes, however, this fact proves to be a great convenience. It makes it possible for us to determine the elasticity of demand for housing without recourse to questionnaires or psychological investigations of any kind. All we need to do is look at the rules imposed by savings banks, and deduce from them the relation between the amount of loans made and the rate of interest obtained. It is a simple matter of turning the crank, and out comes the demand curve for home mortgage loans.

## 6. Elasticity of Demand

The demand for housing has an elasticity of unity.

Whenever people pay the same amount in total for varying quantities of what they buy, the elasticity of demand is equal to one. The lower the price, the more they buy; and the higher the price, the less they buy, but their total outlay remains the same. Their demand curve is then called a *constant outlay curve*. It is shaped like a rectangular hyperbola, and has the equation

$$pq = R \text{ or } p = R/q$$

where $p$ means price, $q$ quantity, and $R$ is a constant.

In the case of housing, $R$ is the constant yearly outlay on rent, or rent-equivalent in the form of interest, amortization, and real estate tax, as fixed by take-home pay.

When savings banks fix an arbitrary limit on mortgage loans, setting monthly payments at 25% of aftertax income, they make families spend a constant amount on housing. whether housing is cheap because interest rates are low, or whether it is costly because rates are high, makes no difference. Total outlay remains a constant. Hence the demand curve for housing displays unit elasticity.

Everybody buys shelter. Nobody is priced out of the market. Shelter is not like airplane travel, where tickets cost so much that most people never fly, even in this day and age. A drastic cut in airline fares would bring travel by plane within the means of many new customers, but such is not the case with shelter. Everybody is a customer already. To the extent that everybody spends 25% of his income on shelter, everybody exhibits a unit elasticity of demand.

The foregoing statement, to be sure, somewhat oversimplifies the problem. Yet it is a convenient first approximation. Some families, of course, pay nothing to a savings bank, since they own their homes free and clear. They stand outside of the market; they never borrow, they never repay. Other families live in rented apartments, but even in this case their pattern of consumption is much the same as that of their friends who live in single houses heavily mortgaged. Consequently it comes close to the truth to say that the demand for housing shows an elasticity of unity.

## 7. A Typical Borrower

Let us consider the case of a home buyer whose salary is $15,000 a year. The cost of the house he can buy will vary from $30,000 to $40,000, depending on the rate of interest he is charged by his bank. In any event, his annual payments will be $2,000 a year for 25 years. In the parlance of the mathematics of finance, these payments are called an *annuity certain*. The present worth of this annuity depends upon the rate of interest at which it is discounted, as shown in Diagram II.

```
                    Mortgagor's Borrowing Power

   Salary                                        $15,000
       Less social security and income taxes      -3,000
   Take-home pay                                   12,000


   Pledgeable fraction, 25% of take-home pay    $ 3,000
    Less real estate tax and fire insurance       -1,000
   Balance for interest and amortization           2,000


   Total payments made during the entire
     25 years, at $2000 a year              $50,000          $50,000
   Present worth of $2000 annuity certain
     for 25 years                      @8%: $21,350    @5%: $28,188

   Down payment @30% of cost       $ 9,150          $12,082
   Mortgage @70% of cost           +21,350          +28,188
       Total cost of house         $30,500          $40,270
```

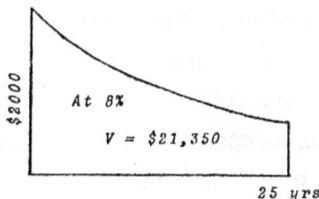

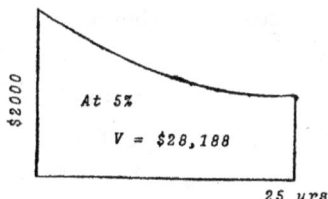

Figure 1       Figure 2

Diagram II. Present Value of Annuity Certain

In this diagram, the area *V* under the curve represents the present worth of the annuity of repayments that the borrower pledges to make in exchange for the bank's loan to him. In Figure 1 this area is smaller than in Figure 2. The higher the rate of interest, the smaller the area *V* will be. In other words, the higher the rate of interest, the less the annuity is worth today.

If a savings bank does not have money enough to meet the demand for loans at one rate, it can always raise the rate more and more until it can just meet this demand. Contrariwise, if the bank cannot find an outlet for all its cash receipts at one rate, it can always lower this rate, and pay more for each annuity. In other words, it can always loan a smaller or larger sum to each applicant, and the applicant can then buy a smaller or larger house, once he has saved enough money for the required down payment. To find the rate that will balance supply and demand, all the loan officer need do is feel his way along from day to day.

Every building boom or slump has two dimensions, namely (1) the total number of housing units constructed, and (2) the average cost of each unit. When interest rates rise, one or both of these dimensions will be reduced. Care, however, is required in reading the statistics, since published figures usually cover dimension (1) but not dimension (2). Thus in the year 1971, the number of units constructed was large despite high interest rates. The average size of each unit, however, was small, for many flats and mobile homes were included in the total for that year. Subsidized tenements also distorted the statistics.

## 8. Statistics on Building Permits

Every building boom or slump has two dimensions, namely (1) the total number of housing units constructed, and (2) the average cost of each unit. When interest rates rise, one or both of these dimensions will be reduced. Care, therefore, is required in reading the statistics, since published figures usually cover dimension (1) but not dimension (2). Thus in the year 1971, the number of units constructed was large despite high interest rates. The average size of each unit, however, was small, for many flats and mobile homes were included in the total for that year. Housing built by public authorities also distorted the statistics. As a result, the figures on building permits did not give a complete picture of the effect of high interest rates.

## 9. Depreciation and Amortization

Forty years and more ago it was not the custom for savings banks to require yearly amortization of their loans. In those days a typical loan ran for only three years, and then was renewed for a new amount at a new rate of interest. If the building was depreciating with age, the borrower was obliged to accumulate cash, and reduce the size of his loan. In effect he amortized his loan in this way, but the process was not as systematic as it is today.

When creeping inflation is under way, houses tend to increase in market value. In the meantime physical aging occurs also. One process may exactly offset the other. Thus it may come to pass that a new house costing $30,000 twenty-five years ago is still worth just $30,000 today. If so, the payments made by the family to amortize their mortgage in the meantime have indeed succeeded in building up their equity in the house. Had no inflation been under way, however, the amortization payments would have gone mostly to offset the depreciation that occurred in the meantime.

Fortunately a house when well maintained does not depreciate down to a residual value of zero at the end of a mere twenty-five years. On the contrary it may take a hundred years for a house to become altogether worthless. In that event only part of the money used to amortize the loan represents true depreciation, and the rest represents the increase in the owner's equity.

## 10. Hidden Saving

If the original owner and his heirs do not live in their house for a hundred years or more, until it goes to wrack and ruin, they can sell the house to another family, who will then sign a new mortgage note, and start paying interest and amortization all over again. Let us suppose the house cost $25,000 to begin with, and that the first mortgage was written for $20,000. If the new buyer pays $18,000 for the house after it is 25 years old, and signs a new note for $15,000, principal payments against this one house will come to $20,000 + $15,000, or $35,000 in all, even though the original cost of the house was only $25,000. Clearly a great deal of contractual saving goes on during all these years. If the second owner sells the house for $12,000 when it is 50 years old, and if his own note has been paid off completely by then, he can take this much money out of the house and reinvest it in U.S. savings bonds. The first owner could do so too with his $18,000 when he sold. Between them the two families would then own $18,000 + $12,000, or $30,000 worth of savings bonds in all. A house costing $25,000 would thus have produced $30,000 in savings bonds after 50 years, and the house itself, though old and much depreciated, would still remain in use.

## 11. Loans on Automobiles, Furniture, and Appliances

Instalment loans on automobiles, furniture, and appliances are not self-liquidating loans in the strict sense of that term. When the borrower buys an automobile he does not turn around and resell it at a profit afterwards in the way that a retail merchant resells his merchandise. Instead the car buyer pays his instalments with money saved from his wages. Automobile loans, therefore, are just like home loans. And like home loans, they require the borrower to maintain an equity in the property he pledges as security against his loan. Thus, if an automobile costs $3,000, the borrower must first make a downpayment of $1,000, let us say, before he can obtain an instalment loan for the balance of $2,000 still due.

The instalments on loans already outstanding, plus the interest thereon, provide an inflow of cash which a bank can then loan out again to other borrowers. This cash inflow on old loans is determined by contract, and is not affected by any change in the rate on new loans. The function of the interest rate, therefore, is to ration the fixed inflow of cash from old loans to the demands of borrowers for new loans.

Since the demand is very inelastic in the case of automobile buyers, because their loans are short and the interest payment is small compared to the monthly amortization, money for automobile loans will always be obtainable at a price, even if it has to be pulled away from other would-be borrowers. A sharp rise in the rate will not curtail the volume of automobile loans. Only a rise in the monthly amortization charge will do so. Such a rise can be brought about by shortening the life of the loan from 36 months to 30 or even 24. The Federal Reserve Board at certain times has had the power to do this by recourse to Regulation W[2].

While all this is true, nevertheless it is also true that the need for automobiles, furniture, and appliances is tied to the need for housing itself. They are all part of the same package. When a family buys a house they commit themselves to these other expenditures too. Their total outlay on the whole package is determined by their aftertax income. If the interest rate is low enough to let them swing a house, it is also low enough to let them buy furniture, appliances, and a car. The result is to make the demand for instalment loans on these items depend on the rate of interest on mortgage loans. Both enjoy the same elasticity of demand in the long run, though not in the short run.

---

[2] See Raymond P. Kent, *Money and Banking* (New York: Holt, Rinehart, & Winston, 1966), 5th ed., p. 560.

# CHAPTER VI
# THE CASH FLOW OF A SAVINGS BANK

## 1. The Workings of a Savings Bank

What really goes on in a savings and loan association, a coöperative bank, a mutual savings bank, or the savings department of a commercial bank?

Let us call every one of these a "savings bank" for short.[1] We shall soon see that these banks operate in a way quite different from what they are usually thought to do.

The purpose of this investigation is to show how changes in the rate of interest bring a bank's inflow and outflow of cash into balance.

Every bank deals with three groups of people, namely, "old borrowers", or *debtors*, a large group, "new borrowers" or *applicants*, a small group, and "receivers of interest" or *depositors*, a very large group.

The primary function of a savings bank is to collect money from the first group of persons and lend it to the second. The money is then used to buy new houses. The third group is entitled to the interest arising from this process.

When an applicant secures a mortgage loan, he signs a contract to make monthly payments of interest and amortization for many years afterwards. He thereby becomes a debtor. He thus changes his role from applicant to debtor for the remainder of the process.

The typical depositor leaves his original deposit in the savings bank to grow at compound interest for years on end. Some large depositors, to be sure, do indeed enter permanent dividend orders with the bank whereby they receive checks each quarter representing the interest earned on their deposits. These large deposits sometimes come from the proceeds of life insurance policies, or from an inheritance. Most deposits, however, are small, and their owners let them grow at compound interest until needed

It so happens that new deposits, on the one hand, and withdrawals of principal and interest, on the other hand, are about equal. The two offset each other. Consequently the rate of growth of assets turns out to be about the same as the rate of interest credited to savings accounts.

---

[1] Some commercial banks, to be sure, put their savings deposits into instalment loans rather than mortgage loans. Such banks are not included in our list of savings banks.

This coincidence, however, is not essential to my theory. If it so happened that a large number of depositors always took their interest out whenever it was credited to their accounts, then the total assets of the bank would grow less fast, but the bank would still function in much the same way.

## 2. Two Ways of Saving

There are two ways to save: either a man can pile up his assets, or he can pay off his debts. Either way results in true saving.

On the one hand, if a man buys a $1,000 bond and receives interest at 5%, he has $50 more to spend each year thereafter. On the other hand, if he pays off a debt of his amounting to $1,000 and bearing interest at 5%, he again has $50 more to spend each year. Both acts give the same result.

Whether a man increases his assets $1,000, or decreases his liabilities $1,000, either way he adds $1,000 to his net worth. This gain in his net worth shows that he has really succeeded in saving $1,000. Hence either process constitutes true saving.

Most saving nowadays consists of debt reduction. The typical saver goes into debt first, in order to buy an asset, and then he pays his debt off afterwards. Homeowners pay off their mortgages month by month, car buyers pay off their instalment loans, and corporations buy in their bonds for their sinking funds. All of these payments are acts of saving.

Saving done to extinguish a debt is usually contractual saving rather than optional saving. Yet it is not always so. If a man goes into debt to buy shares of stock, and then gradually repays his broker with money saved from his salary, he is performing optional rather than contractual saving. Yet he is still saving. Each payment reduces his debt and increases his net worth. The debits and credits are equal. Any credit to net worth indicates an act of saving.

In the less common case where a family saves to increase an asset rather than reduce a liability, they often choose life insurance as their best form of saving. While such saving is voluntary, it is nevertheless contractual rather than optional. Since insurance premiums bear a due date, they are quite unlike the hit-or-miss deposits of unspent salary that a man might put into his brokerage account from time to time.

In grandfather's day it was thought to be highly improvident for a family to go into debt to buy costly items like an automobile, a washing machine, or a sewing machine that the family could not pay cash for. Nowadays no one objects. An auto saves on carfare, and lets a man take a better job. A washing machine saves on laundry bills, and a sewing machine saves on clothing bills. It is sound finance, therefore, to buy these durable consumers goods with borrowed money, going into debt first and saving the money afterwards. Most families do just this. And when the family pays the monthly instalments on its debts, it is saving money just as truly as if it put the money in the bank first and spent it later. The new procedure, like the old, gives rise to the phenomenon of interest, but in a way all its own.

Interest arises because money to lend is scarce, and young people compete for loans. They want to buy houses and cars early in life. Age fifty is too late. They need these goods before they have saved up for them, not afterwards. Raising a family cannot wait on good old-fashioned thrift.

## 3. Financing the Purchase of a Home

In its simplest form, a mutual savings bank is a club whose members use it to help one another buy a house. All members put money into the club repeatedly, but each member takes money out only once.

A typical home buyer first deposits $1,000 in the club each year for six years, and then withdraws $6,000, plus the compound interest of $630 that has accumulated at 4% meantime. He also borrows another $14,100. This lets him buy a house costing $20,730. This member then continues to contribute $1,000 a year for twenty-five years more in order to pay off his loan of $14,100 with interest at 5%. He is thus obliged to save $1,000 a year for thirty-one years in all.

Mortgage debtors who are paying off their loans year by year are saving money at a rapid rate. This makes these persons the most important savers of *money* in the whole community. (The debt reduction, to be sure, is partially offset by the depreciation that accrues on the house meanwhile, and so the net saving is less than the gross debt reduction.)

Traditional theory fails to fit home loans. This theory says the interest rate is set by two forces, namely: (1) the attempt of the borrower to maximize his profit by resort to more plant and equipment, and (2) the attempt of the lender to secure wages of abstinence as a reward for saving. In the case of a home loan, however, the borrower, when he signs a mortgage note, is not trying to maximize any profit of his, for he is not in business. Nor when he saves money and repays his loan month by month, does he seek wages of abstinence. He abstains from consumption, to be sure, but he has no choice; he is under contract to save, and no one pays him to do so. Yet interest is a vital part of the whole transaction. Traditional theory, unfortunately, sheds no light on saving of this sort.

## 4. Loans and Repayments

If a savings bank makes its first loans in the year 1950, let us say, and if these loans run for twenty-five years, then the bank will receive its first repayments in 1951, its second in 1952, and so on, all the way through 1975. If this bank also makes a second set of loans in 1951, it will receive its first repayments on these additional loans in 1952, and so on, through 1976. With two sets of loans outstanding, the bank will receive two sets of repayments each year. And if other new loans are made each year thereafter, then in ten years there will be ten sets of repayments coming in.

These repayments supply money that can be loaned out again. In the year 1951, to be sure, repayments are not large enough to support the same volume of loans as were made in 1950, and so extra funds must be supplied from outside. Since borrowers pay interest, however, as well as amortization, they repay more than they receive. Meanwhile most depositors leave their dividends untouched. In due course, therefore, total repayments will become equal to first year loans. Once this point is reached, no further infusions of outside capital will be needed. The bank can then run on its own power.

To start a bank in the beginning takes more steps than to keep it going afterwards. To make loans in the first few years, a bank needs money from the outside, but to make loans in later years, it needs only the receipts from its first loans. Hence, in the beginning, a bank must have capital supplied by stockholders, or deposits supplied by savers, but afterwards it can keep going on the interest and amortization it receives from loans already outstanding. The problem of getting a bank started, however, is not the problem that concerns us now. All we need to consider now is how a bank works once it becomes a going concern. Start-up difficulties can be overlooked for the moment.

Contractual payments from debtors on their loans already outstanding provide most of the cash inflow of a savings bank. In any given year this inflow is a known constant. It cannot be changed by a rise or fall in the rate of interest on new loans now being made to new applicants.

The cost of running a bank is about 1% of deposits. It is covered by the spread between (1) the average rate charged on loans both old and new, and (2) the current rate paid on savings deposits of all kinds. Thus, when the first rate is 5%, the other will be 4%.

If new deposits, over and above interest earned, exceed withdrawals by a small amount, as usually happens, then the 1% cost of running the bank can be offset by a 1% gain from new deposits, and the bank will then be able to grow at a rate of 5%, the same as the rate it is earning on its invested assets. By coincidence, this is about how things often work out in practice.

## 5. The Lending Power of a Savings Bank

The amount of money that a savings bank can lend each year is fixed by the volume of its net receipts during that particular year. These receipts depend mainly (but not wholly) on the following two factors:

1. The rate of interest being earned on loans already made.
2. The yearly amortization on these same loans.

The loan contract usually provides that interest and amortization will be the same in total each year. If a loan is written for twenty-five years, let us say, amortization will be quite small in the first year, but very large in the last. In the first few years most of the money repaid goes to interest, but as the loan is gradually written down, interest on the unpaid balance becomes less and less. In the last few years most of the yearly payment goes to amortization. In fact, in the very last year amortization comes to almost 100% of the small balance still due.

A bank that has been in operation for many years has some old and some new loans on its books. If all the loans were written for twenty-five years in the beginning, and if the bank were not growing, then the average age of the loans would be twelve and one half years. In this case amortization might come to 4% of the unpaid balances. However, if the bank is growing steadily, it will have more new loans than old on its books, and so the average age of its loans might be only eight years, let us say, with seventeen years more to run. In this case amortization might be 6% of the unpaid balances.

Recently banks have been writing new loans at a much higher rate of interest than that on old loans. If the average rate on new loans is now 8%, whereas the rate on old loans was only 5%, then both together will show an average rate of 6½% or so. In fact, for a growing bank the average rate may reach almost 7%. Interest and amortization together will then add up to some 13% of total loans held by the bank.

## 6. How the Rate Is Reached

Will one dollar ever *equal* two dollars, or two dollars ever *equal* three dollars? No, this will never happen. But something else, almost as miraculous, happens every day. One dollar will often *buy* two dollars, or two will often *buy* three, provided the buyer consents to wait for the delivery of his purchase. This miracle is performed by the intervention of an interest rate and a suitable interval of time for the transaction to run to completion. Thus two dollars today will buy three dollars later, if the interest rate is 6% a year, and if the delivery of the three dollars is postponed for seven years.

Were the repayment to be less, then the interest rate would be less too, while if it were more, the rate would be more. Whenever payment and repayment are both known it is always possible to find some rate of interest that will make the one exchange for the other during any given time span.

Such an exchange is just what occurs when a savings bank makes a mortgage loan. The bank uses present money to buy future money. The interest rate then moves up or down until it reaches the right level to let the amount loaned now just suffice to buy the amount to be repaid later.

Assume that a savings bank enjoys a net cash flow of $10,000,000 in the year in question. The bank must ration this fixed sum out fairly to every man of good credit standing who applies for a loan, and pledges 25% of his present take-home pay for 25 years. If the amount pledged by the group of borrowers as a whole turns out to be quite large, what interest rate must the bank charge to cut the demand down to size? The bigger the demand, the higher the rate must be, of course, or else the bank will not have money enough to go round. The required rate can be found in the table below.

Determination of Interest Rate

| Supply of Money to Lend | Demand for Loans, i.e. Repayments Pledged Yearly for 25 Years | Resulting Interest Rate |
|---|---|---|
| $10,000,000 | $ 400,000 | 0% |
| 10,000,000 | 454,100 | 1% |
| 10,000,000 | 512,200 | 2% |
| 10,000,000 | 574,300 | 3% |
| 10,000,000 | 640,100 | 4% |
| 10,000,000 | 709,500 | 5% |
| 10,000,000 | 782,300 | 6% |
| 10,000,000 | 858,100 | 7% |
| 10,000,000 | 936,800 | 8% |
| 10,000,000 | 1,018,100 | 9% |
| 10,000,000 | 1,101,700 | 10% |

To compute the figures in the middle column, refer to the table of annuities in an actuarial textbook. Such a table will show that the present worth of an annuity of $1 for 25 years at 5% is $12.78. Consequently a much larger annuity, such as $782,300, would be worth much more, namely $10,000,000, as shown in the table above. The figure of $782,300 is obtained by dividing 12.78 into $10,000,000. Figures for other rates of interest can be found in the same way.[2]

The final rate always proves just right to let the savings bank loan all the money it has on hand to lend, now, with none left over, and with no would-be borrowers left unsatisfied at this particular rate. This is how the rate is reached.

The rate of interest thus determined is the rate paid by the homeowner to the bank. This rate is not the same as that paid to the depositors themselves. They get less. The bank first deducts its own expenses, and then pays its depositors whatever is left over.

The rate paid to depositors is not a fair measure of the fundamental rate for the economy as a whole. The really significant rate is the rate on home mortgages. This is the rate that is fixed by bargaining at arm's length between borrower and lender.

## 7. Growth of a Savings Bank

When a bank makes a loan, it pays some money out now in exchange for more money to be repaid later. In the case of a home loan, the repayment is broken into a long series of small instalments. These instalments may be looked upon as an *annuity certain*—in contrast to an annuity contingent on survival, such as a man might buy from a life

[2] See Reitz, Crathorne, and Reitz, *The Mathematics of Finance* (New York: Henry Holt & Co., 1921), p. 323, line 25.

insurance company. The cost to the lending bank of the annuity certain is the amount of money lent, i.e., the face value of the loan made. The value of the loan is thus the *present worth* of the annuity.

Borrowers, when they take out a loan, always promise to repay more in the end than they receive in the beginning. If depositors, meanwhile, leave their money in the bank to accumulate at compound interest, and do not withdraw the dividends credited to their accounts, the lending power of the bank grows larger and larger every year. Each year the bank's receipts on interest and amortization exceed its receipts the year before.

CASH FLOW OF A TYPICAL SAVINGS BANK
in millions of dollars

| No. | Item | Cash Dr. | Cash Cr. | Bonds + Mtges. Dr. | Bonds + Mtges. Cr. | Savings Dpsts. Dr. | Savings Dpsts. Cr. | Surplus Dr. | Surplus Cr. | Income Dr. | Income Cr. |
|---|---|---|---|---|---|---|---|---|---|---|---|
| 1 | Balances, at start of year | 5 | | 100 | | | 95 | | 10 | | |
| 2 | Amortization of loans and calling of bonds | 4 | | | 4 | | | | | | |
| 3 | Interest earned, at 5% | 5 | | | | | 3½ | | ½ | | 1 |
| 4 | Dividends paid by check | | ½ | | | ½ | | | | | |
| 5 | Other withdrawals | | 19½ | | | 19½ | | | | | |
| 6 | New deposits | 21 | | | | | 21 | | | | |
| 7 | Expenses and taxes | | 1 | | | | | | | 1 | |
| 8 | Losses | | | | 0 | | | | | 0 | |
| 9 | Balances | | 14 | | 96 | 99½ | | 10½ | | | |
| 10 | Totals | 35 | 35 | 100 | 100 | 119½ | 119½ | 10½ | 10½ | 1 | 1 |
| 11 | Balances | 14 | | 96 | | | 99½ | | 10½ | | |
| 12 | New loans made = net cash flow | 9 | 9 | | | | | | | | |
|  | Balance | 5 | | | | | | | | | |
| 13 | Balance at end | 5 | | 105 | | | 99½ | | 10½ | | |

The multicolumn journal above shows the cash flow of a typical savings bank for a single year. In this particular case the bank is paying its depositors only 3½% on their savings accounts. Back in the 1950s, before creeping inflation got underway, a rate as low as 3½% was fairly common.

In a quiet year, one not upset by disintermediation, inflation, high interest rates, or a credit squeeze, the main concern of a savings bank is to keep all its money at work. In such a year it usually happens that new deposits are just large enough to cover expenses, taxes, cash dividends and other withdrawals. The balance available for investment in new loans then turns out to be the same as the sum received from interest and amortization on old loans. Call this balance the "net cash flow" of the bank. Its size in no way depends on the rate of interest at which new loans are now being made. Instead it is fixed by old contracts already in force. This makes the supply of funds to lend a constant. As a result the demand for loans, all by itself, determines the outcome and sets the rate of interest. With demand in turn being strictly limited by the aftertax income of borrowers, the interest rate depends ultimately on this income, and on nothing else.

Unless the demand for money to borrow increases as fast as the supply of money to lend does, the rate of interest will decline. The lower the rate goes, the larger the present worth of the fixed annuity pledged by borrowers will become. In this way changes in the rate of interest will keep demand and supply in balance.

## 8. An Imaginary Ideal Savings Bank

Webster defines "ideal" as "existing in imagination only, imaginary, hypothetical, but lacking practicality". The word *ideal* is used in this sense when a physicist talks about Carnot's ideal heat engine, for instance. This engine is purely a theoretical concept, a tool of thought—but an extremely useful tool for all that.

I will now describe an ideal savings bank, analogous to Carnot's ideal heat engine. My ideal savings bank is likewise only a tool of thought. Nevertheless it turns out to be a very useful tool. By means of this tool I will later prove the Growth and Discount Theorem, as I shall call it.

The ideal savings bank suffers no credit losses, sustains no operating expenses, pays no taxes, and holds no uninvested funds. Its depositors leave their money in the bank to accumulate at compound interest; they do not take their dividends out in cash. Whenever any depositor walks into the bank to make a withdrawal, he always meets a friend who is about to make a new deposit of the same amount. They stand arm in arm at the teller's window, with the first man receiving the very same banknotes as his friend deposits. Hence the bank itself need hold no idle cash. This arrangement lets the depositors as a group have their cake and eat it too. (Commercial banks run in the same way. At the end of the day their deposits and withdrawals just about balance.)

My ideal savings bank makes mortgage loans, nothing else. All its loans are the same in length, 25 years for instance. They all run to maturity, none are paid off beforehand. But even if they were paid off beforehand, it would make no difference. If John Dow owns a house for seven years, let us say, and then sells it to Richard Roe, the new owner merely replaces the old. He takes out a new mortgage whose monthly payments are the same as before. While the fraction called interest and the fraction called amortization will differ on the new loan from the old, the total payment will remain the same. It is this total as such that constitutes the cash inflow of the bank. The bank will still receive the same income as before to relend. No change in the rate of interest will occur. Hence the fact that most Americans move from house to house every few years, and do not let their mortgage loans run to maturity, does not change the operation of my ideal savings bank.

This ideal bank enjoys a steady rate of growth, such as 5% per annum, year after year. At the end of 1950, for instance, it receives total interest and amortization of $1,000,000 on its various loans outstanding. At the start of 1951 it lends all this money to a new group of borrowers. Next year it has larger receipts and makes larger loans, 5% larger, since the bank is assumed to be growing at that rate. Income and outgo in this year will then be $1,050,000. In the following year the figure will be $1,102,500, with growth continuing at 5% compounded annually. We assume that the demand for loans, and the supply of money to lend, both grow at this same rate. Growth continues for 25 years, and into the 26th year too. At what rate of interest will loans be written at the end of the 25th year and the start of the 26th?

This rate will be 5%, as I will prove in the pages to follow.

The foregoing is a special case of the general Growth and Discount Theorem. In this particular case the rate of interest $i$ for new loans is equal to the rate of growth $g$ for repayments on old loans.

Although the rate of interest is affected by many factors, it is quite possible for growth alone, in and of itself, to produce an interest rate of 5%, 6%, 7%, or even 10%, as we shall soon see. Usually the rate of growth is the major factor—but not the only factor—in setting the rate of interest.

The following comparison of the ideal savings bank with the ideal heat engine will serve to summarize their essential features, thus:

# THE CASH FLOW OF A SAVINGS BANK

*Assumptions*

| *Ideal Heat Engine* | *Ideal Savings Bank* |
|---|---|
| 1. No heat losses | 1. No credit losses |
| 2. No friction losses | 2. No operating expenses |
| 3. No deviation from full load | 3. No idle cash |
| 4. Temperature measured from absolute zero | 4. Growth measured from start to finish of loan period |

*Deductions*

Efficiency equals ratio of (1) intake temperature less exhaust temperature to (2) intake temperature, i.e.

$$E = \frac{T_1 - T_2}{T_1}$$

Rate of interest on new loans equals rate of growth in repayments on old loans, i.e.,

$$i = g$$

*Diagrams*

pressure

volume

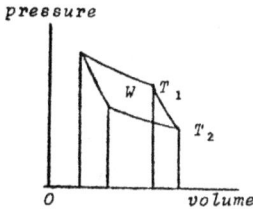

The meaning of this diagram is explained in most college textbooks on physics.

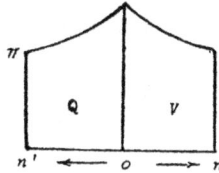

The meaning of this diagram will be explained forthwith.

*Diagram III: Carnot's Ideal Heat Engine and the Ideal Savings Bank*

## 9. The Flow of Repayments

When a bank is serving a growing community, the number of applicants for loans, together with their collective earning power, grows each year. Their demand for loans thus grows too. I assume, of course, that the money supply is allowed to grow enough to support this rising demand—but more on that subject later. Each year an increase occurs in the yearly repayments that a new set of applicants is willing and able to pledge for the right to borrow large sums from the bank. For any one year, this pledge may be represented by a series of 25-year payments, thus:

||||||||||||||||||||||||||

*Diagram IV: Yearly Repayments from a Single Group*

Next year the bars will be higher, and so on, year after year.

When the various series are set one under the other, in staggered fashion, they show that each set of bars is higher than the preceding set, as shown in Diagram V.

A   |||||||||||||||||||||||||||

B    |||||||||||||||||||||||||||

C      |||||||||||||||||||||||||||

D        |||||||||||||||||||||||||||

*and so forth*

*Diagram V:   Yearly Repayments from All Groups*

In any given year, one and only one bar from each series enters the sum of total repayments to the bank for that particular year. These individual bars are shown as heavy lines in the chart.

## 10. The Supply of Money to Lend

In order to see clearly just how the repayments add up, we should take a look at a very simple case, one where the bank makes loans for only five years instead of twenty-five.

At the *start* of the first year the bank lends to a set of borrowers called group A, at the start of the second to group B, the third to group C, the fourth group D, and the fifth E.

At the *end* of the first year, group A makes its first repayment of interest and amortization, at the end of the second year its second repayment, and at the end of the fifth its final repayment. In the sixth year this group drops out.

At the end of the second year, group B makes its initial repayment, and at the end of the sixth year its final repayment.

At the end of the third year, group C makes its initial repayment, and so on for group D and group E.

Group F becomes a borrower at the start of the sixth year, and makes its initial repayment at the end of that year. Group G does likewise in the seventh year, and so on for groups H, I, J. etc. to the end of the alphabet and beyond.

In the sixth year, as noted, Group A makes no repayments, Only groups B, C, D, E, and F do. In the previous year it was groups A, B, C, D, and E who made repayments.

In the fifth year, groups A, B, C, D, and E each make one repayment, or five in all. The total is made up of five separate payments, one from each group, and represented by five bars one under another in Diagram V. If the bars for any given year are now set side by side instead of one under another, then their tops will touch a compound interest curve. This curve portrays the growth side of my Growth and Discount Theorem

Were loans to be made for a term of twenty-five years instead of five right from the start, and were these loans to be 5% larger each year, then repayments would likewise show a growth rate of 5%, just as in the first case. The analysis would remain the same. The curve of receipts would still rise as shown in Diagram VI. The payments in this diagram, be it noted, are made all at the same time, all at the end of the twenty-fifth year.

*Diagram VI: Income to be Lent*

## 11. Growth in the Demand for Loans

Growth in the demand for loans depends mainly on three factors:

1. Growth in population in the bank's market area.
2. Growth in productivity per man-hour, and thus in hourly wages.
3. Further growth in the wage level merely because of inflation.

The total effect of these three factors is to increase the income of wage earners as a class. If the increase is 5% each year, then borrowers in group B will bid 5% more for loans this year than borrowers in group A did last year. Likewise borrowers in group C will bid 5% more next year than those in group B do this year, and so on for D compared with C, E with D, F with E, etc.

In order for demand to grow at 5%, the general money supply must grow at 5% too, if velocity stays the same.

## 12. The Growth and Discount Theorem

Let us assume that growth goes on at a steady rate for many, many years. At the end of any 25-year period, when the bank makes loans at the start of the 26th year, what rate of interest will emerge? With demand still growing at 5% in the 26th year, when group Z borrows, will the rate of interest charged to borrowers in this group turn out perchance to be 5% too?

These latest borrowers, like their predecessors, obtain their loans by selling collectively an annuity certain to the savings bank, with repayments running for 25 years. Must these repayments be discounted at 5% in order that income and outgo shall balance for the bank?

The effect of a discount rate, in contrast to an interest rate, can be portrayed on a diagram as a descending rather than an ascending curve. This curve represents the discount side of my Growth and Discount Theorem, as shown in Diagram VII.

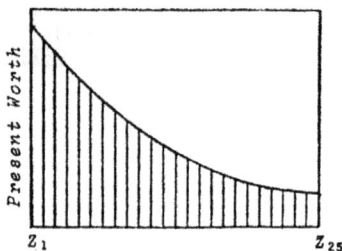

Diagram VII: Payments to be Received, Discounted

By looking at Diagrams VI and VII the reader can see that the total for the bars in one diagram will prove equal to the total in the other diagram if each bar in one diagram just matches a corresponding bar in the other diagram. Such will indeed be the case if the rate of growth in the first diagram is equal to the rate of discount in the second.

The loans here being made are instalment loans. The borrower receives all his money at the *start* of a given year, but he waits until the *end* of this year to make his first repayment. Hence this first repayment must be discounted back for a whole year to find its present worth on the day when the loan is made to begin with. Likewise the second instalment must be discounted back for two years— and so on, all the way to the final instalment.

If demand is growing at 5%, let us say, then borrower Z in the 26th year can pledge a repayment 5% larger than borrower Y in the 25th year did. Nevertheless, when this first instalment $z_1$, is discounted at 5%, its present worth turns out to be just equal to the instalment paid the year before by the earlier borrower, the very man who borrowed in the 25th year. The same process applies to the second instalment $z_2$ for the 26-year man compared with the instalment $x_2$ for the 24th-year man, and so on, one after another.

The argument may now be put the other way around, thus:

In order for the bank to lend all of its cash receipts for any given year, when these receipts have been growing at the rate of 5% a year, it must lend them at 5% the next year, provided growth in demand continues at 5% during that year. In other words, for any rate of growth, high or low, $i = g$.

Each of the 25 bars in Diagram VII represents the *present worth* of an instalment to be paid in the future on a new loan to be made by the bank now. This new loan will be made at the end of the 25th year and the start of the 26th. The *present worth* of each of these future year-end repayments, discounted back to the start of the 26th year and end of the 25th, is represented by this new series of bars. But none of the payments in this new diagram are made at the same time; instead, they are all paid in sequence, one after another.

When the bank makes a loan, it is buying an annuity certain, as noted earlier. The *cost* of this annuity is represented by the total of all the bars in Diagram VI. The *value* of this annuity, in turn, is represented by the total of all the bars in Diagram VII. Cost and value are equal. When the bank makes the purchase, it credits Cash for the cost of the annuity, and debits Notes Receivable for the value thereof. If the face of the loan is $20,000, the debit and credit are each $20,000.

In order to make *present value* in Diagram VII become equal to *total cost* in Diagram VI, the proper interest rate $i$ must first be ascertained, and then used for discounting the annuity purchased. Here $i$ is the unknown we seek to find. If a rate of 6%, for instance, makes the present value come out too small, then a lower rate, such as 5%, must be used. There always exists some rate high or low that will do the trick. This rate is the one at which the new loan will be made.

The foregoing is a statement of an important special case of my Growth and Discount Theorem. A mathematical proof is set forth in the Appendix.

In this special case just described it turns out that the rate of interest is equal to the rate of growth. This is an extremely interesting discovery. It shows that growth in the demand for loans of all kinds is a major cause of interest on bonds and mortgages in modern America. Not demand alone, but *growth* in demand, is what counts.

## 13. Initial Capital

How much capital does it take to get a savings bank started to begin with? The answer depends on how high the interest rate goes in the first few years. In the beginning, when the very first loans are being made, and group A is bidding for money, all of the money lent that year must come from outside. At the very start, the bank receives no repayments of interest and sinking fund on outstanding loans. It has no such loans on its books. If demand is keen and outside funds are scarce, the first loans may be made at 10%, 15%, or even 20%. The money goes to the highest bidders at whatever rate will clear the market. Consequently a very small amount of outside capital will suffice to start a bank if the interest rate stands high enough in the first year.

In the second year, when group B applies for loans, the bank enjoys an inflow of repayments on old loans already made to group A. This inflow is much less than the outflow was in the first year, to be sure, and so new capital is needed in the second year too. This new capital, plus the repayments, is the total amount to be loaned in the second year. The strength of the demand for loans in that year will then determine the rate of interest on these new loans. This rate could well be lower than before. If new capital is as large as before, and if demand is the same as before, the rate will indeed be lower. But if new capital is less, with the result that capital plus repayments come to the same total as before, the rate will stay as high as before. Evidently in the second year, just as in the first, the amount of new capital required cannot be specified as equal to some fixed and inflexible sum. Instead, the bank can make do with whatever amount it can obtain from outside. The interest rate takes up the shock.

The same rule applies in the third year, the fourth, and the fifth.

In the sixth year, however, if all loans run for five years only, the bank can proceed without recourse to outside capital. But if loans run for twenty-five years, it will take the bank twenty-five years to stand on its own feet, and reach a state where the rate of interest on its loans is equal to the growth in demand for them.

Many American savings banks, however have a history going back a hundred years or more, and so it is not necessary to pinpoint the exact year when they could have become independent of new capital. Suffice it to say that independence becomes possible at some point determined in large measure by the length of the loans each bank is making.

In poor countries, where free capital is scarce, it is hard to get a savings bank started. Yet without such a bank men cannot borrow on mortage loans to buy new houses. And without good housing they cannot stay healthy and rested, and perform a good day's work. As a result, the whole country is handicapped.

One way out is for a poor country to seek capital abroad. Seed capital, so called, can be a great blessing. In times past, England furnished a great deal of money for such uses. Yet in the end she got no thanks for it. The recipients accused her of milking her colonies. Although England did indeed take back a large volume of interest on her investments abroad, she also continued to add to these investments on a great scale year after year. Did she ever get back as many billions in the end as she poured out along the way? And was she not entitled to do better than just break even?

## 14. Deviations from the Ideal

Critics of my theory will doubtless say, "What good is it? After all, everyone knows that the ideal savings bank never is seen in practice. Every bank faces costs of operation. Many depositors withdraw their interest, while many others make new deposits. Then there are taxes to consider. So it goes. Deviations from the ideal are many indeed."

Moreover, when we come to apply the theorem to life insurance companies, which, like savings banks, are large sources of new capital, we again find many deviations from the ideal.

At first blush these criticisms seem very damaging. But are they really so bad in fact?

Reverting to Carnot's ideal heat engine, we see that it too is open to similar criticism. Yet it proves to be extremely useful in practice. To be sure, no actual engine is free from heat and friction losses. But how large is each loss? How can it be reduced? Efforts to reduce losses led inventors to go from reciprocating steam engines to turbines, and from one-cylinder gasoline engines to six and eight-cylinder engines. But most of all, the theory showed what really was needed, namely hotter steam for turbines and higher compression for autos. Thus Carnot's ideal heat engine proved to be an extremely useful tool of thought after all.

The same verdict will prove true for the foregoing special case of the Growth and Discount Theorem. Whenever this special case fails to fit the facts exactly, it simply brings to light important forces that affect the rate of interest in practice, influences that heretofore have been swept under the rug. This is all to the good. It only makes the theorem so much the better.

### 15. Effect of a Sudden Rise in Demand for Loans

The fundamental cause of growth in the demand for loans is growth in the demand for housing. Housing explains it all. This rise in the demand for housing may result from various factors, such as an increase in population or a rise in hourly wages, when financed by a sufficient increase in the money supply. In any event it is *growth* in the demand for housing that is the ultimate cause for the payment of interest on mortgage loans.

If a 5% growth in demand and a 5% rate of interest make the income and outgo of a savings bank equal to start with, and if demand now undergoes an increase larger than 5% next year, the supply of funds to lend will nevertheless show no sudden increase during that particular year. Consequently some of the enlarged demand must go unsatisfied at the old rate of interest. Applicants will compete against each other, and will bid the rate up. The successful ones will be those who offer to pay $782 a year, let us say, or interest at 6%, for 25 years in order to borrow $10,000 now, whereas earlier borrowers needed to pay only $710 a year to borrow the same amount at 5%. Whenever the demand for home loans increases more than usual, the interest rate goes up.[3] The mechanism is automatic.

---

[3] At 5% compounded annually, the present worth of an annuity of one dollar a year

High interest rates on home loans are just inflation in another form. When a rise in wages enables consumers to pay more for a leg of lamb, it also enables them to pay more for a bundle of banknotes. This bundle is then used to build a house. Buyers pay for this bundle on the instalment plan. A higher interest rate is simply a new price for a bundle of the old size. Both food and banknotes thus obey the same law. Inflation hits them both alike.

Any family that fails to win a higher wage during inflation must still pay a higher rate of interest. Then it perforce must borrow less, and make do with a smaller house. When inflation sends prices and interest rates up, people whose income is left behind have to economize on mortgage loans along with food and clothing. These expenses are all alike.

## 16. The Propensity to Consume

In prosperous times people find it easier to save money and put it in the bank. But in such times their borrowing power is higher too, and so they spend more for houses and cars, and withdraw more money to make down payments on these purchases. What is the result? When their incomes rise in prosperity, do they really save a large percentage of the final increment, as Keynes asserts when he lays so much stress on the "marginal propensity to consume?"

## 17. Near Money

Savings deposits are often called "near money", but they can't be used to pay the butcher's bill until they are converted into demand deposits. When you make a withdrawal from your savings deposit, the teller hands you a check drawn on the bank's own demand deposit already existing in some commercial bank. Your withdrawal merely takes the money away from some would-be home buyer who would otherwise have been able to borrow it from the savings bank. Now you spend it instead, but total spending does not increase. Evidently, in its effect upon the price level, near money is not real money.

---

paid at the end of each year for 25 years is $14.094, and so the present worth of $710 is $10,000. Likewise, at 6% the present worth of one dollar is $12.783, and so the present worth of $782 is $10,000 also. In the tables of a book on the Mathematics of Finance, the present worth of such an annuity certain is represented thus:

$$a_{\overline{n}|} = (i - v^n)/i$$

# CHAPTER VII
# LOANS ON APARTMENT HOUSES

## 1. Apartments vs. Single Houses

Apartments and single houses are substitutes for each other. They are not perfect substitutes, to be sure, because each has its own good and bad points. Nevertheless they do compete with each other well enough to keep the cost of living about the same in each kind of dwelling.

One difference, however, should now be mentioned. Although a family living in a single house cannot commit itself to monthly payments in excess of 25% of its aftertax income, a family living in an apartment is free to exceed 25% if it wishes to set up its budget in this way. In other words, people living in a mortgaged home are not free to push their outlay on shelter to the point determined by marginal utility, while people living in rented quarters are quite free to do so. But this difference is usually not very important.

Not all apartment dwellers, to be sure, desire to spend more on rent than homeowners do. Some apartment dwellers may in fact spend less. They may curtail their spending because they think apartment life is not as pleasant as home ownership. If they were to buy a house of their own, they might rearrange their budgets and spend more on shelter than they do now, even though this would entail economies in other directions.

A family's preference for a private house over an apartment depends somewhat on the number of children and their age. Many families think that a single house with a wide lawn is desirable for growing children. After the children have grown up, however, the parents may feel that a small apartment requires less housework and is more conveniently located.

To some extent the choice between apartments and private houses also depends upon habit. People who have grown up in the heart of a big city sometimes do not like the suburbs, and vice versa. Much depends on personal taste.

Although some families have strong preferences, there are others who make their choice mainly on dollars and cents. They compare the rental of an apartment with the mortgage charges on a private home. If urban rents go up, they buy a house in the suburbs. On the other hand, if interest rates on mortgages go up, they remain in a city apartment. Because the two different modes of living compete with each other so strongly, their prices must remain nearly the same, quality considered.

## 2. Rigid Budgets

It is a common assumption of economic theory that family budgets are all a matter of free choice on the part of consumers. This rule, however, needs to be taken with a large grain of salt. Custom and convention have a great influence on the way people spend their money. Once a family has decided how much they can spend for a house, they have thereby determined the sort of neighborhood in which they will live. Having moved into a certain neighborhood, they are expected to follow its conventional pattern of consumption.

The home furnishings they put in their house, the kind of cars they drive, the clothes they wear, the entertaining they do, the contributions they make to charity, the schools and colleges they send their children to, all belong to a certain pattern. A man must adhere to this pattern because he is told "People expect it of you". He has little freedom of choice.

Almost the only part of the family budget that is completely flexible is the recreation account. Here is the one place where people can do just what they like. One family can spend its money on a cottage at the beach, another on travel, a third on golf and skiing, a fourth on hunting and fishing, a fifth on gardening and photography, a sixth on boating, a seventh on music and movies, and so forth.

Were it not for flexibility in recreation, as well as diversity in jobs held by breadwinners, we would all become more and more alike. The way we live, the way we spend our time, that is what makes us what we are. The more we act alike, the more we grow alike.

## 3. Comparative Cost

The amount of satisfaction that a family can obtain from its outlay on shelter depends on what it costs to build an apartment house on the one hand, and a single house on the other hand. The land occupied by an apartment house, being located near the center of a city, is more expensive than land in the suburbs. Yet fewer square feet per family are needed. On balance, therefore, land rent per family is usually less for an apartment house than for a single family dwelling. The cost of the structure is also less per family. If the building is ten stories high, one roof will take care of ten families instead of only one. Likewise a single large furnace for ten families is cheaper than ten small furnaces for ten single houses. The same considerations apply to the cellar and the walls. For this reason it is cheaper to house people in apartments than in single houses. If the investment per family is less, the real estate tax ought to be less, except for the fact that tax rates per thousand dollars of assessed value are usually much higher in big cities.

Financing charges are also higher on apartment houses. Banks look on these buildings as business ventures subject to substantial risk, and so they charge a higher rate on the mortgage loan, and require faster amortization. The owner of the apartment house, moreover, must receive a good profit on his equity money, while the private homeowner expects only 4% or 5%, such as he could get in a savings bank. But the real estate operator, with his capital at risk, expects 10% or 15%. This return, moreover, must come after the payment of Federal and state income taxes. As a result, the pretax return must run as high as 20% or 30%. It can be somewhat lower, to be sure, if the profit is to be taken in the form of capital gain, a recourse that is open to the first owner of the building. For all that, financing costs for an apartment house are a good deal higher than for an owner-occupied single family dwelling.

## 4. Migration to the Suburbs

When all is said and done, it is probably much cheaper to house people in apartment houses than in single houses. The accommodations, however, do not seem as desirable to most tenants. For that reason there has been a large migration of families from the cities to the suburbs.

This migration has been held in check by two forces. First, families need to acquire a down payment before they can buy a suburban house, and second, landlords try to keep their properties fully rented even if they have to reduce the rent. This price cutting has been concealed by the effects of inflation in recent years. If landlords had not felt the competition from thousands of new single houses built in the suburbs, they would have increased their rents even more than they have actually done so far. By holding their rents down, landlords have been able to keep their buildings fully occupied. In fact they have created what appears to be a housing shortage in many cities. If rents were higher, this shortage would disappear. Many families would move to the suburbs, others would double up with their in-laws, and in extreme cases a young couple would not get married in the first place.

## 5. The Demand for Loans

As in the case of single houses, the effective demand for apartments is derived from the earning power of the head of the family. Rentals cannot exceed his ability to pay. Nor can they exceed his willingness to pay, because his family will make do with a smaller apartment rather than go hungry or ill clad.

Carrying the argument a step further, we see that the rent received determines the profit of the landlord, and this profit then determines the market value of his apartment house. The market value in turn determines the assessed value, and the latter determines the real estate tax. The market value likewise limits the mortgage loan on the apartment house, and thus limits the interest and amortization payable on it. All of these limits apply, of course, to old buildings already constructed and rented, not to proposed buildings that may never be erected after all. For old buildings, a chain of causation runs from the first limit to the last.

Because the aftertax income of the tenants ultimately determines the size of the mortgage loan, it turns out that apartment houses are just like private homes as regards the way in which they help to set the level of interest rates throughout the whole economy. It makes little difference whether the demand for shelter reaches the savings banks by one route or the other. The application for mortgage loans can come either from the homeowner or the landlord. In either case the size of the demand is limited by the aftertax income of the occupants of the building. For single houses, the rule is that the owner can pledge 25% of his aftertax income to service the loan. For apartment houses the rule is that the tenant can pledge somewhat more if he wishes, but the amount is limited by the other demands upon his budget. In both cases the demand for loans goes back to what families can or will spend on shelter as compared with food and clothing. Throughout the entire field, considerations of the technical productivity of capital, and the advantages of Böehm-Bawerk's famous roundabout method of production, have no place at all.

In order to emphasize the difference between my theory of interest and the traditional Marginal Productivity Theory, I should like to call mine the *Home Loan Theory of Interest*.

## 6. Rent Control and Rent Subsidies

In time of war, if new construction stops, and a housing shortage threatens, then rent control may be required. In time of peace, however, when new construction thrives, rent control is most unwise. Yet in 1974, twenty-nine years after the end of World War II, rent control is still in force in New York City, and has just been launched in Boston.

Rent control hurts the market value of every apartment house already occupied. Assessed value declines, and tax revenue shrinks. Rent control is indeed a shortsighted policy for a city to adopt. Although rent control applies only to old buildings, nevertheless it threatens new buildings too. Any investor who buys a new apartment house now faces the risk that a rise in his rents will be outlawed later. If so, his investment will no longer prove a good inflation hedge. He would do better to put his money elsewhere.

To the extent that rent control discourages the building of new apartment houses, it reduces the demand for mortgage loans thereon, and depresses the rate of interest through out the whole economy.

Rent subsidies, sometimes paid to poor families by the government, let these tenants pay higher rentals for the same quarters they would occupy anyway. In the slums no other people would try to live in these buildings. The result, therefore, is usually to pull rentals up, and raise the market value of the tenements themselves. Their loan value rises too. This increases the demand for mortgages, and sends interest rates up. Thus rent subsidies, if granted because interest rates are too high to begin with, only make matters worse.

# CHAPTER VIII
## THE PRICING OF NOTES, BONDS, AND MORTGAGES

### 1. Current Yield, and Yield to Maturity

The current yield on a note or bond and its yield to maturity are seldom one and the same. Only if an issue is bought at 100, or par as it is called, will the two yields be just the same. Otherwise not.

Consider a 4% bond that was issued many years ago, but still has ten years more to run. If it now sells for 80, its current yield is 4/80 = 5%. But the man who buys it now at a discount of 20 points from par will also make a profit of 20/80 = 25% on his investment in ten years, and so he receives 2½% extra per year. Adding this appreciation of 2½% to the current yield of 5%, he comes out with a total of 7½%. Allowing for compound interest, however, he gets a little less, namely 6.79%, according to the bond tables. Current yield and yield to maturity evidently are not the same.

The contrast is even clearer for a bond selling at 101 and due in only one year. If this bond carries a 6% coupon, its current yield will be nearly 6%. But the buyer will take a loss of one point when the bond is paid off, and so his yield to maturity will be only 5%—or 4.95%, to be exact, according to the bond tables. Here again, current yield and yield to maturity are not one and the same.

### 2. Purchase and Sale of IOUs

Lending money is like making wares to sell. When the lender grants a loan to start with, he buys an IOU. This piece of paper is his raw material. He holds it to maturity, and then he sells it back to the borrower at a profit. When the borrower redeems his note, the lender stamps "PAID" on it.

The profit which the lender makes is called interest or discount. If the profit is collected at the end, with the lender loaning $100,000 today and collecting $106,000 at the end of the year, the profit is called interest at 6%. But if the profit is collected in the beginning, with the lender loaning only $94,000 today and collecting $100,000 later, the profit is called discount. This discount of 6% is equivalent to interest at 6.38%.

Lending money is also like making wine. A winery buys grape juice, lets it ferment for several years, and sells the product at a markup in the end. A bank, for its part, buys an IOU, lets it age, and sells it at a markup too. But the bank, unlike the winery, knows beforehand who will buy its paper when mature. The buyer will be none other than the borrower himself when he redeems his own note. The bank knows the price the buyer will pay, and the date the sale will occur. All of these details are spelled out when the original contract is signed and the bank buys its raw material to begin with. In some ways, therefore, making loans is easier than making wine. Yet both procedures are akin to manufacturing in general, for both convert raw material into finished product.

If a lender buys a long-term bond instead of a one-year loan, the paper he buys consists of a series of coupons as well as the principal itself, with the latter being payable twenty or thirty years hence. The lower the price the lender pays for the bond as a whole, the higher his gross profit will be.

Since the coupons come due one after another, the lender receives a periodic revenue from selling these coupons back to the borrower, and when the principal itself comes due, the lender receives a further revenue, in a lump sum. Call the total revenue R, and the cost Q. The gross profit G will then be $G = R-Q$. The spacing of total revenue piece after piece will depend, of course, on the size of the coupons compared with the principal, but all bonds with the same coupons, principal, and risk should still sell for the same price.

Bonds, even good bonds, if their coupon rate is low and their date of maturity distant, sometimes sell at a deep discount from par. On May 26, 1970, U.S. Treasury 3½s of 1990, for instance, sold as low as 60. For an outlay of $600, therefore, a lender could buy 40 coupons worth $17.50 each every six months, and one stripped bond worth $1,000 on February 15, 1990. The face value of coupons and principal combined was thus $700 + $1,000 = $1,700, or nearly three times the cost of the raw material itself. But to make this assured profit of $1,100 the holder would be obliged to wait twenty years in all.

Some lenders don't mind waiting. Savings banks and insurance companies, for instance, have nothing else to do with their time. Yet they never need pay $1,700 today for an IOU worth $1,700 in the end.

Too many IOUs are offered for sale to them. Competition among sellers of IOUs—among borrowers, that is—drives the price of this paper down.

Lenders have only a limited amount of cash to spend for bonds and mortgages. In any given year the cash intake of insurance companies, pension funds, savings banks, and other institutional investors is fixed by old contracts already in force. It is independent of today's interest rate. Their demand curve is thus a fixed outlay curve. The more IOUs they buy, the less they can pay for each. If Q is the constant cash outlay they can make, and if c is the price per unit of the IOUs they buy, while q is the quantity or number of units bought, then their demand curve is a rectangular hyperbola whose equation is $Q = cq$ or $c = Q/q$.

## 3. Interest and Saving

Most loans involve two acts of saving, not one alone, the first act occurring when money is accumulated to make the loan, and the second when it is accumulated again to repay the loan.

Sometimes the lender is under contract to save in the beginning, but always the borrower is under contract to do so in the end. When the lender buys life insurance, for instance, he is under contract, and when the borrower repays his bond on the due date, he too is under contract. Here neither man saves just to earn interest.

The lender, to be sure, may not always be a contractual saver. Sometimes he is merely a precautionary saver. Only rarely, however, does he accumulate money at age 25 in order to spend the interest on it at age 45. At 45, to be sure, he may prepare for retirement at 65, but at middle age he usually lets his employer do his saving for him, through a pension fund, where he thinks the money comes out of some one else's pocket, not his own.

Sometimes a homeowner may pay interest on his mortgage loans, and amortize this loan too year after year, yet no net saving on his part may occur. If his house depreciates as fast as he pays his loan off—which seldom happens, to be sure—then his house will be worthless by the time it is all paid for, and the homeowner will have saved nothing meanwhile. His outlay will then be *expense*, not saving.

## 4. The Price That Clears the Market

Suppose for the moment that we know how many bonds will be offered for sale in a certain year. (Elsewhere I consider how this supply is determined.) Knowing this supply on the one hand, and knowing the shape of the demand curve on the the other hand, we can then find the price that will clear the market, as shown in Diagram VIII:

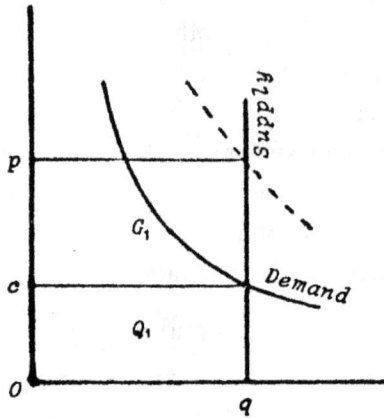

Diagram VIII: Lender's Gain

In the usual case bond interest is paid semiannually year after year until the bond matures, but to simplify the diagram let us assume for now that the interest is deferred, and paid all in one lump sum at the end. Interest will then be included in the redemption price $p$. On long loans of twenty years or more this price $p$ will lie far above the original cost $c$ paid by the lenders when they first buy their bonds.

In this diagram the cost $c$ is determined by the intersection of (1) the vertical supply curve rising from a given point $q$ with (2) the constant outlay curve $cq = Q$. The position of this latter curve depends on the quantity of money $Q$ that lenders have on hand to spend for paper to put into their portfolios. If lenders have more money to spend next year than this, the demand curve will rise, and so will the initial cost $c$ of the bonds. But the final price $p$ will remain the same. As a result the gross profit $G$ will be less in the end, provided the supply of bonds $q$ stays the same as before. And the less the gross profit, the less will be the interest or discount that lenders will earn on their loans, since profit and interest are merely two names for the same thing in this case.

## 5. Changes in the Interest Rate

In Diagram VIII, the interest rate would become zero the second time around if lenders reinvested all their interest received. Were lenders to retain all the gross profit $G_1$ they earned on their first set of loans, and were they to add this extra money to the original sum $Q_1$ which they had lent the first time, then they would send the price of IOUs way up. The second time around they would have on hand a new sum of money $G_1 + Q_1$ to lend. The rectangular hyperbola representing the demand curve for bonds, mortgages, and other paper would shift upwards in this second round, as shown by the dotted line, and would pass through the right-hand corner of the large rectangle whose area is $G_1 + Q_1$. Thus, in the second round, the lenders would pay out as much money for their paper at the start as they would get back in the end. No profit $G$ would emerge this time. The resulting interest rate would be zero.

Two assumptions, be it noted, underlie this special case, to wit: (1) None of the interest received the first time is withdrawn by lenders. Instead, all of it is saved and loaned out again next time. (2) No growth occurs in the number of IOUs sold by borrowers in the second cycle.

If the number of IOUs increases, however, as it will when the country is growing and the demand for money to borrow is rising, then the rate of interest will not fall to zero after all. Zero interest rates are thus a purely hypothetical phenomenon.

For an altogether different special case, Diagram VIII shows that the cost $c$ would stay as low, and the interest rate $i$ would stay as high, in the second cycle as the first, *provided that* the lenders withdrew *all* of their gross profit $G_1$; the first time, saving none of it to relend next time.

In still another case, if part of the gross profit is saved and loaned out again, and if the number of IOUs increases also, then the two changes can offset each other. When growth occurs in both demand and supply, as usually happens, the interest rate can stay nearly the same from one time to the next.

A bank is a firm, just like a farm, a factory, or a retail store. It too is ruled by the Current Assets Mechanism. Its current assets, or its quick assets Q, are spent in the beginning for fixed costs C, and for labor and raw materials M. For a bank, newly purchased IOU's are its raw material. These change slowly into finished goods, the sale of which provides the bank with its revenue R. When the matured notes receivable are collected in cash, they become quick assets Q again. The bank, like other firms, can then embark on a new turnover of its working capital. The gross profit G that the bank makes each time is called interest. All of this is described in my book entitled *The Current Assets Mechanism*, where I use the same symbols as here.

In order to make a net profit P = G - C, a bank like any other firm requires growth in the demand for its wares year after year. Otherwise, if it reinvests all its earnings every time, and if its competitors do likewise, supply eventually catches up with demand, and profits vanish.

## 6. Exchanges, Refundings, and Extensions of Debt

Exchanges, refundings, and extensions of debt do not in themselves cause any rise or fall in the rate of interest. They merely put as much new money back into the market as they take out.

A simple exchange, in fact, does not require the use of any new money at all. Exchanges of this sort are made by the U.S. Treasury many times a year. When a certain issue of bills or notes matures, the Treasury offers a new issue in exchange. The Federal Reserve Banks almost always accept the exchange completely, and most private holders accept the exchange up to 70% or 80% of the total number of maturing bills or notes in their hands. As a result, the Treasury needs to dip into its cash for only a small fraction of the total issue. The net leakage, therefore, is usually quite small.

Most industrial companies use sinking funds to reduce the size of their bond issues before maturity.[1] In this way a 25-year bond issue is often reduced to half of its original size by the time it comes due. The purpose of a sinking fund is to make sure that an issue will be small enough to refund with ease when it matures. If the issue totals $50,000,000, for instance, in the beginning, and is reduced to $25,000,000 by maturity, the sum of $25,000,000 is the final amount then paid back in cash by the borrower. To raise this money the borrower usually sells a new bond issue. Often the new bonds can be sold to the holders of the old bonds. In any event, these holders usually take their money and put it into some other bond issue, the sellers of which then have money available for taking up the new issue. Because

[1] Public utility companies, unlike industrial companies and railroads, often omit sinking funds, as in the case of American Telephone.

a refunding of this sort puts just enough new money back into the bond market to pay for itself, it can be called self-financing. Consequently the new issue does not tend to raise or lower the prevailing rate of interest.

The coupon on the new issue, however, will often be different from that on the old, because interest rates will usually have changed in the meantime. The return on the new issue thus adapts itself to the going rate. But refunding issues do not in themselves alter the general interest rate.

While refundings do not change the interest rate, they may nevertheless have some effect on short-term rates as contrasted with long-term rates. In the case of a 25-year Treasury bond, for instance, this bond just prior to maturity will be a short-term issue even though it was a long-term issue when it was first brought out. Three months previous to maturity its remaining term will be so short that it will compete with 91-day Treasury bills for a place in the secondary reserves of commercial banks. If the Treasury replaces this 25-year bond at maturity with a new 25-year bond, it will be offering a long-term issue in place of a short-term. When the Treasury does this on a great scale, as has happened on occasion, long-term Treasury issues fall in price somewhat. Meanwhile Treasury bills rise in price a little. In other words, when the Treasury undertakes to extend the average maturity of its debt, long-term interest rates go up and short-term rates go down. This effect appears even though the federal budget is in balance, and even though the total volume of government bonds outstanding remains the same. Extensions of debt may be said to affect the pattern of interest rates without affecting their average level.

In the short-term money market, as contrasted to the long-term, a tremendous volume of refunding goes on all the time. Many corporations who sell three-months or six-months commercial paper come back for renewals repeatedly. Each time they renew their paper, the rate may change up or down somewhat. The volume of the new debt, however, being the same as the old, mere refunding of the debt does not change the level of rates in general.

The same rule applies when different companies take turns in borrowing from commercial banks. If Company A borrows for the three months of January, February, and March, while Company B borrows for April, May, and June, and Company C for the third quarter, and

Company D for the fourth quarter, all in one year, and if the same process is repeated in the second year, no shift in rates is caused by this sequential borrowing and replacement. It is only when firms borrow more this year than last, or less than last, that any effect should be expected.

If an old debt is refunded at a new coupon rate, the borrowing power of the debtor will be altered, to be sure. Thus if a public utility company is obliged to refund an old issue of 4% bonds with a new issue of 8% bonds, as happened many times in 1969 and thereafter, then the interest coverage on the new bonds will be only half as good as on the old. This will impair the company's credit rating somewhat. Additional bonds will be hard for it to sell, and new issues will have to be reduced in size. As a result, the growth of the company will be retarded. It will then be the duty of the public utility commission to authorize a rate increase for the company.

### 7. Cash Flow Constrasted With Profit Maximization

Cash flow, as we have seen, is the mechanism that control the demand for bonds and mortgages by insurance companies and savings banks. Cash flow thus rules the rate of interest. But cash flow does much more than that. It also rules the rate of wages and the pricing of all competitive products, as I show in my book entitled *Prices and Wages, Profits and Growth, Taxes and Dividends*. Cash flow, or the turnover of working capital as it is sometimes called, is thus the mechanism that keeps supply and demand in balance throughout the entire free enterprise system. It is the key to understanding how the whole American economy works, with no need for five year plans or other intervention from the central government in Washington.

Standard theory, however, holds a different view of the matter. It says that profit maximization is the correct key to understanding a competitive economy. But this view is mistaken for two reasons: First, it assumes that businessmen possess the data needed to recognize a maximum, when in truth such information is outside their ken. Second, it assumes that such a maximum is attainable, when in truth competitive firms can never *maximize* their profits; all they can do is try to increase their profits, or *majorize* them (to coin a word).

To maximize their profits, firms would need to reach the peak of the curve in Diagram IX. But a rigid credit constraint, as shown by the dotted line, holds all firms in check. Because of this constraint they cannot lay hands on current assets enough, or fixed assets enough, to reach the maximum.

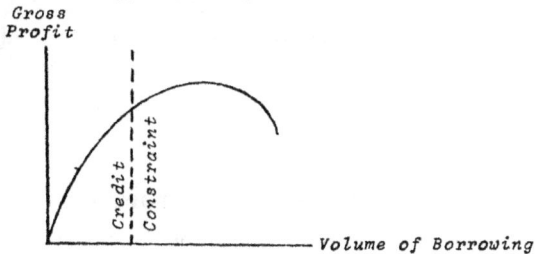

Diagram IX: The Constraint on Profit Maximization

In Diagram IX the term *gross profit* means profit before fixed charges of all kinds; in other words, it means profit before cash outlays for interest, property taxes, repairs, indirect labor, and so forth. In equilibrium, when growth is absent, firms make just enough gross profit to cover this cash overhead, but no more.

When standard theory says that all firms seek to maximize their profits,[2] it is correct, but when it claims they nearly always reach this goal, it is mistaken. To *try* is one thing, to *succeed*, another.

## 8. Interest Rates and Bond Prices

Does the long-term interest rate determine the level of bond prices? Many people would answer yes to this question. The correct answer, however, is no, for changes in the rate do not *cause* changes in prices. Instead interest rates and bond prices are simply two sides of the same coin.

We measure the long-term rate by looking at the price of bonds. There is no other way to measure it. When bonds go up, the rate goes down, and vice versa. Both changes occur at the same time, but neither is the *cause* of the other.

What holds true for the bond market likewise holds true for the stock market. It is not correct to explain a rise in stocks by saying that a lower interest rate is now being used to discount their future dividends, and this has *caused* prices to rise. No such process of cause

---

[2] Cf. Paul A. Samuelson, *Foundations of Economic Analysis* (Cambridge: Harvard University Press, 1947) p. 88: "The first fundamental assumption is that the firm tries to maximize its profits".

and effect is at work. A bull market in stocks must be explained in some other way.

To drive the point home, let us listen to the following silly conversation:

"My roommate, who got married a few years ago, is a lot heavier now than he was in college."

"Why?"

"Because he has put on so much weight."

The foregoing argument still leaves room, however, for the short-term rate to affect the long-term rate, and vice versa, by means of a mechanism to be described in the next chapter.

# CHAPTER IX
# LONG AND SHORT-TERM INTEREST RATES

## 1. Borrowers-Either-Way

Some firms should borrow only long-term, others only short-term, but a few may borrow either way. Public utilities, whose assets consist mainly of plant and equipment, should borrow only long-term (except for construction loans), while merchants,whose assets consist mainly of inventories and receivables, should borrow only short-term. Manufacturers, however, who use both fixed and current assets in their business, may borrow either way. Oil companies and municipalities may also borrow either way. They can sell long-term bonds to pension funds, insurance companies, and savings banks, or they can sell short-term notes to commercial banks. The limit on their bond issues is set by their interest coverage, the limit on their bank borrowings by their current ratio. Within these two limits their choice is set by the gap beween long and short-term rates.

Whenever bank loans are hard to get, or command too high a rate, borrowers who can offer either short or long-term paper are crowded out of the short-term market. These "borrowers-either-way", as I call them, are then obliged to sell fewer notes but more bonds. As a result, long-term bonds of all kinds fall in price. Then with bonds at bargain prices, institutions with long-term liabilities buy them in larger volume, hoping for a capital gain in due course. Money that these lenders would otherwise put into mortgages loans now goes into long-term bonds. Consequently a scarcity of mortgage money develops, and the interest rate on mortgages goes up. Families then buy smaller houses, or postpone their purchase altogether, and young couples continue to live with their in-laws. This behavior of borrowers makes the supply of mortgage notes signed by home buyers turn out to be quite elastic. Meantime public utility companies and the U.S. Treasury, both of whom display a very inelastic demand for loans, copy the interest rate that emerges elsewhere.

Evidently short-term and long-term rates are determined in two interconnected markets, namely the commercial loan market and the home mortgage market, with corporations and private home buyers being the principal borrowers in each case. The two markets are hitched together as shown in Diagram X.

87

| Demand for Loans | Short-term Borrowers | Borrowers- Either-Way | Long-Term Borrowers |
|---|---|---|---|
| Supply of Money to Lend | Short-term Lenders | | Long-term Lenders |

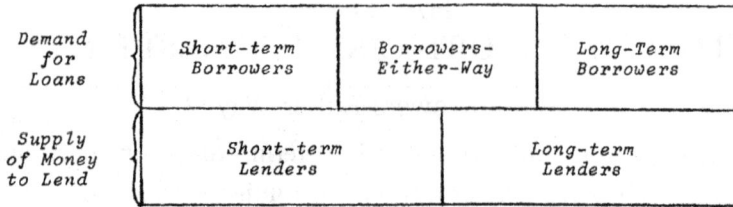

Diagram X:  Borrowers-Either-Way

In order to emphasize that lenders-either-way are much less important than borrowers-either-way, I have omitted such lenders from the diagram.

If the money market were completely unified, all borrowers would deal with all lenders. However as things now stand, the short-term borrowers deal only with the short-term lenders, and the long-term borrowers only with the long-term lenders. Only borrowers-either-way deal with both kinds of lenders.

New bonds of intermediate term, running for only ten years or so, are seldom issued. The available supply of such bonds comes mainly for old long-term issues that have now run part way to maturity. These old issues are often held by life insurance companies and pension funds whose corresponding long-term liabilities have likewise run part way to maturity.

## 2. The Encroachment Theory

Short-term rates are sometimes higher, but usually lower, than long-term rates. It all depends on how low the banks are willing to set their lending rates in order to maintain or increase their loans to borrowers-either-way. Meanwhile these firms make use of their freedom to change the ratio of their short-term to their long-term debt.

Sometimes, to be sure, banks are hard pressed to honor their lines of credit. Then they are forced to sell marketable securities at a loss. Meantime they raise the short-term rate above the long-term. But when banks are calling their borrowers back, they drop the short-term rate below the other rate. Yet merely to retain their present share of the business of borrowers-either-way the banks must keep their own rate lower than new bond issues need. The reasons for this spread will be listed in due course.

In order to put all their legal reserves to work, the banks name a prime rate that will hold their present share of the market as it grows each year. Often they try to lend still more, to encroach, as it were, on the bond market. If they had not encroached so far in the past, they would not enjoy so much of the market as they do today.

The term structure of interest rates, and the "yield curve" of short versus long rates, adjusted for risk, can mostly be explained in this way.

I suggest the new name *Encroachment Theory* for this explanation of the term structure of interest rates.

Sometimes, to be sure, encroachment comes to a halt. It can push no further. In the 1930s, for instance, short-term interest rates fell extremely low, and Treasury bills yielded but a fraction of 1%. Excess reserves were huge. Why were the banks unable to persuade borrowers-either-way to shift to bank loans? Risk was doubtless one answer. Many potential borrowers lacked creditworthiness. Their earnings were poor and their current ratio weak. Other borrowers, hard hit by the depression, were afraid to take on more debt. Still others could find no use for extra money, neither short nor long. Their sales were low, and their plants were partly idle. As a result the banks could find no borrowers to use their extra lending power. They remained flooded with excess reserves, and interest rates stayed low. Encroachment was still hard at work, to be sure, but it was pushing against a stone wall.

The interest rate quoted on customer loans or commercial paper, and received by lenders, is seldom the true rate incurred by borrowers. A gap prevails. Borrowers must maintain a line of credit as a "back-up" for their paper.[1] To keep this line of credit in force, they must carry large idle balances with their home banks, even when they are selling all their paper elsewhere. As a result a prime rate of 5%, for instance, might mean a cost of 6% all told for most borrowers. Such a rate might easily be higher than the long-term rate on bonds already issued by these same corporations. If so, these borrowers would be tempted to sell still more bonds to provide their seasonal working capital, planning to relend the money by purchasing commercial paper in their own slack season, when some other companies might need the money instead.[2]

Whenever the banks have excess reserves, they try to dissuade large corporations from becoming self-financing in this way. To do so, they name a prime rate for short-term loans that is well below the going rate

---

[1] After the Penn-Central disaster in June 1970, Chrysler was obliged to invoke its line of credit to protect its finance paper. Otherwise it might have gone bankrupt too.

[2] See Chapter XV, §9, *infra*.

on long-term bonds. All of this is in accordance with the *Encroachment Theory* for the term structure of interest rates.

The Encroachment Theory, just described, deals with the *supply* of funds to lend, but another theory, known as the Expectations Theory, deals with the *demand* for funds to borrow, as we shall now see.

### 3. The Expectations Theory

The Expectations Theory of long and short-term interest rates is better known as the Hicks-Lutz theory.[3] According to this theory, the long rate is the average of expected future short rates. Joan Robinson, however, makes fun of this whole idea; she says it requires lenders to forecast short-term rates "from now till Kingdom Come".[4] But this difficulty is not so serious as it sounds. The more distant the rate, the less precisely need it be forecast, because distant rates enter the formula of present value less often than near rates do. Thus if $c$ is the coupon and $P$ the principal of a 20-year bond paying interest semiannually, while $i_1$ is the interest rate in the first half-year, $i_2$ in the second, and $i_{40}$ in the last, and if $V$ is the investment value of coupons and principal combined, then the following formula applies:

$$V = \frac{c}{1+i_1} + \frac{c}{(1+i_1)(1+i_2)} + ... + \frac{c+P}{(1+i_1)...(1+i_{40})}$$

In this formula the nearby rate $i_1$ appears 40 times, but the distant rate $i_{40}$ appears only once. Evidently Mrs. Robinson's objection is not so serious after all.

### 4. Putting the Equity in Jeopardy

Not the lender, but the borrower, is the one who takes most of the risk when a loan is made.

[3] I myself propounded the pure Expectations Theory of long and short-term interest rates in great detail before either Hicks or Lutz wrote about it. Their theories, by incorporating liquidity preference or the like, are really modification of my own unadorned theory. Yet many writers now use the term "Hicks-Lutz Theory" to mean the pure Expectations Theory without any modifications at all. See my *Theory of Investment Value* (Cambridge: Harvard University Press, May 1938), chs. X and XX. See also J.R. Hicks, *Value and Capital* (Oxford University Press, Feb. 1939), p. 145, and F.A. Lutz, "The Structure of Interest Rates" in *The Quarterly Journal of Economics*, Nov. 1940 pp. 36-63, and Burton Malkiel, *The Term Structure of Interest Rates*, (Princeton University Press, 1966). See also Irving Fisher, *The Theory of Interest* (New York: The Macmillan Co., 1930), pp 314-315, reprinted by Augustus M. Kelley, Clifton, New Jersey.

[4] Cf. Joan Robinson, "The Rate of Interest", *Econometrica* 19 (April 1951), p. 102 note.

The lender stands to lose but a *part* of his loan, while the borrower risks *all* of his equity. And this equity is at least as large as the loan itself. If a textile mill, for instance, borrows $1,000,000 to buy wool tops, and spends $500,000 of its own money for wages of spinners and weavers, and if it uses another $500,000 in cash for overhead meanwhile, then the total cost of its output will be $2,000,000. Were a business panic like that of 1921 now to occur, causing orders for finished goods to be canceled prior to delivery, the mill might be unable to meet its bank loan when due, and so it would be forced into receivership. The bank would then take over, and would sell the cloth at distress prices, perhaps realizing the full $1,000,000 on its own loan after a few months. The mill itself, however, would lose all its working capital of $1,000,000. Clearly the loss sustained by the mill as a borrower would far exceed any loss suffered by the bank as a lender.

Yet if the mill had been rich enough in the beginning, and had been able to finance its operation without recourse to a bank loan, it could have weathered the panic safely. It could have laid its workers off for a few months, and could have held its finished inventory in storage until the storm blew over. Then the goods could have been sold for $1,500,000, let us say, and only a moderate loss need have resulted. Meanwhile the price of raw wool would have fallen in half, and so the mill, even with its reduced working capital, would still have been able to resume business at its former volume. This happy result would have been due to its freedom from short-term debt.

Anyone who contracts a short-term debt puts his head in the lion's mouth. To finance one's business with a revolving credit is a risky undertaking. Wise men know this. They prefer long-term debt. A 25-year mortgage is much safer than a 6-months bank loan. It gives a firm room to turn round. If interest rates are moderate and profits are good, the mortgage can be refunded a few years before it comes due. This is the safe course. Who knows but what an economic crisis may occur if the borrower waits till the last day? A long-term borrower can choose his own time to refund, while a short-term borrower cannot. Hence long-term debt is much safer to incur.

Firms who are in a position to borrow either long or short—firms, in other words, who hold plenty of unencumbered assets both fixed and current—such firms prefer to borrow long. They dislike to borrow short. Their aversion to short loans reduces the supply of short-term paper. This scarcity tends to hold its price up, reducing the short-term interest rate as a result.

It does not require a very large differential, however, to induce many firms to borrow short instead of long after all. They feel that the saving in interest compensates for the increase in risk, provided their volume of short-term borrowing stays small. But having finally decided to borrow short, these firms must still convince themselves that renewals can be made at an average rate no higher than the present long-term rate. Otherwise it would be cheaper to borrow long to begin with.

During an inflation, when firms need more and more current assets to finance production year after year, the day may come when a borrower-either-way finally loses his right to choose between short and long-term increases in debt. If at first a firm borrows short-term more and more, then its current ratio each year grows worse and worse. In the end the banks refuse to let its loans get any larger. Then the firm is forced to resort to long-term borrowing. It can no longer let its hopes for a future decline in short-term rates determine its choice. When its current ratio shrinks to a certain limit, it is forced into the long-term market. This is part of what happened to Ford and Chrysler in the winter of 1970. Their bankers urged them to sell bonds. Such sales of bonds helped to drive long-term rates up higher than ever.

## 5. Liquidity Aversion

The term "liquidity preference" has been in common use ever since Keynes wrote his *General Theory*.[5] But the contradictory term "liquidity aversion" is unheard of. In fact the very idea seems absurd at first sight. Why should anyone have an aversion to liquidity?

This question is easy to answer if we stop to think that the phrase "liquidity preference" usually does not mean what it seems to mean. "Liquidity preference" seldom means a preference for liquidity or marketability as such. Instead it usually means a preference for short-term issues simply because their price is steady, even though their renewal rate is not.

If we take "liquidity preference" to mean preference for short-term issues, then we can go on to ask if such a preference is always seen, or even usually seen. The right answer would seem to be that such a

[5] John Maynard Keynes, *The General Theory of Employment, Interest, and Money* (New York: Harcourt, Bruce and Co., 1936).

preference is sometimes seen, and sometimes not. Commercial banks, whose deposits are payable on demand, obviously need short-term assets to set against these short-term liabilities. But their own loans to customers, though short-term too, can scarcely be called liquid. Insurance companies, on the other hand, who are saddled with just the opposite kind of liabilities, namely long-term liabilities, need long-term loans. Consequently they eschew short-term paper. They display "liquidity aversion". And so do savings banks and many other lenders.

If a savings bank were to invest all its money in two-year notes paying 9% (a common rate in 1970), and if short-term interest rates were to drop to 4% two years later, then the bank would wish it had bought long-term paper to begin with. In fact, if competing banks had their funds still invested long-term at 8% (a common rate on mortgages in 1970) while the first savings bank could now get only 5% on mortgages, then this unfortunate bank might see a lot of its deposits flow out to its competitors as soon as the two-year period for 9% notes was over, and it became obliged to cut its own dividend rate. For that reason savings banks have a very pronounced "liquidity aversion", to use my new phrase.

What is true of savings banks is also true of many other investors who need to protect themselves against a possible future drop in short-term interest rates. Included among these long-term investors are life insurance companies, pension funds, endowment funds, universities, hospitals, churches and most private individuals. In truth it is hard to find anybody except a commercial banker who has a strong liquidity preference in the sense of needing short-term rather than long-term securities for his portfolio. This being the case, why should "liquidity preference" be considered the true cause of interest? Can Keynes really be right when he says that "interest is the payment for parting with liquidity."[6]

During many months in the year 1970, short-term interest rates were much higher than long-term. On January 28, 1970, for instance, the short-term Treasury 4% bonds due in February 1972 were quoted at 92 bid to yield 8.43% to maturity, while the long-term 4s of February 1988-93 were quoted at 67¼ to yield 6.84% to maturity in 1993. This put the short rate 157 basis points above the long rate. How does this square with Keynes's theory of liquidity preference?

---

[6] Keynes, op. cit, p. 167

So firmly rooted, however, are the misconceptions about liquidity preference that I must elaborate the point. Ever since Keynes wrote his *General Theory*, economists have considered it axiomatic that short-term issues are safer than long-term. These issues carry no risk of a fall in market price. Three-months U.S. Treasury bills are said to be the safest investments in the world. But safest *for whom*? For commercial banks, yes; for savings banks, no. For stock speculators, yes; for widows and orphans, no. For short-term investors, yes; for long-term, no. In fact what good bond is riskier than Treasury bills for you and me today (Dec. 12, 1969)? Bills due on March 5, 1970 yield 7.84%, to be sure, and are absolutely certain to be paid at maturity. Even so, if I were to put these bills into a trust fund for the college education of my grandson in the years 1986 to 1990, with his expenses to be paid out of income rather than principal, and if I required the trustee always to reinvest the money in Treasury bills until 1990, how safe would these bills prove to be? What if a depression got under way in 1986? What if the Federal Reserve Board created huge excess reserves in the hope of reviving business then? Might not yields go down to 1% or less? It has happened before. What a risk for me to take! Can anyone say, therefore, that short-term issues are not extremely risky? Would it not be far safer to invest the trust fund in long-term Treasury issues like the 3½s of 1990, now selling at 65½ bid, with a current yield of 5.35%? These bonds give some protection against inflation, moreover, because they will rise 50% in market price during the next 20 years, while Treasury bills will not rise at all. Meantime the yield on bills may fall way down. Whoever said that short-term bills are riskless, and should command a premium on that account?

Liquidity, even in the non-Keynesian sense of pure marketability, does not pertain to Treasury bills more than to Treasury bonds. Over a stretch of twenty years, money put into 91-day bills would have to be invested and reinvested eighty times, whereas money put into long-term bonds need be invested only once. If we use the spread between the bid and asked prices to measure the cost of rolling the money over each time, and if we take the spread on bills as .03% (it actually jumps to .06% for bills running a shade over 91 days), then the cost of rolling the investment over 80 times is 2.40%. In contrast, the spread for 20-year bonds is 16/32 of a point (it actually is less on round lots for a skillful trader), and so the cost for bonds is only 0.76% of the sum invested. Just compare 2.40% with 0.76%! Clearly the much praised liquidity or marketability of short-term issues is pure fiction as regards the long-term investor.

To avoid the rollover cost on Treasury bills, it is possible, of course, to exchange the old issues for new at the Federal Reserve Bank every three months. Yet this involves risk and trouble. The owner of the bills must carry them through crowded streets, and stand in line for service. Even if he avoids risk by resorting to registration of his holdings, he must still spend time and postage on each exchange. All things considered, therefore, the cost of using Treasury bills would seem to be as high as that for Treasury bonds.

## 6. Treasury Bills

What is the essential difference between Treasury bills, on the one hand, and currency or money in general, on the other hand? Both are issued by the government, yet they are not just alike.

The essential difference is the refusal of the government to make change for Treasury bills on demand, to exchange a single $10,000 Treasury bill for a thousand $10 bills without waiting for the due date on the big bill to arrive.[7] No such refusal is seen for currency in large denominations.

Treasury bills cannot be used for most payments. They are too big to use for the purchase of food, shelter, and clothing day by day. Hence they are not money or currency.

Imagine what would happen if the government were suddenly to enact a new law stating that all $10,000 Federal Reserve notes now in

---

[7] Contrast the views of Hicks (op. cit. pp 164-5) who says,

"We shall get nearest to the true nature of interest if we consider the relation between money and that type of security which comes nearest to being money, without quite being money. This is to be found in the very short bill, a bill payable in the very near future, when that bill is regarded as perfectly safe from risk of default. If we can find a reason why such a bill should stand at less than its face value, at less, that is to say, than money of the same face value, we have found a reason for the existence of pure interest.

"The only possible incentive to hold money is one which we have already touched on in an earlier chapter, but must now explore more fully. If people receive payment for the things they sell in the form of money, to convert this money into bills requires a separate transaction, and the trouble of making that transaction may offset the gain in interest. It is only if this obstacle were removed, if safe bills could be acquired without any trouble at all, that people would become willing to convert all their money into bills, so long as any interest whatever was offered. Under the conditions of our model, *it must be the trouble of making transactions which explains the short rate of interest* (my italics)."

I maintain that bills, even if their purchase involved no trouble at all, would still sell at a discount, because *they come in denominations too large to use*.

circulation could no longer be exchanged for paper money of smaller denominations, and that holders would have to wait 91 days to convert their notes. Then these $10,000 Federal Reserve notes would at once sell at a discount, just as $10,000 Treasury bills do already. The real reason why Federal Reserve notes suffer no such discount now is that the banks will always consent to exchange them for currency of smaller denominations on demand.

To "monetize the national debt", all the U.S. government needs to do is to make large Treasury bills convertible into small Treasury bills on demand.

Treasury bills are widely used by commercial banks as a secondary reserve. If a depositor in a New York bank draws a large check in favor of a depositor in a Chicago bank, the first bank can shift the money by sending Treasury bills for the amount of the check. The usual procedure, however, is for the New York bank to sell its bills to a dealer in government bonds, and for the Chicago bank to buy bills from this same dealer, or some other. The sale of bills gives the New York bank funds on deposit with its Federal Reserve Bank; these funds are then used to cover the large check when the Chicago bank presents it for collection. The purchase of bills gives the Chicago bank a profitable use for the funds it now acquires at its own Federal Reserve Bank; the newly purchased bills now stand as an asset on its books matching the new increase in its deposit liability. The net result, therefore, is the same as if the first bank had sold Treasury bills directly to the second bank.

Treasury bills thus serve as a means of payment between banks. Because they bear interest day by day, and can be bought and sold in huge amounts without upsetting their price, nothing else is quite so good for settling big balances between banks. No wonder dealings in bills are enormous every day!

Since Treasury bills enjoy these unique advantages, it would seem that they ought to command a better price and give a lower yield than any other short-term security. Yet they do not do so. The best finance company paper, like that of the General Motors Acceptance Corporation, sells for the same low yield, once allowance is made for state income taxes. While Treasury bills and finance paper both are subject to the federal tax on their interest, the bills are exempt from state taxes, but the paper is not. Treasury bills, moreover, pay their interest (or discount) in advance, while finance paper pays its interest at the end, and this makes the bond-equivalent return on bills slightly higher than the discount they show. When all adjustments are made, therefore, Treasury bills are seen to command no premium over finance paper. [8]Why?

The answer is that bills enjoy no scarcity. The volume outstanding is enough, more than enough, to fill the needs of the commercial banks. The excess goes begging. It has to be absorbed by investors who don't need its superb marketability, by investors who find finance paper just as good for their purposes. These investors are the marginal buyers of Treasury bills. They are the ones who set the price.

In order to drive this point home, let us consider a similar situation that occurs in the case of silver and gold. Silver has a unique and very valuable property that gold does not. Silver, in the form of silver bromide, is sensitive to light, and so it is required in large amounts for the manufacturer of photographic film. Gold cannot be used instead. Yet silver does not command a higher price than gold. Why? The answer is that there is no scarcity of silver. The photographic industry does not need to buy the entire output. The excess goes begging. It is absorbed by inferior uses, like the manufacture of knives, forks, spoons, and hollow ware. Because stainless steel and chinaware are cheaper than silver, the housewife is often willing to use them instead. These substitutes keep the price of silver down, and make it settle at a figure far less than makers of photographic film would pay were a scarcity to prevail. Tableware, not photographic film, sets the price of silver.

Treasury bills are like silver. They are in excess supply. Hence they do not command a premium price even though they do indeed afford the best means of settling interbank balances.

If Treasury bills often yield a bit less than Treasury bonds, it is *partly* because bills trade in such huge quantities all day long, not because their term is short. The distinction between easy salability and early maturity must not be overlooked.

---

[8] On Jan. 28, 1970, for instance, finance paper was quoted at 8½% for 30 to 99 days, (see *The Wall Street Journal*, Jan 29, 1970 page 23, column 3.) After deduction of the Massachusetts income tax of 8%, the net return was 7.82%. On the same day, Treasury bills, exempt from state income taxes for individuals, were quoted at a discount of 7.91% bid, 7.85 asked, for the maturity on Feb. 28, 31 days later. (*The Wall Street Journal* page 27, column 3.) On a bond-equivalent basis, the discount of 7.91% was equal to interest of 7.99%. Clearly, Treasury bills do not always carry the very lowest yield of any short-term security. Evidently they enjoy no special scarcity value of their own.

## 7. The Supply of Short-Term Paper

Many borrowers are quite able to issue either long-term or short-term paper. In normal times, the U.S. Treasury in particular can shift from long to short with the greatest of ease. The Treasury sells bonds, notes, and bills. Its maturities run from thirty years to thirty days. Only the old law that once set a limit of 4¼% on long-term bonds ever kept the Treasury from tailoring its borrowing to the exact needs of its investors. Were it not for this law, the Treasury could always have said, "we'll give the public just what it wants, we'll sell whatever commands the highest price, we'll borrow in whatever is the cheapest way".

Treasury issues are not the only ones that can be tailored to the whim of lenders. Municipal bonds can also be made either long or short.[9] So can industrial issues much of the time. The market is full of borrowers-either-way.

Moreover, as regards the long-term bonds of the U.S. Treasury, many of its old issues that were brought out twenty or thirty years ago are now close to maturity, and thus have become short-term issues in effect. The same is true of a huge quantity of old long-term corporate bonds now due for payment soon. Investors who prefer short-term issues are faced with an enormous supply of such maturing bonds. There would be no scarcity were it not for the fact that the commercial banks have such large reserves that they are usually hard-pressed to keep all their lending power at work.

An analogy will make the point even clearer. The ice cream companies, for instance, are in the same position as borrowers-either-way. They can make either vanilla or chocolate ice cream. Both kinds cost the same to make. If the public suddenly decides it wants more

---

[9] Competition between long and short paper shows vividly in a report quoting the mayor of Peabody, Mass., published in the *Boston Herald-Traveler,* page 3, on Dec. 30, 1969, as follows:

> The city sought bids for a 20-year loan of $15.9 million for capital improvements, including $12.6 million for a new high school.....7.20 per cent was the lowest bid.... "It would have an immediate impact on our tax rate," said the mayor. He now plans to finance with short-term, one-year bonds. "The sort-term notes will do until the money market breaks," he said.... "Projects planned will go on as scheduled".

When the mayor decided to borrow short instead of long, his action tended to raise short rates and reduce long rates. His choice, therefore, should not be called liquidity preference. That term applies to lenders, not borrowers. Lenders produce the opposite effect from what borrowers do.

See also the article in the *Federal Reserve Bulletin* for Dec. 1971 on "State and Local Borrowing", especially p. 981.

chocolate and less vanilla, the dairy companies can change their product mix the very next day. It's all as easy as that.

This rule holds good in the money market too. If investors want short-term issues, many borrowers can offer short-term notes, while if investors want long-term issues, these same borrowers can offer long-term bonds. As a result, there is a very elastic supply of each kind of security.

Municipal bonds, to be sure, which are often sold as serial notes, are sometimes issued in the wrong proportions. The reason, however, is that the fire and casualty companies, who buy the long-terms, currently are beset with underwriting losses (which they charge against taxable interest), and so they do not need any tax-exempts. As for the short maturities, an artificial demand is created by the fact that the big banks in each city already hold a huge volume of presently maturing notes, and cannot safely refuse to renew them without exposing themselves to the wrath of the local politicians.[10] As a result, short-term municipals usually command a lower return than long-term ones do.

## 8. Idle Money, Hoarding, and Bearishness

It is so easy for individuals to transfer surplus cash from their checking accounts to their savings accounts, using the mails for the purpose, that any rate of interest over 3% is enough to keep most people from letting any of their money lie idle. For large institutions, in turn, it is so easy to telephone the money desk at their commercial bank, and order surplus funds to be invested in finance paper, that any rate over 2% is enough to keep pension funds, insurance companies, and savings banks from letting their own money lie idle. Even when these institutions are bearish on the bond market, and are waiting for prices to fall, they do not need to hoard their money uninvested in the meantime. Consequently low interest rates—unless they go extremely low—do not increase the volume of idle money very much. Is it plausible, therefore, to base the whole theory of short-term interest rates on the bother of putting money to work, as some writers do?[11]

---

[10] To protect the banks and their depositors, and to promote better diversification of risk, a federal law should forbid the banks to lend money to their own cities and state. Tax exemption would then need to be extended to out-of-state municipals too.

[11] Cf. Hicks, *op. cit*, p. 165. "[This] trouble .... Explains the short rate of interest."

## 9. Call Protection

Now in the year 1973 the threat of falling interest rates is so bad that many long-term investors are demanding extended "call protection" on the long-term bonds they buy. Whereas five-year call protection was once considered sufficient, many investors now insist on ten-year protection, or else they demand a very high redemption price. They are afraid that interest rates will fall, with the result that their bonds will be paid off too soon, and they will be forced to accept in exchange a new issue carrying a lower coupon. They want to make mighty sure that they are not stuck with a short-term issue. This certainly does not sound like the short-term liquidity preference that Keynes talks about so much.

Since there is no scarcity of short-term bills and notes, and no superfluity of long-term bonds, how can it be said that liquidity preference makes short-term rates normally lower than long-term rates?

The term structure of interest rates during the past twenty-five years, to be sure, has usually shown the yield curve to have its short-term end lower than its long-term. Yet this shape of the curve does not prove that liquidity preference rather than some other factor was the true cause of this shape. The Encroachment Theory gives a better explanation, as we have already seen. The banks were always encroaching on the bond market.

A further explanation is the Expectations Theory of short and long-term interest rates. According to this theory, a rising yield curve means that borrowers expect short-term rates to rise in the future. These expectations need not be proved correct by the event, of course. If borrowers hold a certain belief at the time a loan is made, that in itself is quite enough.[12]

It is not the expectations of *lenders*, be it noted, that count, for very few lenders enjoy any freedom of choice. The expectations of *borrowers* are far more important. Furthermore, even though many borrowers have no choice but to deal in the short market on the one hand, or the long market on the other hand, nevertheless if an important minority

[12] For arguments pro and con, see J.M. Culbertson "The Term Structure of Interest Rates" in *The Quarterly Journal of Economics*, 71, (1957) pp. 485-517; and D. Meiselman, *The Term Structure of Interest Rates* (Englewood Cliffs, N.J.: Prentice-Hall, Inc., 1962); and J.B. Michaelson, "The Term Structure of Interest Rates, Comment", in *The Quarterly Journal of Economics*, 77 (1963) pp. 166-174.

are free to deal either way, then the final yield curve should reflect the expectations of this minority.

## 10. The Extra Risk of Default in Long-Term Bonds

The risk of default on a long-term bond is not just like the risk of fire on a building covered by a long-term insurance policy, for the risk on a bond is not strictly proportional to the duration of the exposure, to the number of years to maturity. No indeed, because for a bond time introduces new uncertainties. Take the case of the Norfolk and Western Railroad, which hauls huge tonnages of coal to power plants. Today it is one of the most profitable railroads in the country. Its first mortgage 4s of '96 are rated Aa. Yet twenty-five years from now, when these bonds come due, the road may be in trouble. Who can say? Pipelines may carry coal as a slurry by then, or electricity may be generated mostly at the mine mouth. New power plants may be served by barge lines, or nuclear power may replace coal. A higher premium for risk, therefore, should be included in the gross return on its long-term bonds than on its short-term notes. On its short-term notes, little risk is present. Hence the term structure of the interest rates on its equipment trust certificates and its bonds of varying maturities does not give a true reading of pure interest rates short or long.

Long-term municipals likewise involve more credit risk than short-term ones do. A long-term bond gives more time for the finances of a city like New York to go from bad to worse. Risk, therefore, puts yields up on long-term municipals.

In fact, as one peers into the future, only U.S. Treasury issues wholly escape this escalation of risk with time. For Treasuries there is no risk, because the federal government is the one and only borrower than can always print new money to pay its debts. Treasury bills, notes, and bonds, therefore, are the only issues that can give a true forecast of future rates, a true reading of the expectations of borrowers. Yet even here the expectations of borrowers are confronted by the "encroachment" of lenders, as we have already seen.

In any event, however, the fears felt by lenders-either-way have little effect on the term structure of interest rates, for the number of lenders-either-way, unlike the number of borrowers-either-way, is very small. Most buyers of long-term issues have no choice but to buy long-terms despite the extra credit risk that such bonds entail. Hence the lesser credit risk on short-terms is but a minor factor in explaining their price. What really counts is the efforts of the commercial banks to find enough shorts to keep all their lending power at work .

## 11. Uncertainty and Liquidity Preference

Uncertainty may sometimes become so great that lenders and borrowers both lack any conviction about the future of interest rates, and so the Expectations Theory no longer holds sway.

Then uncertainty in and of itself may push both borrowers and lenders into the short-term market. This at last is *true* "liquidity preference", for both parties. But the net effect is zero. Borrowers push the short rate *up* by their increased demand for short loans—not down as required by accepted dogma—while lenders push the rate down— quite in accordance with the Liquidity Preference Theory. Borrowers and lenders thus offset each other. Proponents of standard doctrine fail to see that the usual argument about liquidity preference has *two* sides to it, not just one.

Moreover, the *net* effect may often be quite the reverse of accepted doctrine, for borrowers may be swayed much more by liquidity preference than lenders are. A borrower often lacks diversification. The loan he seeks may be his only debt, long or short, and so he has a strong motive not to lock himself into a long-term contract when he feels highly uncertain about the outlook. If so, he may insist on a short loan, and this very insistence may overpower the mild doubts of lenders. This will send the rate up, not down, exactly the opposite of what we have always been taught to believe.

## 12. Summary

The term structure of interest rates is determined by supply and demand, both together, not one alone.

As regards *supply*, the volume of money offered on loan to borrowers of all kinds is determined by the cash receipts of savings institutions plus the lending power of commercial banks. The institutions receive a fixed flow of contractual savings, a flow that is independent of the prevailing interest rate. Meanwhile the commercial banks are held in check by the fixed amount of their reserves. But if the Federal Reserve Board now increases these reserves, the member banks can make more loans to borrowers-either-way, and can encroach on the province of long-term lenders. To do so, they reduce the short-term rate they charge on customer loans, and set it lower than the long-term rate on corporate bonds, as described by the *Encroachment Theory* of short and long-term interest rates.

As regards *demand*, borrowers-either-way prefer to borrow long; they consider short loans dangerous. Nevertheless they consent to borrow short if given a sufficient inducement. But they must feel sure no future rise in short-term rates will penalize them when the time comes to renew their loans. Their calculations are thus governed by the *Expectations Theory* of short and long-term rates.

Working together, these two theories, with adjustments for risk, show why short rates are usually lower than long rates. They give a much better explanation of the term structure of interest rates than the Liquidity Preference Theory does.

# CHAPTER X
# LOANS TO THE U.S. TREASURY

## 1. Borrowing Either Way

While the Treasury is normally free to borrow either short or long, this freedom, to be sure, has often been absent during recent years, because an old law limited the coupon rate to 4¼% on Treasury bonds running for more than seven years. Maybe this law will be wholly repealed fairly soon. Or maybe long-term rates will fall below 4¼% some day. If so, the Treasury can once more become a borrower-either-way, and will be able to resume its role as an equalizer of short and long-term interest rates. This would be all to the good. The sooner the better.

Meanwhile the very fact that a huge volume of old Treasury long-term debt is still outstanding helps to keep short and long-term rates in line with each other. Lenders themselves are still free to buy either bills, notes, or bonds, making their purchases from the floating supply. The sellers of the old Treasury issues always receive cash, and can invest it in new corporate issues of one length or another, just as they see fit. In so doing these investors guide new savings into eventual uses that can be either short-term or long-term. The presence of so many Treasury issues both short and long makes all this possible.

## 2. Bond Dealers' Inventories

Dealers who buy and sell Treasury, municipal, and corporate bonds in the over-the-counter market carry large inventories financed with money borrowed day by day from commercial banks. The interest they pay on these bank loans is a major item of expense to them. In computing their income taxes, they use this expense as an offset to the accrued interest they collect each day on bonds held for sale. When the prime rate on bank loans is high, the dealers need bonds with a high coupon rate in order to come out even. Otherwise the tax deduction goes to waste.

Discount bonds, like the Treasury 3½s of 1990 that sold as low as 60 in May, 1970, do not afford a current return high enough to "pay their board", as the expression goes. At their low, these bonds had a current yield of $3\frac{1}{2}/60 = 5.94\%$ compared with the prime rate of 8½% on bank loans. The low price was caused in part by the reluctance of dealers to carry discount bonds like these in stock. When the prime rate was cut step by step to 7% six months later, the bonds rose in price to 72¾. Meanwhile, to be sure, the business outlook had changed, and so long-term as well as short-term interest rates would be expected to ease. Nevertheless it would be hard to deny the existence of a strictly mechanical, nonpsychological link between the current return on bonds and the cost of carrying them in inventory. The dealers themselves would surely insist that such a link exists, with income taxes being an important part of the connection. This is one striking way in which the long-term rate is tied to the short-term rate.

### 3. Unlimited Borrowing Power

Since loans to the U.S. Treasury are free from all risk, lenders set no limits on these loans. The Treasury, unlike a manufacturing company, never needs to consider the marginal productivity of new plant and equipment. Unlike a public utility, the Treasury never finds its borrowing power held down by rate regulation at the hands of various state commissions. Unlike a municipality, the Treasury never is held in check by the dislike of its citizens to levy extra real estate taxes upon themselves. Unlike a homeowner, the Treasury never needs to limit its interest expense to a fixed percentage of its take-home pay. There is a special reason for all this, to wit: The U.S. government can always print extra money, directly or indirectly, to pay its interest if it runs a deficit in its budget. Other borrowers cannot. Only the vague fear of inflation ever holds the Treasury in check.

Yet the Federal government may sometimes balance its budget, or even show a surplus. When the budget is balanced, the Treasury borrows no new money. All it does is refund its outstanding bonds and notes as these fall due from time to time. It makes no added demands upon the money market. Under these circumstances its effect upon the interest rate is neutral, or nearly so.

Every time the Treasury refunds its debt, however, it repays an issue that had been due within a few days, and replaces it with an issue due less soon, an issue due in 91 days, six months, nine months, one year, or even five, ten, or twenty years hence. In so doing, the Treasury relieves the scarcity of longer term issues, and tends to depress their prices a trifle.

When the Federal government runs a deficit, and borrows money to pay relief, grant foreign aid, or buy munitions, it gives no thought to the rate of interest now prevailing in the money market. Its demand for loans is completely inelastic. The amount borrowed remains the same regardless of whether the rate is 2%, 4%, 6%, or even 8%. Hence the Treasury's demand curve may be represented by a vertical straight line whose position depends entirely on considerations quite outside the money market itself. While this demand is part of the composite demand for loans in general, it contributes nothing to the elasticity of this composite demand. Whatever elasticity composite demand may have comes from some other source.

Incidentally, when the Treasury does in fact run a deficit, and borrows money to cover this deficit, it uses but little of the new money to pay for productive goods like highways and harbors. Unlike municipal bonds, which usually finance schools and streets, Treasury bonds seldom lead to capital formation.

## 4. Measuring the Interest Rate

The prices of government bonds, and their interest rates both long and short implied thereby, are the most important prices in the whole money market. They are the best indicator of the pure interest rate. So huge are the daily dealings in Treasury issues, and so marketable are these securities, that they render a very accurate reading of the rate that will balance supply and demand.

Yet the balance so revealed is only a putative balance, not a true balance. Today's price only shows what dealers *believe* the right price to be, not what the right price really is. Today's price is merely an expression of opinion—expert opinion, to be sure—but mere opinion nevertheless. It is not a statement of fact.[1] Tomorrow the price will probably change. Although new data will be known by then, new thinking will also have been done by then. Both of these causes, acting together, will make the price change.

The true long-term rate is reflected better in Treasury bonds than in corporate bonds. Treasury bonds have no sinking fund. Most of them are noncallable before maturity, but few corporate bonds enjoy more than five years of call protection after issuance. While the buyer of a Treasury bond is sure of getting his full yield all the way to maturity,

---

[1] Cf. my *Investment Value*, p. 17

even if interest rates ease a lot meanwhile, the buyer of a corporate bond runs the risk of having his bond called meanwhile, and replaced with another bearing a lower coupon rate. The corporation thus enjoys a "heads I win, tails you lose" option. The Treasury does not. Although some Treasury bonds, like the new 8½s of February 1994-99, do indeed display a split maturity, this feature is by no means as bad as the callability of a corporate bond like the Telephone 3⅞s of 1990. The latter bond, issued in 1958, can now be called at prices slightly over par at any time. If interest rates, now so high that the Treasury 8½s sell at 103¾ to yield 8.10%, should fall to 3% in 1979, the Treasury 8½s, with at least fifteen years more to run, would rise to 166 in 1979. The Telephone 3⅞s, however now selling at 59¼, would not rise above their call price of 101.61 for that year. Furthermore, deep discount bonds like these give their return partly in the form of a capital gain. Consequently these Telephone bonds, like most corporate bonds, do not give a true measure of the long-term interest rate.

In comparing long and short-term rates, care should be taken to allow for the greater marketability of Treasury bills compared with Treasury bonds. Bills can be sold in blocks of $10,000,000 with hardly a jolt to their price, but bonds cannot. The Federal Reserve Banks stand ready to stabilize the Treasury bill market at any hour of the day, but the Social Security Insurance Fund declines to do the same thing for Treasury bonds. The Fund ought to be willing to buy or sell in large amounts at any time. It could easily do this without undertaking to support the price too.

Suddenly, late in May 1970, the quotations furnished by the government bond dealers to the newspapers showed a doubling of the gap between the bid and asked prices on long-term Treasury issues. The gap widened from ½ point previously to a full point afterwards. Obviously no such change could suddenly have taken place on the "inside market" that dealers quote minute by minute to insurance companies and other large investors. Perhaps the change was intended to help banks and brokers who were placing orders for small investors "guilty" of withdrawing money from savings accounts to put into government bonds.

When a common stock like General Motors commands a spread of only ⅛ point between the bid and asked, a Treasury bond, entailing less risk to the dealer, surely deserves a spread even smaller. Yet the market on these bonds is so inactive that the spread remains quite wide.

To some extent the price of long-term Treasuries may be held up by a special provision in the law that allows these bonds to be used at par for the payment of Federal estate taxes. The heirs can thus pay a tax of $100,000 with 100 bonds that cost only $63,000, let us say. But if the demand for estate taxes is not enough to absorb the entire supply of these "flower bonds", then the marginal buyer will be an investor who already owns more than enough bonds to pay his tax, and who values the extra bonds purely as income producers.

Such an investor would consider Treasury bonds safer than AAA corporate bonds, because the Treasury, as a last resort, can always print the money needed to pay interest and principal. A corporation, in contrast, must earn this money. Treasury bonds, moreover, are exempt from state income taxes. For both of these reasons, Treasury bonds deserve to sell higher than corporate bonds. And for these same reasons, Treasury bonds afford the best measure of the pure interest rate.

When the Treasury sets out to borrow new money, it names whatever rate of interest is needed to outbid other borrowers. In so doing, it copies the rate that it finds to prevail elsewhere in the money and capital markets. Moreover it displays a completely inelastic demand, because it shows itself willing to pay whatever price, high or low, is necessary. No matter whether the rate is 2%, 4%, 6%, or even 8%, its volume of borrowing stays the same. Consequently its demand curve is a vertical straight line.

## 5. Fiscal Policy

Fiscal policy so-called involves both debt and taxes.

When the Federal government runs a deficit; this deficit is usually so small—except in time of war—that it adds but little to the supply of notes and bonds brought out each year. New borrowing by cities and states, by public utilities, and by the residential sector of the economy, all for the purpose of true capital formation, far exceeds new borrowing by the U.S. Treasury. Hence the Federal deficit, if any, does not dominate the interest rate.

Taxes, however, are quite another matter. Corporate income taxes in particular restrict the ability of corporations to accumulate new equity as a base for new debt. And individual income taxes also reduce the ability of private persons to borrow money and assume business risks. Likewise, if tax receipts are spent for armaments, the nation's labor force cannot produce consumers goods, and so the cost of living rises, making it harder for people to save. These are the ways in which fiscal policy really acts on interest rates.

# CHAPTER XI
## LOANS TO MUNICIPALITIES

### 1. Municipal Bonds

Municipal bonds are usually sold to finance the construction of schools, roads, sewers, water mains, and other public works, all of which are made necessary by the growth of cities and towns. They are an offshoot of the demand for private housing as such. The faster the population of a city grows, and the more new houses that are built within it, the greater will be the demand for all these municipal improvements. When home loans increase in volume, municipal bonds soon follow suit. Municipal borrowing thus belongs to the residential rather than the industrial sector of the economy.

Taxes, not profits, provide the revenues to cover the charges for interest and sinking fund on municipal bonds. In order for the bonds to be issued in the first place, they must be approved by the voters as a special item on the ballot at election time. The voters consent to tax themselves, and thus to reduce their outlays on food, clothing, and shelter. They do this because they believe schools and other such public goods provide more satisfaction than private expenditures would do. Municipal borrowing, therefore, shows an elastic demand, and its volume is quite responsive to changes in the interest rate.

Municipal debt is often held in check, moreover, by state laws that limit borrowing to some fixed percentage of property values. Investment bankers, when asked to underwrite municipal bonds, also set limits of their own. These limits do not reflect the marginal utility of schools, roads, and the like. Not how much cities and towns may want to borrow, but how much investors are willing to lend, often determines the outcome. When lenders thus limit the effective demand for the funds they wish to lend, they thereby depress the interest rate on their own loans. An arbitrary ceiling on the interest rate is the result.

A ceiling on municipal debt is formed in another way too. When savings banks set a limit on their loans to homeowners, and say that monthly payments for interest, amortization, and real estate taxes shall not exceed 25% of the borrower's take-home pay, they thereby limit the sum that is available for the banks and the municipalities to split between them. If real estate taxes go up, mortgage payments must come down. The total stays fixed. Were tax rates to go sky high, home buyers would be forced to buy very small houses. The assessed value of these houses would be small too. Even at a high tax rate, the tax itself would not be large. As a result the total collections of the city would be held down, and its borrowing power would be restrained. All of this would come to pass because the savings banks set an arbitrary limit on monthly payments, fixing them at 25% of take-home pay.

## 2. Interest Received, Tax-Exempt for Lenders

The interest on municipal bonds is exempt from the federal income tax, both for corporations and for individuals, and it is also exempt from the state income tax of its own state. Hence these bonds sell at a higher price and give a lower yield than other bonds do. But what the investor saves on taxes paid he loses on interest received. If the tax exemption were removed, municipalities would need to pay a higher rate of interest, and levy higher taxes on homeowners. The extra money paid to the bondholders would then go to the U.S. Treasury as extra income tax. Homeowners would pay the cost of this "reform".

Municipalities, because they can borrow either long or short, are what we call "borrowers-either-way". They raise money in whichever way is cheaper. They try to guess the future path of interest rates, and are quite willing to sell recurrent issues of short-term notes if they think this is better than selling a single issue of long-term bonds. In fact, they continually belabor their bankers for the best advice they can get on this perennial problem. In so doing, they link short-term to long-term rates in accordance with the Expectations Theory.[1]

Fire and casualty insurance companies are normally large buyers of long-term municipals, and commercial banks of short-term ones. Banks, in fact, can borrow on certificates of deposit at 6%, for instance, and put the money into municipals at 4%, but still turn a profit on the deal. How is this possible?

This feat is possible only when the bank is already receiving a large amount of taxable interest on customer loans, Treasury bills, and the like, against which demand deposits have been credited. Then the bank can use the interest it pays on its certificates of deposit, or CDs, as an offset to the interest it receives from its loans and discounts LD, leaving the interest from its municipals as net profit. The balance sheets and

---

[1] See Chapter IX, §9, supra.

income accounts below show that earnings are larger after the sale of CDs and the purchase of municipals than before:

Balance Sheets

| | Before | | | | | After | | |
|---|---|---|---|---|---|---|---|---|
| LD | 100 | DD | 100 | | LD | 100 | DD | 100 |
| | | | | | Municipals | 100 | CD | 100 |
| | 100 | | 100 | | | 200 | | 200 |

Income Accounts

| Before | | | After | |
|---|---|---|---|---|
| Int. earned @ 6% on LD | 6 | | Int. earned @ 6% on LD | 6 |
| Int. expense | 0 | | Int. expense on CDs | -6 |
| Balance | 6 | | Balance | 0 |
| Fed'l. tax | -3 | | Fed'l tax | 0 |
| | | | Tax-free interest on municipals | 4 |
| Net income | 3 | | Net income | 4 |

Interest expense on CDs, however, must not exceed interest earned on LDs, or else there will be some interest expense going to waste. Usually, of course, the rate on LDs is higher than on CDs anyway.

Even when short-term interest rates on Treasury issues were higher than long-term rates, as in 1969, municipal bonds nevertheless often failed to follow suit. Tax-exemption explains this paradox in part. Short-term municipals are usually sold to banks, while long-term ones are sold to insurance companies. Banks can always use current expenses to offset taxable income, but fire and casualty companies, who have recently been faced with heavy underwriting losses, cannot always do this nowadays. Bond dealers, therefore, in order to get rid of their long-term issues entirely, are forced to sweeten the yield on them. Short-term municipals, in contrast, require no such sweetening.

Credit risk also makes the long-term yield on municipals higher than the short-term. Lenders to New York City, for instance, knowing that the city is running a deficit year after year, demand a large premium for risk on the long-term bonds, but ask little on the short-term notes. They believe that no financial crisis is likely soon, but such a crisis may occur eventually, causing debt service to be interrupted for a while.

Many new issues of municipal bonds are underwritten by large commercial banks, who then sell the bonds to other banks, and to insurance companies also. When a city raises money by issuing serial bonds, the bank that underwrites the whole new issue sometimes fails to dispose of the long maturities. As a result, in its Annual Report the bank may show heavy holdings of long maturities, with a bad paper loss thereon, all in apparent defiance of the usual rules for prudent investment. This departure from good banking practice is purely the result of miscalculation by the underwriting department. The banks sometimes get stuck with the wrong bonds.

One way for the underwriters to get rid of their long-term bonds is to cut the price and raise the yield. The higher the yield, the more the bonds will appeal to small investors, to buyers who are not in a high tax bracket. If a tax-exempt bond has a yield of 4½%, it can compete with a corporate bond that has a yield of 6%, when offered to investors in the 25% tax bracket. There are a great many such investors. But if a tax-exempt bond yields just 3%, only those investors who are in the 50% bracket or above will be potential buyers. There are few such investors. Inasmuch as there are many more investors in the low tax brackets than in the high, the demand for tax-exempt bonds is very elastic.

Tax-exemption, to be sure, does not explain the entire demand for municipal bonds. Some of these bonds are bought by the retirement funds set up for public employees even though these funds do not need the tax-exempt feature. The money could be invested at a higher return elsewhere, but the law often gives the fund no choice.

### 3. Revenue Bonds

Revenue bonds, though tax-exempt, are not protected by the full faith and credit of the borrowing governmental agency. The safety of their principal and interest depends entirely on the success of the venture they finance. Thus the Triborough Bridge in New York might serve a demand so insistent that it could earn its cost several times over, while a bridge across Chesapeake Bay might fail to cover its fixed charges fully. No two issues of revenue bonds, in fact, are exactly alike in risk.

When a city or state undertakes a new venture financed with revenue bonds, it supplies no equity capital of its own to protect the borrowed capital. In contrast, a private corporation engaged in a commercial enterprise would usually display a debt-equity ratio of one to one (or less), with only half of the money being furnished by the bondholders, and the rest by the stockholders. To this extent, corporate bonds are better than revenue bonds.

Municipalities, however, enjoy two offsetting advantages. In the first place, their venture pays no income or real estate taxes. In the second place, it enjoys a monopoly, or at least a partial monopoly.

Customers who decline to patronize the tunnel or bridge must use another road that is much longer. The monopolist is thus free to set an arbitrary price on his service that will maximize his profit. Since a road or a bridge has little variable operating cost to pay, maximizing profit means maximizing revenue.

To maximize revenue is not easy, however. Nobody knows for sure what the demand curve looks like. Its elasticity is a matter of guesswork. If a tunnel or bridge does not show a profit, should the toll be raised or lowered? If so, how much? And is demand growing? How long would it take volume to respond in full to a change in price? No one can say.

Most ventures financed with revenue bonds are almost unique. Comparisons with other tunnels, bridges, and toll roads give no reliable estimate of likely revenue. Consequently new issues of revenue bonds are often quite speculative.

Sometimes revenue bonds are issued to finance ventures that never should be undertaken in the first place. Should Boston, for instance, sell revenue bonds to build a sports stadium for its professional football and baseball teams? If the proposed stadium cannot pay its way as a private venture, why should it use public funds? If sport lovers do not enjoy the games enough to fill most of the seats day after day, and pay prices for tickets high enough to cover all costs, why should the venture be granted tax-exemption on its real estate? Could not the capital needed for this enterprise be used to better advantage elsewhere? Should not some taxpaying firm in private industry borrow the money, and put it to work in its own business?

All told, however, the volume of revenue bonds is small in comparison with the total of municipals as a whole. While these bonds do contribute somewhat to the composite demand for loans of all kinds, their importance is insignificant. They are only of curious interest to us therefore.

## 4. Credit Ratings

A merchant who hopes for repeat sales will do his best to satisfy his customers. If he wants you to keep on buying his brand of bread week after week, he will make sure you get good bread in the beginning. The same rule applies to borrowing and lending. If a city borrows $5,000,000 on six-months tax anticipation notes in May 1971, it will move heaven and earth to keep its promise come November, because it wants to borrow again in May 1972, and so on, year after year. Repeat business keeps the borrower both honest and prudent.

With revenue bonds this safeguard is sometimes missing. Suppose a tax-exempt authority is organized to sell revenue bonds and build an aquarium, with the proceeds of ticket sales pledged for interest and sinking fund. The borrower in this case has no plan to build still more aquaria year after year in the future. He is tempted, therefore, to overestimate his expected revenues in the beginning, so as to tell the lender that interest coverage will be ample. Sometimes he proves to be mistaken.

A city or town that sells municipal bonds should use the money for fixed assets only, not for current expenses too. If the money is put into a new high school that will last for fifty years, so that no such huge outlay will be needed again for a long time, then the town is not overstepping the bounds of prudence when it sells bonds to pay for the school. The sinking fund, of course, should extinguish the debt long before the school itself becomes obsolete and has to be replaced. Nevertheless no equity money need be provided by the town to protect the borrowed money provided by the bondholders.

If the town borrows for a different purpose, however, and uses the money for current expenses, the borrowing is unsound. Salaries of school teachers, for instance, which go on year after year, should not be paid with borrowed money. Yet some municipal borrowing nowadays serves only to replenish the bank accounts of cities that labor under a chronic operating deficit.

High outlays for relief, for doles to people who cannot or will not find jobs, often create continuous deficits. Many of these people are really refugees, driven out of the South by the mechanical cotton picker. Although the tractor and the gang plow replaced the man with the mule long ago, and although the corn picker replaced the human harvester, nevertheless the blacks were still needed for many years to pick the cotton. Not until this last farming operation was finally mechanized did their livelihood vanish.[2] Then they became refugees from famine. They fled north to the cities that paid the highest relief. In effect these cities, without knowing it, engaged in competitive bidding for refugees. The higher the dole the cities paid, the more "clients" they enticed and

---

[2] Cf. Richard H. Day, "The Economics of Technological Change and the Demise of the Sharecropper", *American Economic Review*, June 1967, pp. 427-449.

put on relief. When these clients voted, they all voted for doles still higher. And the more the cities paid, the worse their deficits became. Meantime the old taxpayers fled to the suburbs, taking their prudent votes with them.

When will it all end? Not until the supply of refugees is exhausted, it would seem, and the cities have scraped the bottom of the barrel for new voters.

Many of the refugees can hardly read and write. They never learned to do so in school. Perhaps they had no incentive. It requires no "book larnin" to pick cotton. Now in the North, where it takes an education to get a good Job, black boys and girls may try harder in school.

Meanwhile the volume of municipal borrowing promises to remain very heavy. It will absorb a huge volume of savings. Most of the money will go into schools, roads, bridges, water and gas mains, sewers, incinerators, municipal housing, city hospitals, asylums, slum clearance, parks, and the like. Almost none of the money will go into profit-making tools of production. Marginal productivity will not enter the equation. The national interest rate, however, will feel the full weight of all this municipal borrowing.

# CHAPTER XII
# LOANS TO PUBLIC UTILITY COMPANIES

## 1. Distinctive Features

Because public utility companies are the largest borrowers in the corporate bond market, their influence on the level of interest rates in general deserves our most careful study.

Borrowing by public utility companies is quite unlike that by industrial companies. These companies are really quasi-governmental organizations. They buy plant and equipment, and devote these assets to public service.

In order to protect their borrowing power, the regulatory commissions put a floor under their earnings, and in order to protect their customers from exploitation, the commissions also put a ceiling over their earnings. The two limits lie close together. No such floor and ceiling exist for industrial companies.

When public utilities borrow money, they pay whatever rate of interest they must. They are never "priced out of the market". Their demand is completely inelastic, and their demand curve is a vertical straight line. And the rate they pay is simply copied from elsewhere, merely copied, never originated independently by the commissions themselves.

In many cities the electric light company, the gas company, and the telephone company find that their assets serving the residential area exceed those serving the industrial area. If this is true, their borrowing is dominated by considerations of satisfaction to householders rather than profit to their industrial customers. Neither directly nor indirectly does profit maximization control their borrowing.

With electric utility companies today, government regulation is still confined to the question of a "fair return on a fair value" of their invested assets. Regulation does not yet require these companies to render a huge volume of unprofitable services like those furnished by the railroads when they ran passenger trains nearly empty. But regulation of utility companies is creeping further afield every year. The fate of the railroads, for whom it is now impossible to design a schedule of rates that will yield them a fair return on their invested assets, shows what could happen to other regulated industries eventually. All of this is a far cry from what the old Marginal Productivity Theory of Interest would lead us to expect.

## 2. Limits on Borrowing

A public utility company is a regulated monopoly. Its borrowing power depends upon what the public utility commission will let it earn. These earnings then determine the interest coverage on its bonds. The larger the earnings, the larger the debt that can be serviced.

Investors want past earnings to be large enough to cover interest on new debt, with plenty to spare. What counts is not the company's hopes for the future, but its record in the past. Moreover, investors want the company to put new equity capital behind each new issue of bonds. Investors will not buy these bonds if the debt-equity ratio is too high. For many companies, in fact, this ratio is limited by a special clause in their charter of incorporation. As regards interest coverage, the Securities and Exchange Commission also insists on a two for one ratio for new issues of holding company debentures. In the end, therefore, the size of bond issues is set, not by how much the company *would like to borrow*, but by how much investors *are willing to lend*. Because the borrowing power of a public utility company is limited in this way, its demand upon the loan market is also limited, and the rate of interest for the nation as a whole is held down somewhat thereby.

Part of the money these companies spend for new plant is furnished by their stockholders, to be sure. The stockholders receive dividends, but their dividends are limited by the ceiling that regulatory commissions place on the companies' return on investment. As a result, dividends are really a disguised form of interest on the stockholders' equity.

Since the stockholders' claim on earnings is secondary to that of the bondholders, the stockholders are entitled to a higher return than the bondholders get. This return compensates them for the risk they assume in their junior position. Were it not for the fact that common dividends tend to rise as a utility company grows, its common stock would always show a higher yield than its bonds do. Expected growth in the future, however, usually puts the price of the stock up at once, and depresses the yield in the present.

## 3. Long-Term Debt

The balance sheet of a public utility company always shows fixed assets far in excess of current assets. As a result such a company is obliged to borrow at long term rather than short term. Any bank debt it may report is due to be replaced by long-term bonds in the very near future. A public utility company certainly is not what we always mean by a "borrower-either-way".

Money borrowed by a public utility company is not a self-liquidating loan such as a retailer or a farmer might obtain. Instead the money goes into plant and equipment and other assets that provide earnings for many years afterwards before they are completely worn out. These earnings furnish the money to amortize the debt gradually, and pay the interest meanwhile. The debt is represented by a bond issue. Its amortization takes the form of the repurchase of some of the bonds for the sinking fund each year. In the meantime the lender continues to receive interest on all the other bonds still outstanding. If the lender is an insurance company, both sinking fund and interest are then available for relending, and the lender thus enjoys a flow of cash that can be used to purchase new bonds issued by some other borrower.

The money wherewith to pay amortization comes from charges for depreciation made by the borrower. Usually the borrower pays off the entire debt before the plant and equipment against which it was issued have worn out completely. Useful plant, with good earning power, free from debt, then remains. In this way the public utility company engages in contractual saving. This saving occurs when charges for depreciation exceed actual wear and tear. Excess cash from depreciation goes into still more plant and equipment, all of which is devoted to public service. For the country as a whole, a huge volume of saving takes place in this way.

Still other saving occurs through the reinvestment of surplus earnings, a process known as "corporate saving". Surplus earnings, however, are aftertax earnings, and so they are severely restrained by the corporate income tax. Hence amortization of debt and reinvestment of excess depreciation remain the more important forms of saving.

Inasmuch as a public utility company, like any other borrower, must supply equity capital to protect its borrowed capital, the borrowing power of a utility company is always held in check in this way. Even if demand for electricity, for instance, is very keen, the company cannot go ahead and sell bonds faster than its retained earnings permit. Nor can it commit itself to interest charges larger than its earning power warrants. Bonds should not exceed 50% or 55% of total capitalization, as a rule, and interest charges before income taxes should be covered several times, the exact ratio depending upon the peculiarities of the business.

All of these requirements are carefully weighed by the services that rate bonds and pronounce upon their investment quality. The very best bonds are rated AAA. The principal rating agencies are Moodys Investment Service and Standard and Poor's Corporation.[1]

When a utility company makes a profit and reinvests this money in new plant, it increases its future earning power. The debt-equity ratio improves, and so does the interest coverage. This lets the company sell more bonds and make still further additions to its rate base.

If reinvested earnings do not accumulate fast enough, however, a company may be forced to sell preferred stock instead of bonds to finance its growth. Preferred stock counts as equity capital. Additions thereto improve a company's debt-equity ratio, and permit the sale of new bonds, dollar for dollar. Unfortunately preferred dividends must be paid out of net income after corporate taxes, not out of pretax income. To pay a 7% dividend, a company must earn 14% pretax on the proceeds of new preferred stock. It would be much cheaper to finance the company's growth with new bonds. But investment bankers won't underwrite the bonds, and insurance companies won't buy them, unless the debt-equity ratio comes up to the legal standard.

The tax law, however, contains an offset that helps public utility companies sell preferred stock at a good price. This law specifies a tax rate of only 15% on intercorporate preferred or common dividends, contrasted with 48% on bond interest. As a result, a 7% preferred stock yields a corporate investor 5.95% net, whereas a 9% bond yields only 4.68% net. Fire and casualty insurance companies, therefore, being owned in most cases by their stockholders rather than their policyholders, and thus being subject to higher taxes than mutual life insurance companies must pay—these stock companies, to repeat—afford a large market for public utility preferreds.

---

[1] See Forbes, September 1, 1970, pp 10-20.

Since the inflow of cash to life insurance companies and most other large buyers of utility bonds is set in any given year by contracts already outstanding with debtors and policyholders, it follows that the supply of funds for these investors to lend is fixed at a certain limit too. Meanwhile the annuity of interest and amortization that public utility borrowers can pledge to institutional lenders is fixed at another limit. Neither limit depends on the rate of interest itself. Both limits are set by outside factors. It is the ratio between these two limits that determines the rate of interest. The interest rate is not *equal* to this ratio, of course, but it is still determined by it.

If this interest rate does not coincide with that in the mortgage market, money will flow out of the mortgage market into the bond market, or vice versa. In other words, savings banks and life insurance companies will shift their purchases of bonds or mortgages from one field to the other. When the interest rate is the same in both fields, after adjustment for risk and cost of supervision, the market is in equilibrium.

## 4. Financing with Rights

The volume of utility bonds offered for sale each year is limited by the amount of new equity capital put into the business each year. Most of this equity capital comes directly from current earnings, from profits not paid out as dividends. Some of it, however, may come from the sale of common stock in addition to preferred stock. This new common stock is usually sold to present stockholders, who are offered the right to subscribe for it at a price lower than the current market. Stockholders who refuse to subscribe suffer a dilution of their share in future earnings, and the value of their holdings declines when their stock goes ex rights. The device of offering rights, therefore, is a way of coercing stockholders, of forcing them to put new money into the company. The word "rights" is only a euphemism for "assessment".

By omitting all dividends, of course, and reinvesting all earnings, managers could build equity capital up without offering rights. Interest coverage, however, would not be improved by shifting from assessment to reinvestment. The omission of dividends would also hurt the company's reputation with investors.

To get around this difficulty, directors often vote a liberal dividend, and then assess the stockholders to get most of the money back again. American Telephone, for instance, has followed this practice for a great many years. Its net dividend—the excess of its gross dividend over its assessments—has remained very small. But the company has succeeded in building up its equity capital and its bonded debt much faster than it could otherwise have done. As a result, it has sold a huge volume of bonds, and has depressed their price and hurt the general interest rate somewhat. Meanwhile, innocent stockholders have paid large personal income taxes on the money they received with one hand and returned with the other.

A stock like Telephone can be either a growth stock or an income stock, but not both at once. If you take up your rights, you get hardly any net income, but you do get steady growth; while if you sell your rights, you get satisfactory income, but hardly any growth. You can't have it both ways.

Moreover, whenever you sell your rights and spend the proceeds, you are living on your capital. Every time the stock goes ex rights it falls in price. The company has to grow year after year to offset this fall, but you do not participate in this growth.

## 5. Earnings and Growth

To make an offer of rights a success, a company's stock must enjoy a good standing in the market. Earnings must be satisfactory to investors. New equity capital can only be raised when earnings are ample.

Moreover, the larger the earnings, the faster the growth of capital, surplus, and bonded debt can be; but the smaller the earnings, the slower the growth must be.

This rule is obvious in the case of a company that has no bonds at all, and pays no dividends on its common stock. If such a company is allowed a return of 6%, let us say, it will earn just enough to build up its rate base 6% a year. If it earns 7%, its reinvestment rate will be 7%. Regardless of the growth in the demand for its services, its growth will be held down to exact equality with its allowed return.

For companies who finance with bonds as well as stock, the process works out somewhat differently. For example, consider a company with total assets $A$ on which earnings at the rate $a = 7\%$ are allowed. This company has \$100,000,000 of bonded debt $B$ outstanding, on which it pays interest at the rate $b = 5\%$. It also has \$100,000,000 of stockholders' capital $C$ outstanding, on which earnings at the rate of $c$

can therefore be reported. Total assets are $A = B+C$. If it pays a net or "pure" dividend $\pi$ equal to 5% of the book value of its common stock $C$, then its reinvestment ratio $r$ will turn out to be 4% of $C$, as shown below. This reinvestment ratio of 4% will support an increase of 4% in bonded debt $B$ each year, as shown in Diagram XI below.

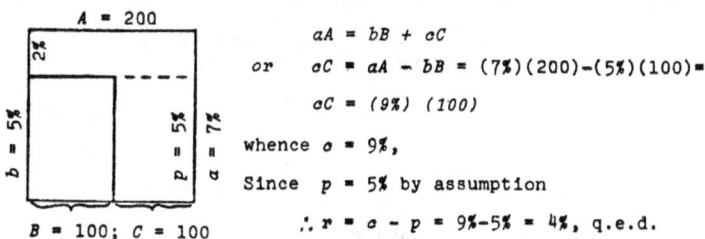

$$aA = bB + cC$$

or $\quad cC = aA - bB = (7\%)(200)-(5\%)(100) =$

$$cC = (9\%)(100)$$

whence $c = 9\%,$

Since $p = 5\%$ by assumption

$\therefore r = c - p = 9\%-5\% = 4\%,$ q.e.d.

*Diagram XI: Rate of Return on Equity*

The following table shows how the return allowed on a company's rate base $A$ limits its reinvestment ratio $r$ and its overall growth $g$. So long as the debt-equity ratio $B/C$ remains the same, a company's growth $g$ will be equal to its reinvestment rate $r$.

| Cause | Effect | | |
|---|---|---|---|
| Allowed Return, $a$ | Equity Earnings, $c$ | Reinvestment Rate, $r$ | Growth Rate, $g$ |
| 5% | 5% | 0% | 0% |
| 6% | 7% | 2% | 2% |
| 7% | 9% | 4% | 4% |
| 8% | 11% | 6% | 6% |
| 9% | 13% | 8% | 8% |
| | Given: $b=5\%$, $p=5\%$, $B/C=1$ | | |

If a company is allowed to earn 8% instead of 7% on its assets devoted to public service, it will grow at a faster rate than a 7% company will grow. The actual rate in any case will depend on the factors listed in the table below.[2]

In this list $a$, $b$, $l$, and $p$ are known parameters, while $c$, $r$, and $g$ are unknowns whose value can be deduced from the equations below.

---

[2] See my *Investment Value*, p. 132, formula 52a.

Let $a$ = allowed rate of return on total assets $A$
$b$ = interest rate on outstanding bonds $B$
$c$ = rate of earnings on equity capital $C$
$l$ = leverage = $A/C$, by definition — derived from the debt-equity ratio $B/C$
$p$ = pure dividend rate = gross rate less assessments
$r$ = reinvestment rate = $c - p$
$g$ = growth of rate base

The formula for $c$ is derived thus:

| | | |
|---|---|---|
| (1) | $A = B + C$ | by definition |
| (2) | $l = A/C$, or $A = l C$ | "        " |

whence

(3) $\qquad l = (B+C)/C$
$\qquad\qquad lC = B + C$
$\qquad\qquad B = lC - C$

Moreover
(4) $\qquad aA = bB + cC \qquad\qquad$ by definition
or $\qquad cC = aA - bB \qquad\qquad$ "        "

Insert (2) and (3) in (4), and get·
(5) $\qquad cC = alC - b(lC-C)$
$\qquad\qquad = alC - blC + bC$

whence
(6) $\qquad c = al - bl + b$
or
$\qquad\qquad c = l(a-b) + b \qquad\qquad$ q.e.d.

Knowing $c$, we can then deduce
(7) $\qquad c-p = r = g$, the growth rate

## 6. Escape from Regulation

Although public utility commissions are empowered to limit the rate of return that companies may earn on their assets, and although these commissions are often slow to lift the allowed return when interest rates rise, nevertheless it is sometimes possible for companies to escape from this regulation in part.

Suppose interest rates rise suddenly, as in the spring of 1970, when the New Jersey Bell Telephone Co., with new construction already under way, was forced to sell $100,000,000 of AAA bonds at the outrageously high yield of 9.35%, a yield far above the company's allowed return. Yet if the company could perchance invest this incremental money at 20%, let us say, the new money would lift the average return on the company's entire rate base. Should this average return now rise above the old prescribed limit, the commission, in the light of current costs for borrowed money, could hardly insist on a cut in phone rates to bring the return back to where it was before. If the commission did so insist, the company could sue in the courts, and would probably get a stay of execution on any such rate cut. In this way it might come to pass that the company's average return would respond somewhat to the rise in the market rate of interest despite any lack of cooperation from the regulatory authorities.

## 7. The Rate of Growth

It is usually said that the growth of an electric light company depends on the growth of the demand for electricity, and likewise for a gas company, a telephone company, and any other public utility company. This statement, however, does not tell the whole truth, not by any means.

Suppose we start with an electric utility that has long been earning a "fair return on a fair value", and has been keeping well abreast of the growth in demand for many years. Let us further suppose that the regulatory commission suddenly cuts the company's rates drastically, as occurs on occasion in some Latin American countries, with the result that earnings cease altogether. The company then has no net income to reinvest in more plant. Nor can it sell new stock, for it pays no dividends. It cannot even sell bonds, because their interest coverage is now too small. Meantime the drastic rate cut stimulates the demand for electricity. In short order the company is running at 100% of capacity every day, with no reserve to draw on in an emergency. If profits reappear because operations are now far above the break-even point, let us assume they are taken away by another rate cut. Growth in plant and equipment, therefore, becomes impossible. Yet demand continues to expand. Evidently it is the rate of return allowed by the public utility commission, not the growth in demand for electricity as such, that determines the growth of the company's rate base. While its output of electricity may grow for a while, its rate base will not.

Something like this can happen even if a company is allowed to earn a rate of return more than zero. Any return that is very low will prevent the company from keeping abreast of demand. Just what is the correct return is often hard to say.

Suppose we consider another company, and let its allowed return be suddenly increased. The company then raises its charges to consumers. When the price of electricity goes up, consumption may not go down, to be sure, but it will certainly not grow as fast as before. Meantime the company's earnings will rise, and the high return allowed on its rate base will induce the management to reinvest as much money as possible in the enterprise. Wires will be put under ground rather than on poles, extra reserve capacity will be installed for use in extreme emergencies, service will be extended to unprofitable customers, hydroelectric and nuclear power will be used even where coal is cheaper, and other measures will be employed to build up the rate base. Meantime the use of electricity will grow quite slowly. The rate of return rather than the growth of demand will thus control the company's growth in assets, in this case just as before.

If for some special reason a regulatory commission wanted to make a public utility company grow very fast, it could set the allowed return very high. The commission might permit a return of 10%, for instance, when the prevailing interest rate was only 5%. Then the company would sell new bonds and stock as fast as it could, and would put the proceeds into new plant in a most extravagant way. Borrowing new money at 5%, and offering its shareholders the right to subscribe to an equal amount of new stock, the company could earn 15% on its equity capital. Total assets would then increase with great speed. In fact, assets might increase even faster than 15% if stockholders could raise cash to take up their rights in such large amounts. Or preferred stock might be issued for awhile. This case, however, is purely hypothetical, and is mentioned only to show the factors involved.

On the other hand, if the issue of rights were held in check somewhat, and made just equal to cash dividends, then the stockholders would pay back with one hand just what they received with the other. A 10% return on total assets, and a 15% return on equity capital, would result in growth at a rate of 15%, but no more. Moreover, if no rights at all were offered, and dividends of 5% were paid, then only 10% would be left for reinvestment, and growth would be held down to 10% also.

Evidently the rate of growth of a utility company is determined by the rate of growth of its equity capital. This in turn is determined by the (1) the allowed return, (2) the cost of borrowed money, (3) the debt-equity ratio, (4) the cash dividend policy, and (5) the volume of new stock offered on rights to shareholders. Contrary to the usual belief, the rate of growth in the demand for service by the customers themselves has nothing whatsoever to do with the outcome.

The perfect rate structure for a public utility company is very hard to define. Such a rate structure should encourage the growth of demand, on the one hand, and must attract plenty of capital, on the other hand. Yet even when a company has a very good rate structure, many of its customers may refuse to believe this fact.

As we have just seen, when a regulatory commission sets the rate of return a company can earn, it thereby sets the rate of growth the company can achieve. By the laws of mathematics, one follows from the other, through a chain of cause and effect. What happens, then, if the commissioners seek to accomplish too much at once? Using a single mathematical equation, they can solve for only one unknown at a time, not two or three together. What if they try to make investment grow faster than earnings grow, and faster than new money can be raised in the bond market? This can easily happen. Yet public utility companies can finance new plant and equipment, including new outlays on pollution control, new lines to unprofitable customers, and extra standby equipment, only just so fast. No amount of denunciation from their critics can speed the process up. Once the rate of return has been fixed, all the rest is predetermined.

The foregoing rule about growth is not meant to imply that managers of public utility companies are irresponsible, and would run wild if their allowed return were set too high. On the contrary, these men take pride in their work, and try to operate their companies in a prudent and economical way, just as if they were engaged in a competitive enterprise. Nevertheless they remain keenly aware of the benefits that additional investment can bring, and so they usually try to make their companies grow as fast as earnings permit.

## 8. Inelastic Demand for Loans

What will turn out to be the true rate of return on new money—incremental money—invested in the public utility industry in the future? Who can say? If the temporary return proves to be 20%, the regulatory authorities will take steps to cut it down; if it is 2%, they will take steps to lift it up. Knowing this, management goes ahead and invests new money regardless of the true return. No one can assert, therefore, that the Marginal Productivity Theory of Interest correctly describes the way in which capital flows into the public utility industry. Instead, this huge industry is a law unto itself.

For clarity in exposition I may have overstated this argument a little, but not much. Managements do make estimates, to be sure, concerning the earning power of new plant and equipment, and they are rather cautious about increments that promise only 2% to start with. But they also know they are under legal obligation to serve the public, and so they often make unrewarding investments. They hope to offset the poor return on these by making more profitable outlays elsewhere. If the allowed return on their rate base is 7%, let us say, the management then shoots for an average return of 7% on new money as a whole.

An average return of 7%, be it noted, is not the same as a marginal return of 7%. Moreover, an *average* return of 7% could easily be higher than the *marginal* return actually achieved by many firms in private industry operating in a freely competitive market. Be that as it may, however, we can always say marginal productivity bows out when regulated monopoly takes over.

A public utility company, unlike an industrial firm, can never say "No!" to its customers. If interest rates go up, and carrying charges on new plant become very heavy, a public utility company cannot say, "We refuse to give you service; it would involve us in a loss to do so." An industrial company, however, can say, "We are raising our prices at once, enough to cover our added costs; perhaps you will refrain from buying at all, therefore." Since a public utility company cannot say no, it cannot respond to a rise in interest rates by decreasing the volume of its new borrowings. Yet such a refusal to borrow flies in the face of orthodox theory.

So long as the allowed return to a public utility conpany is in line with the prevailing rate of interest on bonds and stocks elsewhere in the market, the volume of new capital demanded by a regulated monopoly is the same whether this rate of interest is high or low. In other words, the demand is completely inelastic with respect to the interest rate, and the demand curve is a vertical straight line. Consequently the public utility industry, unlike the housing industry, does little or nothing to take up the shock when interest rates fise or fall.

Elsewhere in the economy our usual rule applies, to wit: the rate of growth determines the rate of interest. For regulated public utilities, however, this rule is reversed, thus: the rate of return determines the rate of growth.Cause and effect are turned right around.

## 9. Loans to Railroads

While railroads can usually borrow with ease to buy rolling stock, they find it very hard to borrow for way and structures. If they had the necessary borrowing power, they could invest new capital very profitably in many of the following assets:

improved classification yards
better grades
easier curves
stronger bridges
higher tunnels
longer passing tracks
better ties and ballast
heavier rail
grade crossing elimination
centralized traffic control
cab to caboose radio
hotbox detectors
roller bearings
coal piers
ore piers
grain elevators
gantry cranes for trailers on flat cars
better machine tools in repair shops
better office appliances
electronic computers
air conditioning
burglar and fire alarms
new office buildings
exploitation of air rights over tracks
trackside real estate

The railroads, unfortunately, with their land and buildings already encumbered by old mortgages, cannot borrow new money on these same assets. Instead, to finance improvements they are forced to depend on their cash flow from earnings and depreciation. But only the most prosperous roads enjoy enough income of this kind. The rest fall further and further behind each year.

Unlike the electric light companies and the gas companies and the telephone companies, the railroads often suffer from a poor credit rating. Even though new money put into classification yards, centralized traffic control, and radio communication systems would often earn a yearly return of 30% or 40% before taxes, many roads cannot find anyone to lend them the money for this purpose. They are receiving too poor a rate of return on their old assets to show proper interest coverage on any new bonds. Many railroads, in fact, are now hard pressed just to meet their forthcoming maturities on old bonds issued years ago. Still more bonds, therefore, are quite out of the question for these roads.

Yet a few railroads are fortunate enough to have large earnings already, and these roads can borrow all they want. But these few roads have surplus earnings to reinvest in their property already, and so they do not need to borrow after all. As a result it comes to pass that marginal productivity does not rule the investment of savings in railroad plant for the industry as a whole. The poor roads are quite unable to push their investment out to the same margin as the rich roads can.

Not only railroads but also many industrial corporations exhibit this unevenness in marginal productivity. If the margin were the same throughout the entire economy—which it certainly is not—then the Marginal Productivity Theory of Interest would be more convincing. The unevenness of the margin, however, seriously undermines the whole theory.

Competition between the railroads, the truck lines, the barge lines, the pipelines, the city busses, the airlines, and private passenger cars is so severe that the Interstate Commerce Commission cannot devise any schedule of rates for the railroads that will provide them with enough earnings to let them borrow as much money as they need to bring their roadway and structures fully up to date. Moreover Congress insisted until recently that the railroads furnish passenger service at a loss. The net result once more is that marginal productivity fails to control the allocation of the nation's savings in the railroad industry.

Since the railroads, like other public utility companies, have no work in process, and use only a small amount of current assets in their business, they cannot raise money by borrowing against current assets in the way that industrial and merchandising companies can do.

Loans secured by new rolling stock, however, in contrast to loans secured by immovable rails, tunnels, bridges, and so forth, are easy for the roads to obtain. A poor railroad can borrow money for freight cars and locomotives almost as cheaply as a rich road can. In both cases the equipment trust certificates carry a lien on the rolling stock. If interest and sinking fund are not met on time, the trustees can take possession of the equipment, and haul it off for use on some other road. As a result, it comes to pass that there is no scarcity of money to lend on rolling stock, and so for most railroads the last dollar invested in equipment earns a much lower return than the last dollar invested in roadway does.

When the railroads issue equipment trust certificates to pay for rolling stock, they usually sell serial bonds, and plan to retire these with cash arising from charges for depreciation each year. The complete repayment usually takes fifteen years or so, while the rolling stock itself often lasts twenty-five or thirty years. Since some of the certificates are specifically designated for repayment in one, two, or three years, while others are not due till thirteen, fourteen, or fifteen years, this procedure makes the railroads borrow both short and long.

The prices of the various certificates vary with the time to maturity. Buyers and sellers both make estimates about the future of interest rates. All of this is in harmony with the Expectations Theory of short and long-term interest rates.[3]

## 10. Loans to Airlines

Most of the money that airlines borrow is used for the purchase of new planes. The airlines raise the money by selling serial notes running for twelve years or so. Commercial banks take the short maturities, and insurance companies the long ones.

The airlines, like the railroads, the telephone companies, the gas companies, and the electric light companies, are public utilities. Their fares are set by a regulatory commission, in this case the Civil Aeronautics Board, or C.A.B. for short. Unlike other public utilities, however, the airlines enjoy no monopoly. They share important routes with each other, routes like those between New York and Miami, or Chicago and San Francisco. Each airline is then free to schedule as many flights a day over its allotted routes as it sees fit. A line that schedules six flights a day over a given route can expect to pick up more business than a line that offers only four. And if the first line drops a flight, some of its business will go to its competitors. Therefore each line feels compelled to offer as many flights as it can.

In order to offer more flights, airlines must buy more planes. But more planes mean more charges for interest and amortization of debt.

---
[3] See Chapter IX, §3.

Meanwhile the number of passengers per day for all lines together increases very little, despite the increase in total service offered. The load factor for every plane declines, and finally falls to the break-even point. Competition brings this all about. The airline business is thus much more competitive than the telephone business or the electric light business, where each company enjoys a local monopoly.

In the airline business, as in so many others, new money is often invested just to protect old money. Thus an airline, insistent on holding its present share of the market, may buy still more planes if it sees its competitors scheduling more flights per day. The airline industry as a whole may do this even though the new investment damages its present earning power. This process can go on and on until the lenders themselves refuse to take part in it any longer.

When lenders lay down arbitrary rules about interest coverage and the debt-equity ratio, they unwittingly limit the borrowing power of the airlines.[4] In other words, they limit the demand for the very loans they are trying to make. And by limiting the demand, they limit the rate of interest these loans can earn.

If the growth of the airlines should subside, it would be very hard for the C.A.B. to name any schedule of fares that would keep the rate of return on invested assets from shrinking towards zero. Only when demand is growing is there a scarcity of planes. And only when planes are scarce do earnings rise and provide the new equity capital that permits the sale of new bonds.

## 11. Loans to Truck Lines

Motor trucks make good collateral for term loans granted by commercial banks, because trucks can easily be repossessed by a bank, and resold to a new user if the original borrower defaults on his loan.

The long-distance trucking companies, though seldom called public utilities, are nevertheless closely regulated by the Interstate Commerce Commission, which assigns their routes and fixes their rates. Their earnings, however, are not limited to a "fair return on a fair value", because they do not enjoy a monopoly like that of the electric light

---

[4] Cf. *Aviation Week* (New York: McGraw-Hill Publications Co.) Issue of Jan. 5, 1970, p. 67, col. 3: "The problem with weakened earnings ... is the discouragement it gives to equity capital as a source of financing. This, in turn, raises debt/equity ratios, and lowers the ceiling on borrowing as a source of capital."

companies. Instead they are more like the airlines and the railroads in their exposure to competition.

Each trucker offers as much or as little service over his assigned route as he sees fit. In order to perform this service, he must buy tractor-trailer rigs, or trucks as they are usually called. He gives this equipment hard use. After five or six years these trucks become worn out and must be replaced.

The money invested in these trucks can be looked upon as a revolving fund. If profits are good, the fund grows, while if profits are bad, the the fund shrinks. If it shrinks, it cannot finance as many new trucks as before. Consequently fewer trucks are kept in use, and total mileage must be reduced. A trucker who formerly scheduled five trips a week from A to B can now schedule only three or four. Load factors then improve, and profits reappear, for it costs but little more to dispatch a truck full to the roof than one half empty. An automatic mechanism is thus at work to control the profits of the trucking business.

Since long-distance truckers compete with railroads and private trucks, their freight rates are held within bounds, and cannot be raised very high by the I.C.C. Furthermore, when the I.C.C. sets both rail rates and truck rates, it thereby decrees a division of business between the two competing modes of transport.

Both railroads and truck lines are heavy borrowers for rolling stock. Neither borrows nowadays for its right of way, however, because the railroads lack creditworthiness, and the truck lines use public highways. The truckers, to be sure, do pay heavy user taxes, but these taxes are not assessed exactly in proportion to the usage of the highways by each truck line. Moreover, the money to build the highways is obtained by the sale of tax-exempt municipal bonds, and the votes to authorize these bonds come from private motorists rather than public truckers. Therefore it cannot be said that this borrowing for the truckers' right of way is closely tied to their earning power.

When the regulatory authority—in this case the I.C.C.—names a schedule of freight rates, it thereby determines the size of the nation's inventory of motor trucks. And when banks lay down certain arbitrary credit rules before they undertake to finance this inventory, they thereby limit the volume of debt issued against the inventory. The smaller the debt, the less the demand on lenders in general, and the lower the rate of interest everywhere will be.

## 12. Summary

We have now surveyed four important types of lending whose volume is closely tied to the growth of the demand for housing, namely home loans, apartment house loans, municipal bonds, and public utility bonds. Housing itself is a consumers good, a durable consumers good. It is bought for the satisfaction it renders, not for its physical productivity. The same rule holds to a large extent for the assets of municipalities, and indirectly for those of gas, electric light, and telephone companies too. This huge sector of the loan market seldom considers profit maximization. Hence the orthodox theory of interest fails to describe it.

The basic needs of men are food, clothing, and shelter, of which the first two are labor intensive, but the third capital intensive. All three of these goods require machinery for their production, to be sure, but only shelter is a durable good still financed with loans even after it is finished and sold. Would it be at all surprising, therefore, to find that shelter has a much larger effect on the rate of interest than food and clothing have?

Statistics support this view. Raymond W. Goldsmith, in his survey entitled *The National Wealth of the United States in the Postwar Period*,[5] lists nonmilitary assets in order of importance thus:

Table V.   Composition of the National Wealth

| | | |
|---|---|---|
| Residential structures | 24% | |
| Consumer durables | 11% | 45% |
| Public (nonprofit) structures | 10% | |
| | | |
| Nonresidential structures (including public | 15% | |
| Producer durables           utilities, however) | 11% | |
| Inventories | 7% | 34% |
| Livestock | 1% | |
| Land, gold, foreign assets, etc. | 21% | |
| | 100% | |

Goldsmith, op. cit., Table A-9, for 1958.

Most of these assets are covered by loans, with the ratio of loans to value being very high on private homes. This table shows, therefore, that loans to households, and all that goes with them, are much more important than loans to competitive industrial firms. In other words the Home Loan Theory of Interest, as I call it, covers a much wider field than the Marginal Productivity Theory of Interest does.

---

[5] Princeton: Princeton University Press, 1962

The table includes only non-military assets. Yet military assets are very large too. Money borrowed to pay for them does not go into tools of *production* but into tools of *destruction*. Here again the orthodox theory of interest, with all its talk about the *productivity* of capital, fails to fit the facts. This grand old theory, though correct in logic, nevertheless covers too little of the whole field to be of much use. It leaves too much out.

Not until we come to manufacturing, retailing, the petroleum industry, and other industrial enterprises do we find any good examples of borrowers who indeed consider the marginal productivity of capital when they seek a loan. Even then we see that marginal productivity fails to exert much effect on the rate of interest. These firms generate most of their new capital internally, and borrow very little. Furthermore, if their assets have but a short life, amortization outweighs interest. All in all, then, industrial borrowing cannot possibly rule the rate of interest. Instead, residential borrowing and all that goes with it is far more important.

# CHAPTER XIII
# LOANS TO INDUSTRIAL COMPANIES

## 1. Characteristics of Industrial Companies

Industrial companies, unlike public utilities, enjoy no monopoly, and face no price control. Economists often complain that many of them are oligopolies, able to obtain prices higher than free competition would permit. Their managers reply, "How we wish this were so!" In truth, their prices are usually controlled by the Current Assets Mechanism, [1] and their rate of profit depends on their industry's rate of growth. Their profits are nowhere near so high as genuine oligopolists or monopolists could earn.

There are three kinds of industrial companies: (1) those who use mostly current assets, and borrow on short term, (2) those who use both fixed and current assets, and borrow either long or short, and (3) those who use mainly fixed assets, and always borrow long. Examples of the first kind are wholesalers and retailers, importers, building contractors, motion picture producers, book publishers, and investment bankers; their short-term borrowing will be discussed in the chapter on commercial banking. Examples of the second kind are manufacturers, miners, lumbermen, farmers, and oil companies, all of whom are borrowers-either-way; their borrowing will be discussed in this chapter. Examples of the third kind are investors in real estate and the like. Their holdings include subdivided land, office buildings, store buildings, shopping centers, motels, hotels, lofts, theaters, garages, parking lots, warehouses, piers, steamships, and fishing vessels, all of which rely on long-term loans; their borrowing will be discussed in this chapter too.

Industrial companies, when they are looking for loans, do not think like homeowners, municipalities, and public utilities. Their motives are different. Industrial companies borrow money in order to make a profit, as much of a profit as they can. They borrow to buy plant and equipment, to purchase raw materials, to pay wages, and to extend credit to their customers. Industrial companies then produce commodities like food and clothing that are sold outright. The profits

---

[1] See my article in *The Quarterly Journal of Economics* for May 1967 entitled "The Path to Equilibrium".

on the sale of these goods are the source from which these companies meet their sinking funds and pay the interest on their bonds.

Since manufacturing, mining, farming, and so forth are not monopolized like the public utility business, these industrial enterprises can never be sure they can sell their wares at a profit in the end. When they borrow money to build a new plant, they go ahead on hope, mere hope. Therefore they must make careful calculations about the productivity of each new increment of money they put into plant and equipment. Investors who buy their bonds also go ahead on hope. They know that the industry will lose its earning power if it erects too much new plant and becomes overexpanded. Hence to protect themselves they demand that earnings on present plant be ample to service the debt on new plant.

This new money goes into producers', not consumers', durable goods. Its earning power is crucial but uncertain. This uncertainty is one of the factors that limits the volume of loans that lenders are willing to grant to industrial companies.

Most of the money invested in new plant, as a matter of fact, does not come from new borrowing at all. Reserves for depreciation, and aftertax earnings, are much more important. For industrial firms, bond issues are but a small source of funds.

When borrowed money is used at all, it can only be repaid in small instalments stretching over many years. The instalments take the form of purchases of bonds for the sinking fund. Although charges for depreciation (which come before income tax) normally provide the money for these instalments, nevertheless the instalments must be paid whether or not the borrowing company earns enough to cover its depreciation. Fortunately these depreciation charges are usually much larger than the instalments themselves. Depreciation applies to the entire plant, whereas the sinking fund applies to borrowed capital only. Consequently there usually emerges an unused portion of the depreciation charge that becomes available for reinvestment in more plant. In fact, the cash flow from depreciation is usually so large each year that only a little occasional borrowing is needed to finance expansion.

The balance of undistributed earnings after the payment of income taxes and dividends also helps to finance plant expansion. As a result, manufacturing companies in the United States can indulge in capital outlays amounting to $30 billion a year, let us say, without needing to borrow more than $7 or $8 billion to help pay for these outlays.

Although statistics for 1969 showed that U.S. corporations of all kinds, both manufacturing and nonmanufacturing, planned to spend as much as $72 billion for plant and equipment in that year, nevertheless these statistics gave an exaggerated impression of the amount of borrowing that would be undertaken for producers durable goods of the special kind that must pay their own way in a competitive industry. Much of the $72 billion total would not go into competitive industry at all. Instead it would go into public utility companies that enjoyed a regulated monopoly. Even in this case depreciation and reinvested earnings would supply a large share of the requirement. For manufacturing companies, depreciation and reinvested earnings would supply an even larger share. The balance that remained to be borrowed, and that must bow to the law of marginal productivity, was small indeed.

Even then, the strong companies would reach out to a lower margin than the weak. Consequently the Marginal Productivity Theory of Interest, though correct in logic, is misleading in practice. In the capital market other considerations are far more important than marginal productivity. We must not let the tail wag the dog.

Many industrial companies are afraid to borrow as much as they can. They know that their industry is subject to severe ups and downs. In a bad depression firms cannot earn their interest charges. If their bonds came due at that time, it would be hard to sell a new issue to replace the old. Bankruptcy might ensue. Clearly it places the stockholders' equity in jeopardy to issue bonds now that might come due on a bad date in the distant future. This risk keeps many companies from using borrowed money to help them reach the margin defined by the old theory.

## 2. Corporate Long and Short-Term Borrowing

When firms who need money for working capital, but not for plant, and who have little or no long-term debt already outstanding, find the short-term rate very high, and likely to stay so, they often turn to the long-term market instead, and sell bonds to insurance companies and savings banks. In so doing, they draw funds away from the mortgage market, and produce a shortage there. The demand from homeowners being elastic, borrowing shrinks in this market, and interest rates rise somewhat. But if firms continue to sell more and more bonds rather than borrow from commercial banks, rates on mortgage loans finally rise a good deal, and carry bond yields up so high with them that long-term borrowing by corporations diminishes too. The rise then comes to an end.

Some firms, when they turn to the bond market, sell more bonds than necessary for the time being. If so, they reverse themselves afterwards, and relend the extra money in the short-term market, buying commercial paper and Treasury bills with their spare cash. This procedure works very well if short-term rates are higher than long-term. And it has the overall effect of keeping the short rate in line with the long. It causes the short rate to be derived once more from the long rate. Since the supply of bank credit is fixed by the policies of the Federal Reserve Board, and since the demand for short-term accommodation from business is highly inelastic, the short-term market badly needs to be able to draw upon the long-term market, or else its own rates might shoot up extremely high at times.

## 3. Limited Borrowing Power

Many industrial firms, especially those whose growth is slow, could still use new borrowed capital to great advantage if only they had the equity capital and the current earnings to support more debt. In this case, as so often, it is not what the borrower would like to borrow, but what the lender is willing to lend, that sets the limit to the flow of new capital into the enterprise.

In order to raise new money, a firm must report good earnings. Not high hopes for the future, but hard facts from the past, are what convince investors. Without good earnings, no bonds can be sold. But with such earnings, plenty of bonds can be sold. Yet the debt-equity ratio must always remain much lower, and the interest coverage much better, than for public utilities.

As a first approximation, we might set up our model in such a way as to make it show that industrial firms borrow up to the limit of their earning power, just as public utilities, municipalities, and even householders often do. Then it could be said of all borrowers, "The more they earn, the more they borrow; the less they earn, the less they borrow." Such a model would be quite simple, and would come somewhere near the truth.

In this model, the demand from manufacturers for loans would not be ruled by the marginal productivity of the new plant that could be built with newly borrowed money. While expected profit would still furnish the *motive* for borrowing, it would not rule the *amount* of borrowing. Creditworthiness rather than rosy hopes would set the limit, and would hold borrowing in check. Earnings on plant already in place would determine the interest coverage on present debt plus any additions thereto. But nowhere in these calculations would the precise marginal productivity of additional plant find expression.

For the typical company engaged in a competitive industry, growth goes on at the same rate as in the entire economy. If this rate is 5%, let us say, the equity capital and the earning power of a typical company will grow at 5% too. As a result borrowing power will grow at the same rate. Growth in borrowing power will then permit growth in debt outstanding. New bond issues will continually be offered to investors in modest amounts. These new issues will soak up a little of the cash flow of insurance companies and pension funds, and will thus help to support the rate of interest on bonds and mortgages in general.

When business is booming, to be sure, and interest coverage is excellent, borrowing may exceed the average for the business cycle as a whole. Yet in the long run the volume of new issues will be determined by the rate of growth in the national dividend measured in current dollars. Once more we find that the rate of growth rules the rate of interest.

Both demand and supply enter into the determination of interest rates. If demand and supply both increase at the same rate, the gap that existed between them to start with will remain open, and the phenomenon of interest will persist. Borrowers will promise to repay more in the end than lenders loan in the beginning. The profit that lenders make on the deal will be called interest.

## 4. New Plant and Equipment

In any given year some firms, to be sure, do not find themselves already mortgaged up to the hilt. They still have some elbowroom left. These fortunate firms are then able to consider the sale of bonds in order to construct new facilities.

Bethlehem Steel was a good example of such a firm in 1967 and 1968. In these years this company sold one issue of $150,000,000 of

5.4% debentures and another issue of $100,000,000 of 6⅞% debentures. Much of the money went into the construction of a huge new steel plant at Burns Harbor, Indiana, built to serve the Chicago market. Here is an excellent example of money being borrowed under circumstances where the marginal productivity of new plant was indeed a vital consideration.

But is borrowing of this sort large enough throughout the country as a whole to have much effect on the interest rate? Statistics show that new issues floated by manufacturing and mining concerns came to $7.5 billion in 1972, compared with $26.5 for home mortgages, $9.5 for apartment house mortgages, and $17.5 for municipal bonds, or $53.5 for the residential sector as a whole.[2] Other borrowers took very large sums too, but their demand curves were highly inelastic, and so they absorbed none of the shock of changes in composite demand.

The only two demand curves that reveal any elasticity at all are those for manufacturing, mining, and oil companies, on the one hand, and those for housing and all that goes with it, on the other hand. In this comparison, housing outweighs competitive industry seven to one. That is why I maintain that the rate of interest for the economy as a whole is closely tied to the demand for shelter.

Every demand curve for loans, to be sure, whether it be sloping or vertical, pushes the rate of interest up or down whenever it shifts to the right or left. Only the sloping curves, however, absorb the shock of a change in total demand. In the end, supply and demand must be equal, of course. Yet most of the components involved can neither stretch nor shrink, as we have seen. There are only two components that can do so, the industrial and the housing. These two are the ones that must do all the work alone.

## 5. Interest Expense, Tax-Deductible for Borrowers

Borrowers usually feel that the federal income tax reduces the burden of interest on their new issues of corporate bonds because this interest is an allowable deduction in computing their taxable income. Thus, if the tax rate is 50%, and the interest expense on $100,000,000 of new bonds at 5% is $5,000,000, then this expense by itself will reduce their pretax income $5,000,000. Consequently their taxes will decline $2,500,000, and so the net cost to them as borrowers will be

---

[2] See Chapter III, §4 entitled *Statistics on Loans and Lenders*

only $2,500,000. The cost, in other words, will be only 2½% of $100,000,000.

This result is correct, however, under one set of circumstances but not another. It depends on whether we are talking about (1) an increase in the size of the debt at a given rate of interest, or (2) an increase in the rate of interest on debt of a given size. In other words, are we talking principal or interest?

*Case 1*: If a company is already mortgaged up to the hilt, and then borrows $100,000,000 more at 5%, let us say, but matches this new debt with another $100,000,000 of new preferred stock, then a return of only 7½% pretax on the entire $200,000,000 of new capital will let it show a pretax interest coverage of 3 to 1 on the new debt, after income taxes at 50% on the extra taxable income, as shown in the table below. But if the company had foregone new debt, and had relied on new preferred stock alone, then it would have needed to earn a full 10% on this new money, in order to add the same $200,000,000 to its fixed assets, and pay a dividend of 5% on the new preferred stock.

*Financing with Equity plus Debt, or With Equity Alone*

|  |  |  |
|---|---|---|
| New debt | $100,000,000 | none |
| New preferred stock | 100,000,000 | $200,000,000 |
| Total | $200,000,000 | $200,000,000 |
| Pretax earnings @ 7½%: | $ 15,000,000; | @10%:$ 20,000,000 |
| Less interest expense | -5,000,000 | none |
| Taxable income | $ 10,000,000 | $ 20,000,000 |
| Income tax @ 50% | -5,000,000 | -10,000,000 |
| Net income | $ 5,000,000 | $ 10,000,000 |
| Preferred dividends | -5,000,000 | -10,000,000 |
| Pretax coverage | 3 to 1 | No interest paid |
| Return needed on total investment | 7½% | 10% |

*Case 2*: If a company's old 5% bonds fall due, and must be replaced with a new 6% issue, then none of the rise in interest charges can be said to fall on the Treasury. Instead the company needs to achieve a good-sized increase in its return on investment, or else the interest coverage on its bonds will shrink, and they will suffer a cut in their investment rating from AAA to AA or lower, thus:

*Refunding at a Higher Rate*

|  | Interest @ 5% | Interest @ 6% |
|---|---|---|
| Debt | $100,000,000 | $100,000,000 |
| Equity | 100,000,000 | 100,000,000 |
| Total | $200,000,000 | $200,000,000 |
| Pretax earnings @ 7½% | $ 15,000,000 | @ 9%: $ 18,000,000 |
| Less interest expense @ 5% | -5,000,000 | @ 6%: -6,000,000 |
| Taxable income | $ 10,000,000 | $ 12,000,000 |
| Income tax @ 50% | -5,000,000 | -6,000,000 |
| Net income | $ 5,000,000 | $ 6,000,000 |
| Pretax coverage | 3 to 1 | 3 to 1 |
| Return needed on total investment | 7½% | 9% |

Evidently the higher the interest rate on the bonds, the higher the pretax earnings must be to provide the same interest coverage. A 5% coupon requires earnings at the rate of 7½% on total assets, while a 6% coupon requires earnings at the rate of 9%. In neither case does the U.S. Treasury shoulder any of the burden when the coupon rate goes up. The corporation carries it all, the entire burden, not just 50%.

Even in 1972, when business is good and getting better, federal, state, and municipal governments are nevertheless at their wits end to find new ways to raise taxes. Corporate income taxes, state and federal combined, already take more than half of a company's earnings. Yet these taxes threaten to go still higher. The higher they go, the less there remains to reinvest for future growth. Since borrowing power depends on the debt-equity ratio, if equity is slow to grow, debt must be slow too, and the demand for loans will lag. A rise in the income tax, therefore, by retarding growth tends to depress the interest rate in due course.

## 6. Marginal Productivity

(Laymen may skip this section. It is addressed to those experts who are loath to abandon standard theory.)

Marginal productivity plays but a very small part in fixing the interest rate.

Although the interest rate is largely set outside of competitive industry, do most competitive firms nevertheless watch this outside rate carefully? Do they reinvest their earnings inside their company up to the point where their last dollar earns the same return after taxes as prevails in the bond market? Do they simply copy the bond rate?

Such a policy for retained earnings may be the one that firms ought to follow. Yet they seldom do. Competitive firms, fighting to preserve their share of the market, and spending new money to protect old money, often disregard marginal productivity altogether. Regulated public utilities, for their part, are a law unto themselves; they often try to build their rate base up as fast as they can. Moreover, in the residential sector of the economy, considerations of profit do not apply. Yet the residential sector dominates the whole loan market. Hence considerations of marginal productivity are very weak at best.

146

For all that, can it still be said that bond money is intramarginal money, while equity money is true marginal money? Is it a fact that many firms do indeed plow their earnings back until they reach the point where their return on the final increment is just equal to the long-term interest rate? And when promoters float a new venture, do they usually employ equity capital out to the point where the last dose earns no more than this interest rate?

The following two cases will shed more light on this problem:

*Case 1.* An aluminum smelter is planning to have a subsidiary company build a hydroelectric power plant in a canyon on a large river. In order for the dam to create a storage lake of ample size upstream, so as to provide a steady flow of water in the dry season, the dam must be made high enough to reach to the top of the canyon. One and only one size for the whole power station is correct. With a dam of this particular height, everything else must be made to fit. Penstocks, turbines, generators, transformers, switch gear, and transmission lines are all fixed by the height of the dam. No marginal adjustments can be made. In this case the capital structure and projected income account of the power plant might look as follows:

| | | | |
|---|---|---|---|
| Bonds | $20,000,000 | Gross earnings @12½% of plant | $5,000,000 |
| Stock | 20,000,000 | Real estate tax @2% " " | - 800,000 |
| Total | $40,000,000 | Balance | $4,200,000 |
| | | Bond interest @5% of debt | -1,000,000 |
| | | Pretax income | $3,200,000 |
| | | Income tax @50% | -1,600,000 |
| | | Net income, after taxes | $1,600,000 |
| | | Dividends @6% on stock | -1,200,000 |
| | | Retained earnings | $ 400,000 |

```
 _____
| Real Estate Tax   |
|_____|
|                   |
|    Income Tax     |
|_____|     12½%
|    Retained       |
|    Earnings       |
|_____|_____|
|  Bond   |  Divi-  |
| Interest| dends   |
|_____|_____|
   $20        $20
 million    million
```

Interest coverage
    pretax            4.2 times
    aftertax        1.6   "
Dividend payout          75%
Reinvestment ratio,      25%
    with retained earnings being used to
    buy bonds for the sinking fund.

The gross earnings of this power plant come to 12½% of invested assets. This 12½% is both the marginal rate of return and the average rate. The marginal rate is thus way above the interest rate of 5% on the bonded debt.

The net income on the common stock comes to 8% of the equity investment of $20,000,000. Here too the return is well in excess of the 5% rate paid on the bonds. This high return is needed in order to give the bonds adequate interest coverage. It is also needed to give a margin of safety for the common dividend, and to provide money for the sinking fund. It is assumed that physical depreciation is zero if maintenance is good.

Because a hydroelectric plant cannot achieve any growth, no reinvestment of earnings can be made for that purpose. Instead, all surplus earnings can be applied to the retirement of the bonds. With purchased bonds being kept alive in the sinking fund, and with interest thereon paid semiannually, about twenty-five years would be needed to complete their retirement. At the end of this period the stockholders would own the plant free and clear. Then they could pay themselves a dividend of 10½% instead of 6%.

The retained earnings that are used to buy the 5% bonds for the sinking fund do indeed earn precisely 5%, and so here is one instance, to be sure, where equity money earns the same return at the margin as borrowed money does. Nevertheless the earnings reinvested in this way are not so used by choice. Instead they are spent in response to a contractual obligation, an obligation that forces the company to buy its own bonds back. Otherwise the parent company would pay itself higher dividends, and could get a better return than 5% on the retained earnings.

In this example, equity money in the beginning earns the same rate as borrowed money does, but in the end it earns much more.

*Case 2.* A large hotel is to be erected in a downtown area. If the hotel were to be only twenty stories tall, it could look forward to a very high occupancy rate summer and winter. Costing $10,000,000, it would yield an estimated profit of $2,500,000 after property taxes, or 25% on the investment. But if the hotel was made thirty-five stories high, and equipped with banquet halls, conference rooms, a large underground garage, and a swimming pool, it would cost $15,000,000, and yield an estimated profit of $3,300,000. The extra $5,000,000 invested would thus add $800,000 to the total profit, and this increment would show a return of 16% instead of 25%. The total investment of $15,000,000 would earn 22%.

With these estimates in hand, the promoters might well decide to build the taller hotel in order to put extra money to work at a good profit. If the small hotel carried a mortgage of $6,000,000 and the large a mortgage of $8,000,000, both at 7½%, the two hotels would earn a pretax profit of $2,500,000 and $3,300,000 respectively. Since the proposed hotels have no record of past earnings to show to lenders, they cannot borrow money at a low rate. Resort to accelerated depreciation, however, might keep the income tax rates down to 42% and 41%, and give returns on equity capital at the rates of 30% and 23%, all as shown in the accounts below:

*Small Hotel*

| | Capital | Income | |
|---|---|---|---|
| Cost | 10,000,000 | @25% = | 2,500,000 |
| Mortgage | -6,000,000 | @7½% = | - 450,000 |
| Gross income | | | 2,050,000 |
| Income tax | | @42% = | - 850,000 |
| Equity | 4,000,000 | @30% = | 1,200,000 |

Interest coverage:
| | |
|---|---|
| pretax | 5.5 times |
| aftertax | 3.7 " |

Debt-equity ratio: 1.50

*Large Hotel*

| | Capital | Income | |
|---|---|---|---|
| Cost | 15,000,000 | @22% = | 3,300,000 |
| Mortgage | -8,000,000 | @7½% = | - 600,000 |
| Gross income | | | 2,700,000 |
| Income tax | | @41% = | -1,100,000 |
| Equity | 7,000,000 | @23% = | 1,600,000 |

Interest coverage:
| | |
|---|---|
| pretax | 5.5 times |
| aftertax | 3.7 " |

Debt-equity ratio: 1.14

*Increments*

| | Capital | Tax | Income | |
|---|---|---|---|---|
| Cost | 5,000,000 | | @16% = | 800,000 |
| Mortgage | -2,000,000 | | @7½% = | -150,000 |
| Gross income | | | | 650,000 |
| Income tax | | 250,000 | @39% = | -250,000 |
| Equity | 3,000,000 | | @13% = | 400,000 |

In this hotel the marginal outlay might be that for the swimming pool. How large should the pool be? How much money should be spent on it? How effective is a pool in attracting guests in the summer when the occupancy rate is otherwise low? The promoters would probably decide that this marginal increment of investment should yield at least 10%, in view of the fact that first mortgage money earns 7½%. Other items in the $5,000,000 extra cost of the large hotel would need to yield much more than 10% in order to bring the average yield on them up to 13%. While the curve describing the marginal productivity of successive doses of money put into this hotel would indeed show a downward slope, nevertheless the curve would not fall below 10% even at its end. Such a return is well above the 7½% earned by mortgage money. Evidently marginal productivity and the interest rate are *not* equal to each other, as sometimes claimed. Yet they move in sympathy with each other, of course. In particular, when the interest rate goes up, the cutoff point on investment in plant and equipment goes up too.

This hypothetical example is true to life when it shows an estimated return of 23% on equity capital compared with 7½% on borrowed capital. This figure of 23% makes full allowance for risk. It is an average of upper and lower estimates that forecast a top return of 30% and a bottom return of 15%, both deemed equally probable.

If allowance for risk brought the return on equity down to a mere 7½%—or the same as the rate on the bonds—then investment bankers would pronounce the common stock unsalable, and would refuse to underwrite it. Such a low return on equity capital as a whole would mean that the marginal increment thereof was expected to earn next to nothing. Hence the entire scheme would be deemed unsound. No equity capital at all could be raised.

Furthermore, a return of only 7½% on equity capital would mean that mortgage interest would be covered scarcely twice before taxes. Such a low margin of safety would make the mortgage too risky for a life insurance company to accept. For this reason too, the scheme could not be financed, because no borrowed capital could be raised.

Clearly, equity money must earn more than borrowed money. Therefore it is wrong to say that businessmen normally push their investment of stockholders' funds out to the point where its marginal productivity is barely equal to the general rate of interest. Yet this policy is just what orthodox theory claims to be the right one and the customary one. The old theory is definitely in error.

Moreover, even if the old theory were right, the result would be inconsequential. Very little money is raised by industrial firms through the sale of new common stock priced at market. (Stock sold on rights, at a discount, is an assessment, and does not fit the case of the hotel just described.) Other borrowers are far more important than industrial firms are. The demand from public utilities, municipalities, homeowners, and others for borrowed money swamps the demand from industrial firms for equity money as such.

In conclusion I maintain that considerations of marginal productivity are so weak as to have little or no effect upon the rate of interest. Such evidently is the rule for firms launching new ventures like the dam and the hotel just described. But for old firms with ample earnings available for dividends a different rule may apply. Let us see:

## 7. Dividend Policies

Where should the reinvestment of earnings stop, and the payment of dividends begin? The answer depends on the rate of interest at which stockholders can reinvest their dividends for themselves. If this rate is 8%, for instance, then their corporation would need to do better than that.

A corporation is often called a capital compounding machine. Yet its ability to compound money is cut in half by the corporate income tax. Stockholders, to be sure, are likewise handicapped by their own income taxes when they reinvest their dividends for themselves. Most stockholders, however, do not earn enough to reach the 50% bracket, and so they can compound their money easier than a corporation can.

Yet firms often reinvest large sums without hope of any return at all. The automobile industry today is about to embark on just such a profitless program of reinvestment. The companies are now tooling up for the new Wankel rotary engine to replace the old piston engine. This new engine, however, offers no hope of an increase in the number of cars sold or the profit per car. Nevertheless it is a necessity, because imported Japanese cars already offer a rotary engine, and American manufacturers must meet this competition. In other words, they must divert hundreds of millions of dollars from dividends to reinvestment, even at no profit, just to stay competitive.

The new tools required for the Wankel engine will only replace old tools made obsolete by this same engine. They are not good security for a bond issue. Unlike a nuclear power plant erected by a growing public utility company, they carry no promise of larger earnings. Instead they are purely defensive.

A large share, in fact, of the reinvestment performed by firms in competitive industry is defensive. It defies the standard rule that capital outlays are always pushed to the point where their marginal productivity is just equal to the prevailing rate of interest. This well-known rule sheds little light on what takes place. Instead, a better rule states that companies who remain competitive always prosper and grow at the rate required by the growth of demand for their products. The Current Assets Mechanism brings it about that earnings just suffice to finance growth at the required rate.[3]

Firms in competitive industry face a much higher risk than public utilities do. They are not guaranteed a "fair return on a fair value" for the assets they invest in their business. They enjoy no monopoly. Their market is not so highly diversified as that of an electric light company or a telephone company, and the demand for their product does not hold up so well during a business depression. Consequently their bonds need higher interest coverage and a stronger debt-equity ratio than suffices for public utilities.

When an industrial company does indeed see a chance, however, to invest new money in plant and equipment at a high rate of return, it can often obtain part of this money from the sale of bonds, and the rest from the retention of undistributed earnings. Under these circumstances, what is the best dividend policy to pursue?

Let us assume that the cash flow of lending institutions is strictly limited. Borrowers competing for this money drive the interest rate up to 8%. Each company gets a share whose size is fixed by the amount of equity capital that it is willing to reinvest alongside of borrowed money, dollar for dollar. Thus, if a company can use $200,000,000 of new plant, it would borrow $100,000,000, and reinvest $100,000,000 out of last year's earnings, while if it needs still more new plant, it would borrow more and reinvest more.

In a large company the engineers, the cost accountants, and the market analysts prepare a list of likely capital outlays, and rank them in order of their estimated profitability. The highest may promise a return of 24% pretax, let us say, and the lowest zero. Assume that total earnings are enough to finance all these outlays with plenty of money to spare. Obviously no money will be invested at 0%. Even at 8% pretax, and 4% aftertax, the company does no better for its stockholders than they could do for themselves if they invested their dividends in 8%

---

[3] See Chapter VIII, "Profits", in my *Prices and Wages, Profits and Growth, Taxes and Dividends* (in preparation).

bonds, and paid personal taxes at the rate of 50% on the interest from these bonds.

The question can now be framed as follows: If a company earns $240,000,000, let us say, how much should it reinvest, and how much should it disburse in dividends?

The correct answer is shown in Figure 2 of Diagram XII, where the cutoff point is shown to be $100,000,000 for reinvestment and $140,000,000 for dividends. At this point the last dollar reinvested earns 8% pretax, 4% aftertax, or the same as the controlling stockholders can get for themselves in the outside bond market.

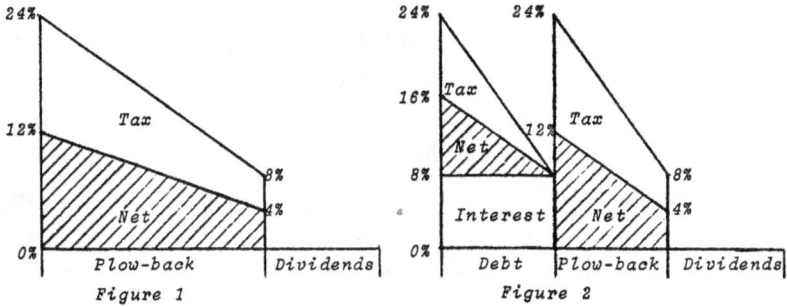

Diagram XII: Marginal Rate of Return

In Diagram XII, the sloping lines at the top of each figure show the falling productivity of various increments of new plant and equipment, one after another. Figure 2 displays two peaks instead of one, because in this figure debt and equity are invested dollar for dollar each time. (I use this one-to-one ratio for simplicity only.)

In both figures of Diagram XII the shaded areas represent after-tax or net income on new plant only, not on new and old combined.

The sloping line at the top of each figure applies to an industrial firm, but not to a public utility. When a regulatory commission sets an upper and lower limit on the earnings of a public utility, and prescribes an *average* rate of return of 8% or 9%, for instance, on assets both new and old, then a *horizontal* line like that in Diagram XI in the previous chapter shows what goes on. In a public utility, if perchance the line were to shift upwards, the company could bring it back down by resort to less profitable increments of new plant and equipment, financed partly with bonds. Such a move would also increase the rate base.[4]

---

[4] Cf. E.E. Zajac, Note on "gold plating" or "rate base padding", in *The Bell Journal of Economics and Management Science*, Spring '72, vol. 3, no. 1.

In Figure 2 of Diagram XII, one half of any new money comes from debt and the other half from equity. Interest coverage pretax turns out to be four times fixed charges, and aftertax two and a half times. The ratio of additional net income to plowback alone is 12% aftertax when debt is present. In Figure 1, however, where debt is absent, the ratio is only 8% on the average. Were the stockholders in Figure 2 to provide all the money—debt as well as equity—they could earn 8% pretax on their extra funds, but only 4% aftertax. This 4% is no more than they can get for themselves in the bond market.

When the interest rate on new money borrowed by a firm is the same as that earned pretax on the marginal increment of newly reinvested earnings, the firm is in equilibrium. If the borrowing rate were higher (say 9%), the firm could lay plans to divert an extramarginal increment of earnings from dividends to reinvestment. Confronting the lending institutions one by one, the firm could threaten to replace bond money with stock money at a rate better than 9%. This process would drive the bond rate down, and set its upper limit at 8%.

The lower limit would be set in another way, but it would still come to 8% pretax. Assume that the total supply of money available for competitive firms to borrow is a constant, fixed by the cash flow of insurance companies and other institutional lenders. (If this fixed sum were to be split between business borrowers and homeowners, a more complicated model would be needed.) No rise in the rate of interest would enlarge this fixed cash flow in the current year. Once the amount of available cash flow is specified at $100,000,000, let us say, for a given borrower, then the total of new debt plus new equity is likewise specified, at $200,000,000 in this case. This total, when applied to the engineering estimates, shows that the marginal increment of new money can earn 8% pretax, and 4% aftertax. Competition from all firms seeking to borrow money will then drive the bond rate up to 8%. In this way the lower limit will become the same as the upper limit. Both will be 8%.

In a great many cases, however, firms cannot borrow enough money to reach their point of equilibrium at 8% or thereabouts. If their earnings on old plant and equipment are low, their interest coverage on old debt will be low too. Then they cannot sell new debt, no matter how promising their new projects may be. Moreover, unless they have net income to spare, they cannot even use reinvested earnings to finance these new projects. In this case the Marginal Productivity Theory of Interest fails us even for firms in a competitive industry.

## 8. Loans to Farmers

Farming, like manufacturing, is a business that requires a great deal of capital. Farmers have a large investment in land and buildings, in machinery, and in work in process. They can use three different kinds of loans to finance their operations, namely mortgage loans on their real estate, instalment loans on their farm machinery, and short-term credit to pay for their seed, fertilizer, insecticide, herbicide, and gasoline. Sometimes they even borrow from their banks to pay the wages of their farm hands. All of the short-term borrowing comes due for repayment when the crop is sold. Short-term loans of this sort are self-liquidating. Long-term loans on real estate and machinery, however, are not self-liquidating. Money spent for barns, drains, fences, roads, and so forth does not add enough to profits in any one year to pay the debt incurred on its behalf. Nor does a tractor or cotton picker earn enough in a single year. Hence real estate and farm machinery are financed with mortgage loans and instalment contracts.

Sometimes a mortgage loan is used to supply money for all three uses. The farmer spends the money for fertilizer, machinery, or buildings in any combination he sees fit. Country banks often make long-term loans like these for purposes partly short-term. If a farmer has excess equity in both his fixed assets and his current assets, he can be a borrower-either-way, just like a manufacturer. Then he can borrow in whatever way will minimize his interest cost.

Farming, however, is a risky business. A crop failure can make a farmer lose all the money he spent for seed, fertilizer, insecticide, and labor. If he has no crop to sell, he has no money to pay his bills. Mere honesty is of no avail. Farmers, therefore, dislike to contract short-term debts, with the whole principal coming due at harvest time. Even long-term debts, with only a small payment due each year, are somewhat risky. Banks, for their part, restrict their mortgage loans to a moderate fraction of the market value of each farm. Even if a farmer could make some extra money earn a high return, he cannot borrow it. Marginal productivity does not rule the outcome. Not what the borrower might dare to borrow, but what the lender is willing to lend, sets the limit on loans to farmers.

When mortgage or instalment contracts are use to finance the purchase of farm machinery, there is still another reason why the rate of interest does not govern the volume of borrowing. This reason involves the fact that farm machinery suffers from a short life. Whenever a capital good, such as a tractor or a motor truck, wears out in only eight or ten years, the need to earn the depreciation on this investment far outweighs the need to earn the interest on it;

A farmer is seldom deterred from buying a tractor because the interest on his loan is 8% or 10% instead of 6%. He does not think in terms of the rate of interest. Instead he asks how long the machine will take to pay for itself. Will it add enough to his profits to return its cost in three years? or five years? Or will ten years be required? Calculations like these show that a farmer's demand curve for short-term loans is very inelastic. Price—in this case the interest rate—has little effect on quantity demanded.

Even if a farmer gets his money by signing a mortgage note on his farm as a whole, and thus contracts a long-term debt, this act does not upset the argument. Not how a farmer gets his money, but how he spends it, is what counts. When he buys farm machinery, it is the rate of depreciation rather than the rate of interest that rules his decisions.

When farmers borrow, they pay whatever rate they must pay. In so doing, they draw funds away from the residential sector of the economy. It is only in this sector that the demand for loans is elastic. Whatever rate emerges there is then copied in the market for farm loans (with adjustments for risk, cost of supervision, etc.). The rate on home loans thus sets the rate on farm loans.

The foregoing argument applies to all short-term loans. Its mathematics are spelled out in detail in the Appendix.

Not all farm mortgages, of course, are written for the purpose of financing the purchase of machines and supplies. Some are written to finance the purchase of neighboring land. Their effect on interest rates then depends on how the *seller* of the land uses the money he receives. Does he use it to buy a house in the city? Or does he go to Florida to spend his declining years, and use his capital to pay his living expenses? In either case, however, the amount of money involved for the nation as a whole is too small to detain us here.

## 9. Loans on Office Buildings

Mortgage loans on office buildings absorb a very large volume of savings, and help to support the interest rate in this way.

Office buildings are like apartment houses and private homes in some respects, but not in all. They afford shelter, they last a great many years, and they entail high fixed costs for interest, amortization, and real estate taxes. But they are a producers' good, not a consumers' good; tenants hire them to make a profit in their business, not to enjoy the pleasures of life. Marginal productivity, therefore, not marginal utility, governs the demand for office space.

Yet an office building is not a factory. What few machines it contains are portable, and use little power. Its usefulness is not restricted to a single company or even a single industry. If a lawyer, for instance, lets his lease expire, the same space can be rented to an architect or an advertising agency. As an investment, therefore, an office building is less risky than a factory. It can safely carry a higher mortgage than a steel mill, a rubber works, or a tannery can support.

If office buildings are well located, the land on which they are built often rises in value as fast as the buildings themselves grow obsolete. Real estate taxes, to be sure, may also go up as time goes on, but rentals in competing buildings go up too, unless there is a serious vacancy rate throughout the whole city. All in all, therefore, a first mortgage of moderate size on a good office building entails little risk. Insurance companies, with their huge cash flow, make large investments in these mortgages.

The supply of new mortage loans offered to the life insurance companies each year depends on the volume of new construction undertaken. Entrepreneurs known as real estate operators "manufacture" office buildings, so to speak. They buy the land, sign up the tenants, secure a construction loan from a bank, arrange a mortgage with an insurance company, and let the contracts to the builders. The builders then make subcontracts for concrete, steel, brick, plumbing, electrical equipment, elevators, and labor of all sorts. In the ideal situation, everybody signs on the dotted line before any work at all begins. In practice, of course, many delays and emergencies occur, and add a good deal to the final cost of the building. Yet if the building is completed and made ready for occupancy while vacancy rates in older buildings are still low, the operator can often make a very large profit on the small equity that he must provide to protect his mortgage loan. If he doubles his money in two or three years, he is able to finance a much bigger building next time. He then takes a fresh look at the market, and decides whether to gamble again or wait awhile.

When inflation is absent, the cost of construction of a new building is about the same as that of an older building completed a few years ago. The new building must earn enough to cover all its costs, including interest, amortization, real estate taxes, maintenance, janitor service, and renting expense. It also must show a net profit after income taxes, so that it can be sold to some investor, and yield the original operator a capital gain. If the building promises to do all this, its construction will be undertaken, otherwise not.

The cost of construction, obviously, is an important factor in the calculation. So long as the cost remains low, more and more buildings will be erected. Construction will continue until the supply of office space, both new and old, becomes so large that rentals sag and profits vanish.

The demand for office space usually is very inelastic. This demand is a derived demand. A large increase in office rent adds very little to the total cost of making a refrigerator, for instance, sold by General Electric, or an automobile sold by General Motors. Consequently tenants like these will not economize on space very much when rents go up, nor use more space when rents go down. For office space, therefore, the demand is much less elastic than for dwelling space in a private home or an apartment house.

The demand for office space is tied to the number of white-collar workers employed in a city. This demand probably grows at about the same rate as clerical employment itself grows. If this employment grows at 2% a year, then the demand curve will shift to the right 2% a year. Meantime, in the absence of inflation, the demand for space can be satisfied by new construction at a constant cost.

Using these assumptions, we could estimate the volume of mortgage loans offered to insurance companies and others for investment year by year. These loans offer strong competition for the new bond issues, the new home loans, and the new Treasury issues that also are competing for the cash flow of the insurance companies, the savings banks, and other long-term lenders. All of these separate demands can be added together to get the composite demand from borrowers of all kinds. This composite demand is then matched against the composite supply of funds to lend. In the end, a rise or fall in the interest rate brings supply and demand into balance.

Whenever demand is highly inelastic—as it seems to be for office space—then the ups and downs in price prove no deterrent nor incentive to users. Tenants pay whatever they must for rent, and borrowers pay whatever they must for interest. In so doing, borrowers draw funds away from the residential sector of the economy. The argument here is thus the same as it was for farm loans. Whatever rate emerges in the residential sector is copied (with adjustments for risk, taxes, cost of servicing, etc.) in the market for loans on office buildings. The marginal productivity of office space, in and of itself, has little effect upon the outcome. The rate of interest for the nation as a whole is determined elsewhere.

Land values in the business districts of most cities rise a great deal over the course of many years. A property with land and building worth $100,000 in 1900 may now be worth ten times as much just for the land alone. If the owner spends $200,000 to tear the old building down, and puts up a new structure costing $4,000,000, the property as a whole may be worth $6,000,000 once it is fully rented to good tenants signing long-term leases. Then it can be mortgaged for $4,200,000, or enough to pay the cost of demolishing the old building and erecting the new one. In the process, new capital formation to the amount of $4,200,000 occurs, but this is partly offset by the demolition of the old building. This capital formation is financed with the savings of the policyholders in the insurance company that makes the mortgage loan. If the owner sells the new building several years later for $6,000,000, he will be richer to the extent of $1,700,000, for his net worth will have risen from $100,000 to $1,800,000. His capital gain will be financed with the savings of the buyers of the building. Although part of his gain will go to the state and federal governments in taxes amounting to $600,000, let us say, and will be used by them for current expenses, nevertheless the remaining $1,100,000 of profit plus the original $100,000 of equity can be kept by the seller to use again in his own business. In this way additional capital formation of as much as $1,100,000 may take place for the economy as a whole.

The terms on which the new owners can borrow will vary from year to year. Sometimes they can secure a 20-year mortgage on the new building, with the interest rate specified for the first 10 years, and subject to renegotiation after that. At other times they may be obliged to give the lending bank or insurance company a slice of the equity in the building—"a piece of the action"—so that the lender can make an extra profit if rents go up in response to inflation. In either case the effective rate on a mortgage loan for an office building is not as firmly fixed as for a private home.

# CHAPTER XIV
# THE STOCK MARKET

## 1. The Yield on Stocks

Does the stock market help set the interest rate? Or does this market just take the rate as it finds it, using whatever rate is determined elsewhere, quite outside the stock market itself? That is the question we need to answer.

Moreover, is the net interest rate in the stock market the same as in the bond market and everywhere else? When all is said and done, and risk, inflation, taxes, and growth have all been considered, does it really make no difference to the average investor whether he puts his savings into stocks, or into bonds, or savings banks, or savings certificates of the U.S. Government?

These questions are not easy to answer. To begin with, the stock market refuses to stand still. Which price shall we take, then, in trying to measure the yield on a typical stock like U.S. Steel? Furthermore, in looking at a stock like duPont, which long enjoyed the reputation of being a growth stock, how can we estimate its growth in the future? And who knows what risk its business really entails, now that it has felt obliged to license nylon to its competitors? As for inflation, we can hear the wildest guesses. And taxes themselves are open to revision at any time. What, then, do we find the interest rate to be in the stock market? How can we measure it?

It is hopeless to try to solve our problem by seeking the answer to this question. Furthermore it is a mistake to say that the stock market reflects the collective wisdom of investors all over the world, and that this wisdom brings it to pass that interest rates are equalized for all kinds of investments. If the market were as wise as all this, why should it change its mind so often, and sometimes rise or fall 50% in a single year? The sad truth is that most investors are only guessing when they buy stocks. They cannot foretell the future with certainty. Perhaps the best that can be said is that stock prices are made partly by truth, partly by myth and partly by forces purely mechanical.

## 2. Balance Between Stocks and Bands

If the stock market and the bond market worked together as they should—which they seldom do—then money would always flow freely from one market to the other, and the two sets of prices would be kept in line with each other. When speculators pushed prices up too high in the stock market, conservative investors would sell their stocks and buy bonds with the proceeds. Likewise, when stocks fell too low in a panic, bondholders would sell their bonds to banks or frightened stockholders, and buy stocks with the proceeds.

Certain forces, however, tend to build a dam between the two markets. The capital gains tax on profits in stocks dissuades owners from shifting from stocks into bonds when stocks get too high. Moreover, the fear of inflation makes these owners of stocks unwilling to buy bonds instead.

Most stockholders are confused. They fail to see that stocks are no hedge against inflation if stock prices go up beforehand, but fail to rise still more during inflation.[1] Furthermore, creeping inflation may be offset by creeping taxation, with the result that dividends fail to rise as fast as money depreciates. When stockholders overlook these facts, stock prices can rise a great deal without causing stockholders to sell out and buy bonds instead, as they ought to do.

Sixty or seventy years ago, when investors were not afraid of inflation, the stock market and the bond market stayed more nearly in tune with each other than now. Before the First World War private investors used to compare stock and bond yields carefully. Whenever stock yields fell too low because stock prices rose too high, many investors would sell their stocks and buy bonds instead. In this way the flow of money that threatened to flood the stock market when the general public became too bullish was drained off into the bond market. New issues in the bond market then sold fast, and plenty of new capital became available to corporations for investment in plant and equipment. As a result, a sudden inflow of money into the stock market did not produce such a steep rise in prices years ago as it does now.

If money will not flow freely out of the stock market into the bond market then savings that go first into stocks cannot finally reach corporations who want to finance with bonds, but refuse to finance with stocks. This happens often. Firms in need of new capital often decline to sell stock, because they do not like to dilute their earnings per share. Their stockholders do not want to cut the public in on a good thing, and so they prefer to raise money by borrowing. Meantime the

---

[1] See my *Investment Value*, pp. 103-6.

public dislikes bonds. The result is to create a demand for stocks without a corresponding supply thereof. Prices rise too high. Yet the capital gains tax and fear of inflation prevent old stockholders from selling.

Mutual funds only make matters worse, because there are so few balanced funds. Most funds specialize in the purchase of stocks rather than bonds. They collect the savings of millions of small investors, and use the money to buy common stocks. Pension funds do likewise much of the time. Were it not for the steady selling of shares that goes on month after month to meet estate and inheritance taxes, and were it not for the even larger selling that goes on to meet capital gains taxes—were it not for all this selling—there would be very few shares indeed coming onto the market for the mutual funds to buy. Yet if the funds were willing to buy bonds as well as stocks, they would be of some use in providing needed capital to industry. As it is, though, mutual funds achieve very little in the way of promoting true capital formation by corporations in general.

## 3. Private Capital Formation

Although the stock market is but a minor source of new capital for corporations, as the Bankers Trust Co. tables show, nevertheless it is a large factor in the process of capital formation for individuals.

If John Doe plans to buy a house someday, and puts his savings into the stock market meanwhile, a rise in the market will help him carry his plans out. Suppose he buys a hundred shares of General Motors at 60, and sells them to Richard Roe at 90 several years later. He enjoys a profit of $3,000, and is able to make a down payment of $9,000 instead of $6,000 on his house. Where does the extra money come from?

The money comes from Richard Roe, who bought the stock with money he saved himself. Every year a huge volume of new savings flows into the stock market in this way, and an equally huge volume flows out, because for every buyer there must also be a seller at the same price. Most of the money that thus flows in and out is used for the purchase of durable consumer goods like houses and cars. Somebody's savings pay for these purchases. Consequently it is correct to say that the stock market is often involved in the process of capital formation for private persons.

Incidentally, we should not feel sorry for Richard Roe, and think he was cheated when he puts his savings into General Motors at 90 instead of 60. So long as he holds the stock, he will receive his dividends. Over the years these dividends may rise, and he may find they give him an excellent return on his investment. Nor should we feel sorry for John Dow, who is missing out on these dividends, for he needs a house more than he needs the dividends. Thus there is nothing sinister about the way in which the stock market collects savings and guides them into new private durable goods.

## 4. Corporate Capital Formation

In the stock market the flow of personal savings into corporate plant and equipment is very small. In this respect the stock market is quite unlike the bond market. When an investor buys a hundred shares of stock in the Southern Railway, for instance, he does not buy the stock from the company itself. Instead he buys it from another stockholder, who is selling out his own holdings. No capital formation occurs. But in the bond market, the reverse is true.

In the bond market, new savings usually go straight into plant and equipment. Bond money goes to buy equipment trust certificates, for instance, offered by the Southern Railway, and is spent by the railroad to buy rolling stock. These equipment trust certificates, moreover, are repaid by a sinking fund year by year, and the investor thus gets his money back again. In the meantime the rolling stock wears out. When it is scrapped, new money is borrowed, and new rolling stock is bought. Money spent by an investor for common stock, however, is not used and repaid in this same way.

If the Southern Railway sells mortgage bonds instead of equipment trust certificates, it again receives the money itself. The money may then be spent for an improved freight yard to speed the classification of cars received from connections and bound for a variety of destinations. The money will go into steel rails, wooden ties, and copper wires, all subject to weathering and obsolescence. The company will set money aside from depreciation charges to meet the sinking fund on these bonds, and will pay the balance at maturity, perhaps with the proceeds of a new bond issue of smaller amount. Thus at the start money flows into the bond market on one side, and at the end it flows out on the other side, with true capital formation occurring meanwhile. Little of this ever takes place in the stock market.

It is seldom that a very large new enterprise is financed by the direct sale of new stock to outsiders. When sales are made in the new issue market, most of the ventures involve only a small number of shares and a low price per share. These new issues do not soak up enough money to have much effect on interest rates.

Sometimes a new venture is financed at first by private subscription. Many years later it may go public, after the venture has proved itself to be a huge success, and its principal owners can liquidate some of their holdings at a price that may be a hundred times their original investment. This latter transaction certainly shows no capital formation of the kind we see in the bond market, where money is borrowed first, and then spent afterwards for new capital goods, with the loan itself being an essential part of the whole process. Instead the sale by the original owners is much like a sale by a small stockholder in General Electric who needs money to put his son through college. Cash changes hands, but no capital formation occurs.

A little of the money that flows into the stock market, to be sure, may reach the corporations themselves, for their managers may sometimes take advantage of high prices to offer rights to stockholders. The money so raised will go into bricks and mortar, machinery and equipment. It will thus lead to a little capital formation. But the amount so spent, as the statistics of the Bankers Trust Co. show, remains small indeed compared to the huge sum that flows through the bond market meanwhile.

The amount will even be small in relation to the other outflows from the stock market for such purposes as commissions, taxes, donations, and spending on houses and cars. These outflows far exceed the sale of new common stock by corporations themselves.

The fact that stock prices are helped by the reinvestment of undistributed corporate earnings should not lead us to confuse reinvestment with voluntary saving. Reinvested earnings come from customers as consumers, not from stockholders as savers. The customers who provide the money for reinvestment have no say about how much shall be obtained in this way. Reinvested earnings, therefore, though given the name of "corporate savings", do not obey the rules of traditional theory.[2]

## 5. The Flow of Funds Through the Market

The flow of new savings into the stock market differs in a special way from the flow of such savings into the home mortgage market or the bond market. Nobody buys stocks because he is in the clutches of the law; nobody in the stock market is under the threat of seeing his mortgage foreclosed. Nobody in the stock market saves because he must keep his life insurance in force lest his family lose their protection. The stock market, to repeat, is not fed by a flow of *contractual* savings. Optional savings are all that go into the stock market. These savings may be systematic, to be sure, as happens when small investors buy shares in a mutual fund and make monthly payments thereon. Yet these periodic payment plans remain optional, and carry no such heavy penalties for default as mortgage payments and life insurance premiums do. Is it any wonder, then, that the flow of money into the stock market is small compared with that into other reservoirs for savings?

Although all the stocks in the stock market display a total value much greater than all the bonds in the bond market, this does not mean that the stock market ranks higher than the bond market in the determination of interest rates. The stock market is a stagnant pool like Great Salt Lake in Utah, whereas the bond market is a body of flowing water like Lake Mead above the Hoover Dam on the Colorado River. Great Salt Lake is many times bigger than Lake Mead in area, but not in flow. This comparison shows why the stock market can be a minor factor in setting the level of interest rates in general.

## 6. Bull Markets

In a bull market, contrary to what is often said, no extra money is needed to put stocks up. They can rise without it. Just buying and selling between traders themselves will do the trick. If John Doe owns General Electric, and Richard Roe owns General Motors, with both stocks priced at 60, let us say, then John Doe can sell 100 GE at 60½ to Richard Roe for $6,050, and this will give him money enough to buy 100 GM at 60½ from the same man on the same day. Neither man need put extra money into his brokerage account. The two simply swap

[2] See Chapter III, §2, on Self-Financing.

their stocks at the new and higher prices. Other traders with other stocks can join in the swapping too, causing prices in general to rise everywhere. These new prices will then be printed in the newspaper, and readers will see that the market is going up.

To put prices up or down, no rigging of the market need occur, no illegal manipulation is required. Just a bedlam of trading is enough.

No real wealth is created by the rise in prices, and no capital formation occurs. People just feel richer, that's all. Likewise, when investors trade the market down, no real wealth is destroyed. Yet they all feel poorer.

If, after all, some new money does indeed flow into the market, it must flow out as fast as it flows in. It cannot stay there. A rise in prices will not soak it up. Something else, like commissions, taxes, the issue of rights, and the withdrawal of profits, is needed. Let us call this factor *evaporation*.

### 7. Evaporation

As we have seen, the reason why Lake Mead, despite the huge inflow of the Colorado River, never rises to flood all the country round about is that this lake enjoys an ample outlet downstream toward the open ocean. Great Salt Lake, on the other hand, enjoys no such outlet. The only way it can get rid of its water is by evaporation. In our analogy with the stock market, evaporation represents the payment of taxes and the encashment of paper profits, a process that goes on quite slowly.

When investors switch from one stock to another at a profit, they pay a rollover tax, otherwise called a "capital gains tax". And when rich men die, their estates pay a death duty. These taxes are a sort of capital levy. Investors raise the funds to pay these taxes by selling some of their holdings to savers who are making new purchases in the stock market. The money then evaporates out of the market and rains into the U.S. Treasury.

Were a great flood to occur in the valley of the Bear River, which drains into Salt Lake, this small stream would carry a huge volume of extra water into the lake. Very soon the water level there would rise enough to cover the wide salt flats along the western shore. Even a moderate amount of water could easily double the area of the lake. Once this happened, evaporation from its surface would double at once too, and restoration of equilibrium would get under way very quickly.

In the stock market the same thing can happen. If a great deluge of hope and optimism sends a flood of new savings into the stock market, its level will rise and its area will increase a great deal. Evaporation will then increase greatly too. With prices higher, estates will be assessed at higher values, and taxes on them will reach into a higher bracket. Investors, seeing new visions for profit, will switch from one stock into another and swap them back and forth, incurring capital gains, and paying taxes thereon. Confident of the future, they will withdraw money from the stock market to buy houses, autos, boats, furs, and pleasure trips. They will also donate shares to colleges, churches, and hospitals, who will sell these shares and use the money to erect buildings, or even to pay current expenses. Thus most of the flood of new money will finally evaporate out of the market. The higher the level of the lake, the wider its surface will be, and the greater its rate of evaporation will become.

Once prices stop rising after a flood of new money flows into the stock market, a few stockholders find themselves dissatisfied with the new and lower yields now prevailing. They then decide to switch their investments into bonds or savings accounts, or into the repayment of any personal debts they may have outstanding. When they try to take their money out of the market, they soak up the final part of the flood that is still trying to flow into the market. Soon prices fall. Then the area of the lake shrinks, and evaporation subsides. In this way the rise and fall of the stock market is automatically held in bounds.

## 8. Pension Funds

Pensions large enough to let a retired man and his wife live in a home of their own, with a car of their own to drive, are something new in recent years. Years ago such a couple would have sought shelter with their children. Adequate pensions for every workman are going to put an extremely heavy burden on the economy as a whole.

Sometimes a pension fund is like a profit sharing plan in that it refrains from making specific promises to pay. It pays whatever it can. It puts much of its money into common stocks, hoping they will increase their dividends as time goes on, and rise in price too. When chronic inflation is under way, stocks offer some hope of maintaining the purchasing power of the contributions made by members of the fund. Definite rules are needed, of course, to show just how much each member is entitled to gain from the rise in the value of his share in the fund during the twenty or thirty years while he remains a contributor. He must also accept his share of the loss if a great bear market like that of 1929-32 occurs. He must take the bitter with the sweet, all according to rule.

### 9. Mutual Funds Sold by Insurance Companies

Few investors in 1968 were worried about a bear market. Everyone feared unending inflation. Savers wanted to own common stocks to take care of them in their old age. Ordinary life insurance, paying a fixed sum at death, or an endowment policy paying such a sum at age 65, seemed too vulnerable to inflation. As protection against premature death, term insurance seemed enough. To provide for ones old age, the purchase of common stocks early in life, plus term insurance carried meantime, seemed like the best combination.

Since this combination is what the public wanted to buy—and still wants to buy—the life insurance companies are getting ready to provide it.[3] They are now selling stock in their own mutual funds. The result may be to divert a huge flow of savings from the bond market to the stock market. Will there be stocks enough to go 'round? Or will the price of stocks go through the roof? Will stock prices rise out of all proportion to dividends paid? Will the attempt to outwit inflation prove self-defeating?

The plan need not be a failure if corporations revise their method of financing in the right way. These companies should shift from bond financing to stock financing. They will need to do so. If policyholders won't buy ordinary life and endowment policies, which require the accumulation of large reserves, then the premium income from such policies will dry up, and the insurance money that used to flow into bonds will no longer be forthcoming. To finance their growth, therefore, the public utility companies and other large borrowers will need to sell stock instead. They can do so by offering rights to their present stockholders. When these assessments become too large for present stockholders to meet, the rights will be sold in the open market. Insurance companies can then buy these rights, and subscribe to new stock with them. The new stock can go into the mutual funds whose shares the life companies are selling to their policyholders. In the end

---

[3] Written in 1968

everything can still come out even for the corporations who need to raise capital and for the insurance companies who have always furnished this capital heretofore. The steady increase in the number of shares outstanding can keep stock prices from going up excessively. And the steady increase in the size and earnings of the borrowers can permit their dividends to rise, and give savers what they seek. In the end it can turn out that the sales of mutual fund shares by the life insurance companies, and their purchase of stocks with the proceeds, will not send prices through the roof after all.

If stock money replaces bond money, however, then dividends paid by erstwhile borrowers must replace interest paid by them. Dividends, however, come out of a company's aftertax earnings, while interest comes out of its pretax earnings. To keep the one as large as the other, and pay income taxes too, a company's pretax earnings must rise a lot. Its customers will then have to pay more for service, and Uncle Sam will pocket the increase as corporate income taxes.

Some insurance companies are now selling shares in real estate investment trusts. These may represent excellent value. Yet they lack liquidity. The assets behind them are not quickly salable. In a panic, how can these trusts redeem their shares?

## 10. Bear Markets

A bear market in stocks has an indirect effect on bonds and mortgages.

When stocks go down in price, corporations who need to raise more capital refrain from selling new shares to their own stockholders by offering rights to them. Corporate managers and security underwriters fear the market will fall still further, and make the rights become worthless. Because of this fear, companies sell bonds instead. Then bonds fall too. Thus a bear market in stocks leads to a bear market in bonds. This bear market may last as long as companies still need to sell new bonds in order to complete plant expansion already underway.

A bear market in stocks affects bond prices in another way too. After stocks have fallen a good deal, and look cheap, some investors in bonds shift into stocks instead. They often sell their bonds in a hurry, in order not to miss the lows on stocks, and this puts bond prices down and bond yields up. The fall in stocks thus causes a rise in interest rates everywhere. It was this mechanism that helped to make stocks and bonds hit bottom at the same time in May 1970.

In the mortgage market, as contrasted with the bond market, a fall in stocks works in a different way. Since home buyers often use money invested in stocks to pay for a house, persons with stock to sell find it easy to raise the money for a down payment when stocks are high. Demand for new houses is then keen, and prices are firm. But if stocks collapse, buyers have less money for down payments, and so residential property declines in price too. The lower the price of houses, the less the mortgage loans thereon will be. Smaller loans then mean lower interest rates on mortgages. Savings banks must always find an outlet somewhere for their persistent cash receipts.

## 11. Dividends

Dividends, since they are paid out of corporate net income, are usually considered the main route by which business profits flow to the entrepreneurs who control the allocation of capital to the economy as a whole. Dividends are supposed to be the carrot that makes the donkey plod along. But scarcely half of the dividend payout of industry serves this purpose. Dividends on preferred stock fail to fluctuate with profits. Even dividends on common stock fail to arouse the profit motive in the case of public utility companies, because if profits rise above a fair return on invested capital, the regulatory commissions cut the rates charged to the public for service. As a result, it is only the common dividends of industrial companies that serve as an inducement to the managers of business. These particular dividends come to scarcely one per cent of the national income. This small sum seems a very low price to pay for the principal incentive that makes the whole capitalistic system so aggressive and efficient.

Undistributed earnings reinvested in a business cannot properly be considered a second form of payment to its owners. The money thus diverted remains at risk. It may finally fail to earn any profit at all. Unless it produces dividends sometime in the future, it comes to nought. Thus it is only actual dividends as such, paid in cash on common stock by companies not subject to regulatory ceilings on their earnings—it is only these particular dividends, to repeat, that drive the whole engine of industry.

All of these dividends, moreover, are taxed at high rates when they reach the hands of stockholders. If the socialists were to nationalize all competitive industries, and put a stop to common dividends, they would lay their hands on very little extra money to pay out to the wage earners of the country.

In the United States today most workers are employed by corporations and private business firms. When men are hired by industrial concerns, their employers expect to make a profit from their labor. Part of this profit is then paid out in dividends. The remainder is reinvested, to be sure, but the purpose of this reinvestment is to maintain and increase cash dividends in the future. As a result it comes to pass that most workmen owe their jobs to the dividends their labor makes possible. If dividends were forbidden by law, no one would have any incentive to hire workers in the first place. In other words: no dividends, no jobs.

Every employee, from beginner to foreman to president, owes his job to the quest for dividends. The competition to succeed, to win a promotion and get to the top, is all tied to the goal of dividends. Dividends are what make the whole machine run at full speed.

The market value of a common stock is set by marginal opinion concerning true worth. Investment value, however, is set by the present value of future dividends. The two seldom coincide. To forecast dividends and estimate their present value is the task of the investment analyst.

Dividends rather than assets or earnings are what really count. After all, what good are assets without earnings, or earnings without dividends either now or later? If Congress were to levy a tax of 100% on dividends, with no hope of repeal, all stocks would become worthless. No matter how large their assets and their earnings, their price would be zero. Clearly dividends determine value.[4]

Statistics show that dividends and interest together claim much less than half the gross profits of business. Taxes claim more. Every firm must pay local real estate taxes as well as state and federal income taxes. The balance not paid out to any claimant, but reinvested, is meant to increase future earning power, for the benefit of all claimants jointly. From this reinvestment—if successful—the government will be the biggest beneficiary.

---

[4] See my *Investment Value*, chs. III and V.

Let us define socialism as government ownership of the means of production, or as the claim on the earnings thereof. From this definition it follows that the United States is now more than half socialistic.

Is monopoly capitalism, as some critics assert, the curse of modern America? To answer this question we must first answer three others, to wit:

1. Are food, shelter, and clothing, which together account for most of consumers spending, made and sold under conditions of monopoly, or of free competition?

2. Are profit margins, measured as a percentage of sales, and checked by the Internal Revenue Service, as high as a true monopolist would set them to maximize his profits?

3. Who receives the larger share of gross profits, the government or the capitalist?

Let the reader decide for himself if the answers to these questions support the charge of monopoly capitalism.

# CHAPTER XV
# LENDING BY COMMERCIAL BANKS

## 1. Creation of Deposits

When a bank makes a loan, it creates new money. It buys an IOU—a piece of paper—and pays for it by crediting the checking account of the borrower. The bank debits Loans and Discounts on its books of account and credits Demand Deposits. The borrower himself debits Cash in Checking Account on his own books, and credits Notes Payable for the amount of the loan received. In this way new money is created by a mere stroke of the pen.

Two restraints, however, hold the process in check. First, the lending bank must hold excess reserves on deposit with the Federal Reserve Bank of its district. Second, this bank must also hold secondary reserves like Treasury bills that it can sell to another bank when the borrower draws checks on his new deposit, as he surely will, and causes the new money to move into this other bank. The net effect of this second restraint is to make it necessary for growth in demand deposits to go on uniformly among all banks in the country at the same time. Then the new money that moves from bank A to banks B, C, and D will be offset by other new money that comes in from banks B, C, and D to bank A.

## 2. Banking as a Service Industry

Commercial banking is a service industry. It provides the means of payment used to run the whole economy. The task of the banks is to originate demand deposits and handle checking accounts. Although in olden days it was the king who coined gold and silver for his subjects, nowadays it is commercial banks who supply the money needed by a country for its commerce. This is the service they render.

Bank earnings come from fees of all sorts. Every deposit that is made, every check that is drawn, must pay a service charge unless the depositor carries a large idle balance. Every sum that is borrowed must also pay a service charge of another kind, the charge in this case being called interest or discount. Thus the earnings of the banking system consist of service charges on checks drawn plus interest on loans made.

The two sets of fees combined must suffice to cover the cost of running the checking account system for the nation as a whole. Unlike the U.S. Post Office Department, which also renders a nationwide service, the commercial banks cannot look to the Federal government to make up any deficit they may incur.[1] The banks must make both ends meet themselves. To do so, they adjust their fees from time to time. If the return on Treasury bills and commercial paper goes down, they must make up the shrinkage elsewhere. Failure to do so would cause their capital to shrink, and the crucial ratio of capital to loans would become dangerously low. If this should happen, borrowers would find bank loans hard to get, and the interest rate charged to customers who have no accounts in competing banks would go up. Then the gross income of the banks would rise too, and let the banks earn enough to meet their large payrolls once more, and cover all their other expenses too.

### 3. The Interest Rate on Bank Loans

Commercial banks, as we have seen, are the main short-term lenders, and merchants are the main short-term borrowers (other than the Treasury). Commercial banks must keep liquid; hence they cannot make long-term loans. And merchants themselves, because they usually have no fixed assets, must borrow against current assets; hence they cannot get long-term loans. Banks and merchants thus fit together hand in glove.

The *supply* of short-term funds to lend, however, far exceeds the *demand* for short-term funds to borrow. Therefore banks also solicit the business of borrowers-either-way. They draw off as much of this other business as they can get. The rest of the demand from borrowers-either-way goes into the long-term market, where it adds to the demand already present from borrowers who can sell only long-term paper.

Competition tends to bring the rate on customer loans into equality with that on other earning assets. Were the customer rate lower than the outside rate, banks would decline customer loans, and would buy short-term bonds instead. Since a huge volume of old long-term bonds is always outstanding, with some of them approaching maturity every year, an ample supply of such short-term issues is always available for banks to buy. As a result, the rate on customer loans cannot fall below the open market rate on other short-term paper.

---

[1] Even though the Post Office has recently been divorced from the government, it can still rely on the government to raise the price of stamps if necessary.

Nor can the bank rate go much above the open market rate. Were it to do so, banks would sell other short-term paper and scramble to make more customer loans. They would undercut each other on the rate to big firms who carry accounts in more than one bank. As a result, the rate on customer loans cannot rise much above the rate on bonds due to mature soon.

It is only the prime rate, of course, namely the rate paid by large and well-known firms, that is thus held down by competition among the lending banks. The rate paid by other borrowers can and does go higher. In fact, many small and little known firms are often the victims of price discrimination by their own banks. The rate charged to the best borrowers, however, the so-called prime rate, is controlled by the open market.

The prime rate that banks appear to charge their customers is not the true rate they actually charge, to be sure, because customers are always required to keep some idle money on deposit in their checking accounts. Thus, if a firm borrows $100,000 at 5%, and maintains an idle "compensating balance" of $20,000, the actual rate on spendable money comes to $6\frac{1}{4}\%$. In this case the interest charge of $5,000 is being paid for the use of only $80,000.

When banks, fearing adverse publicity, do not want to raise the prime rate, they often raise the compensating balance required of the borrower. Thus in 1969, when the prime rate was held down to $8\frac{1}{2}\%$, the compensating balance was lifted from 20% of the loan to 25% in many cases. This made the actual rate $8,500 \div $75,000 = 11.33\%$.

When long-term rates rise, borrowers-either-way stop selling bonds, and seek bank loans instead. As a result, short-term rates rise too, and the banks make a large profit. The banks then raise their dividends to their stockholders. They also open new branches, and compete harder for deposits. This sends overhead up, and reduces earnings.

Whenever the Federal Reserve Board holds the total deposits of the banking system as a whole in check, banks as a group cannot create new deposits. It does them no good to open new branches in order to acquire such deposits; they only take deposits away from each other. These branches inflate expenses and devour earnings. They thus put a stop to the rise in dividends. Unless the banking industry is growing—as it now is—the time soon comes when the banks just barely make both ends meet. What with higher dividends and higher overhead, they just cover their outlays. Then they sink back into stationary equilibrium.

Whenever the Federal Reserve Board permits a rise in legal reserves, however, the member banks hasten to increase their loans and investments. If loan demand remains unchanged, the banks buy open market paper, much of which comes from borrowers-either-way These borrowers then sell fewer long-term bonds to the life insurance companies. The insurance companies, in turn, then compete harder with the savings banks for mortgage loans. A a result, the rate charged to home buyers falls temporarily. Later the mortgage rate rises because demand increases so much. Thus an increase in bank reserves affects the whole money market eventually.

## 4. Derivation of the Short-Term Rate

The short-term interest rate is determined in a very roundabout way. The prime rate on bank loans does not simply slide up and down along a demand curve all its own. We cannot simply say that the demand for bank loans is very inelastic, and so a slight change in the quantity of such loans outstanding will produce a large change in the rate on them. No such simple answer will suffice.

Commercial banks do not confine themselves to customer loans and Treasury bills. In order to use up all their lending power, they also buy corporate bonds of near maturity, and tax-exempt municipals. These investments constitute the marginal outlet for bank funds. They tie the bank rate to other rates.

Whenever the demand for customer loans increases, on the one hand, the banks sell some of their corporates and municipals to dealers, who resell them to savings banks and fire insurance companies. The price the commercial banks get for the bonds they sell then determines the rate they charge on the money they lend. The more bonds they sell, the lower the price will fall and the higher the yield will rise, and thus the higher the prime rate on customer loans will go.

Whenever the demand for bank loans decreases, on the other hand, the banks look elsewhere for ways to put their excess reserves to work. They buy short-term corporates and municipals from the savings banks and the insurance companies. The savings banks thus receive extra money to put into mortgage loans; they can always lend all this money by reducing the interest rate they charge to home buyers. Meanwhile the supply of long-term municipal bonds tends to increase too, because cities and states can afford to borrow more heavily at 3%, for instance, than 5%. The commercial banks also consent to reach out to longer maturities, buying eight and ten-year tax-exempts as well as one and two-year issues. In this way they encroach on the long-term market.[2] This process raises the price and lowers the yield on municipals, and then on corporates. Rather than accept these lower yields, the commercial banks now compete harder for whatever customer loans they can find, and cut the interest rate on these loans too in the process.

Meanwhile a few firms who are borrowers-either-way, and who plan to build new plant, can avoid the flotation of new bond issues if they are willing to finance their inventories and receivables with bank loans. These borrowers compare the rate on bonds with that on bank loans, and so it is the bond rate that sets the bank rate. Here is the one place where a cut in the prime rate will succeed in enlarging the volume of bank loans, not just other assets only.

The net result of these maneuvers in the bond market is to tie the short-term rate to the long-term rate. The prime rate at commercial banks is thus derived, step by step, from the mortgage rate at savings banks. Home buyers and apartment house builders are the borrowers who take up the slack when rates change, because their own demand for loans is elastic, as we have seen in Chapters V and VII.

Apartment houses, like private homes, are very sensitive to the rate of interest on mortgage loans. Real estate investors, who in effect are agents for their tenants, erect more apartment houses when interest rates are low. The lower the rate, the lower their rentals can be. Thus the whole residential sector of the economy behaves in the same way as homeowners themselves do.

The home buyer or his agent always stands at the end of the line. He is the one borrower whose demand is truly elastic. Indirectly he sets the rate everywhere, even on short-term loans made by commercial banks. He is the marginal borrower for the whole economy.

## 5. Lines of Credit

A line of credit is a promise made by a bank to a depositor saying that the bank will grant him a loan in the future under certain conditions. Often the bank promises to make the loan at whatever

---

[2] Cf. Chapter IX, §2, *supra*.

prime rate happens to prevail when the time comes, but sometimes a slightly higher rate is specified. Occasionally the expectant borrower pays a commitment fee for keeping the line of credit open. He is not required, however, to exercise the line of credit unless he sees fit. As a result, the bank can never be sure beforehand just how large the demands upon it will be in the end. If all of its customers suddenly decide to borrow, the bank can be hard pressed to meet its commitments. Yet competition forces banks to extend lines of credit to most of their large customers beforehand in order to get and hold their business in the meantime.

For many customers a line of credit is far more than a mere anchor to windward. It is not just a precaution, but a necessity. An airline, for instance, that places an order for twenty jet planes costing $15,000,000 apiece needs to be assured that it can borrow the money to pay for them when they are delivered one after another. The airline will plan to repay its borrowings out of the annual depreciation earned on the planes after they are put in service. A schedule of serial repayments will be set up, with the short-term notes being sold to commercial banks and the long-term notes to insurance companies. Not until this financing has all been arranged will the airline sign on the dotted line with the manufacturer of the planes. And the manufacturer himself will doubtless resort to a line of credit of his own with another group of banks, who will agree to advance him money week by week to pay for labor and materials while the planes are under construction. Meanwhile the manufacturer will depend on still another set of contracts whereby his union labor agrees to work at specified wages, and his subcontractors agree to furnish parts and materials at specified prices. If production now goes ahead with no unexpected delays, so that overhead does not pile up to an unexpected degree, then a profit to the manufacturer is assured right from the start. Everything being tied together by a network of contracts, the outcome is predetermined. In this network of contracts, the lines of credit granted by the banks are of vital importance.

Not all business is done with such precision, of course. When goods are offered for sale to the general public, the retail buyer seldom enters into a contract beforehand. Not many consumer goods are like tailor-made suits, cut to measure, with the buyer placing his order before the garment is produced. Most consumer goods are manufactured first and sold afterwards. As a result, the producer cannot be sure how many to make. Hence he cannot tell beforehand how much of his line of credit he will need to exercise. Likewise the bank cannot tell beforehand how large the demands upon it will turn out to be in the end. This uncertainty makes it hard for the bank to manage its lending and investing in the most profitable way. Always some profit has to be sacrificed to safety, so that the bank will be able to meet any unusual demands that may suddenly be placed upon it.

The major hazard of banking is seldom a demand from depositors for currency, but more often a demand from borrowers for loans in fulfillment of their lines of credit.

In order to qualify for a line of credit, a would-be borrower must keep a satisfactory balance on deposit with his bank at all times. Such a deposit is called a "compensating balance". If a firm maintains an average balance of $1,000,000 during twelve months of the year, and if its earnings and current ratio are good, it can feel itself entitled to borrow as much as $5,000,000 for several months each year. If this loan runs for three months, an interest rate of 6%, for instance, would mean an interest charge of $75,000. Loss of interest at 5%, let us say, on the idle balance of $1,000,000 for the whole twelve months would amount to $50,000, and would bring the total cost of the loan to $125,000 for the three months while the loan was outstanding. This sum implies an effective interest rate of 10% a year.

Discussions of the "demand for money" should always mention the huge sums tied up in compensating balances. While these deposits do indeed enjoy a moderate turnover every month, they are nevertheless maintained at a higher average level than convenience requires. Furthermore, high interest rates cannot induce the owners of these demand deposits to invest them in securities. Instead the money must be kept more or less idle in order to hold the lines of credit open.

## 6. Changes in Compensating Balances

When the prime rate on bank loans is already high, as it was in 1970, and when political pressure is exerted on the banks to keep them from raising the rate still higher, the banks often respond by raising the compensating balance they demand. Does this move do the banks any good? Or does it only add to the squeeze on borrowers?

Let us start with a situation where the banks are already fully loaned up. They hold no excess reserves. Whenever they resort to rediscounting at the Federal Reserve Banks, they are told they must repay these loans promptly. As a result, they cannot increase their own loans to customers.

Under these circumstances large borrowers, if pressed for money, may try to sell more commercial paper. Rates on this paper will rise well above the prime rate. Borrowers will then ask for additional loans from their own banks in accordance with the lines of credit already granted them. To avoid compliance with these requests, the banks will raise their interest rate indirectly by resorting to the device of requiring larger compensating balances.

When a firm borrows $1,000,000 at 8%, the cost is $80,000 a year. If the compensating balance is 20% of $1,000,000, the idle balance amounts to $200,000, and only $800,000 remains for the firm to use. The effective rate on the usable money is $80,000 ÷ $800,000 = 10%. Offhand it would seem that the device of compensating balances lets the bank earn 10% too on this transaction. But this is not the case, because the bank earns interest on its loans, not its deposits.

Moreover, if the bank now stiffens its rules on compensating balances, and requires the borrower to keep $250,000 idle, leaving him only $750,000 to use, then he finds his effective rate to be $80,000 ÷ $750,000 = 10.67%. With $50,000 less to spend, he now needs to borrow still more, namely $66,667 more, since 75% of $66,667 = $50,000. Evidently, when a bank raises its requirements on compensating balances, and increases the ratio from 20% to 25%, it thereby increases the demand for bank loans by 6.67%.

If we assume that the demand for short-term funds is completely inelastic, because interest is very small compared with gross profit on sales, then the banks who demand higher compensating balances will be confronted with a sudden increase in demand which they cannot meet.

Why cannot the banks meet this demand? The answer is that they are already loaned up to start with. They have no excess reserves. Hence they cannot grant more loans and create more deposits. Lines of credit be damned, the banks are in a jam. The Federal Reserve Board will have to come to their rescue.

Under these circumstances the banks tell their customers to forego loans, and sell bonds instead. If these customers are able to borrow either long or short, they can tap the long-term market. Ford and Chrysler, for instance, did just this in 1970. The bonds they sold were bought by insurance companies and savings banks with money that would otherwise have gone into home mortgages. A shortage of mortgage money then put interest rates up in the home loan market, and residential building fell off.

Meanwhile the commercial banks remained unable to increase their own loans and deposits. The requirement of higher compensating balances did them no good. It simply increased the burden on borrowers. It kept money idle in one place, and drew it away from another. The effect was deflationary.

For some individual banks, to be sure, higher compensating balances seemed to be a money-making device. But for the banking system as a whole it was not. It only made the credit squeeze worse.

The Federal Reserve Board, in its efforts to control inflation, may have been glad to see this happen. In fact, changes in compensating balances are a powerful device for credit control. As such they stand on a par with changes in bank reserves and reserve requirements. Like open market operations, they affect the spending power of the general public.

Is it good money management, however, to leave the rules on compensating balances entirely in the hands of the commercial banks? Should not this ratio be subject to the specific control of the central bank itself? And how can control best be transferred to the Federal Reserve Board?

### 7. Compensating Balances and Deposit Velocity

Imagine a commercial bank that grants a $5,000,000 line of credit to each of six firms A, B, C, D, E, and F under the condition that each firm must keep a compensating balance of $1,000,000 on deposit at all times. Loans are made to the various firms one after another in response to the seasonal need of each firm. Each loan runs for two months, or one sixth of a year. In the beginning, Firm A borrows and repays, then Firm B does so, followed in turn by C, D, E, and F, with no two firms borrowing both at the same time. Even after a firm repays its loan, it keeps its compensating balance on deposit in order to retain its line of credit for use next year. The money thus kept on deposit is not available for spending, but remains idle.

For simplicity in exposition, let us assume that the money now on deposit as a compensating balance came from sales of goods to the Federal government. In the previous year the U.S. Treasury made payments of $1,000,000 to each firm, using checks drawn on a Federal Reserve Bank. Treasury bills sold by the Treasury to the Reserve Bank provided the government with funds to draw upon. When the six firms deposited their Treasury checks in a commercial bank, and this latter bank collected the checks at the Federal Reserve Bank, the commercial bank acquired legal reserves of $6,000,000 in all. Against these reserves stood $6,000,000 of demand deposits payable to the six firms.

At the beginning of the new year Firm A needs money to meet its payroll and other expenses, this being the busy season in its own industry. Accordingly, the firm borrows $5,000,000, the full amount allowed by its line of credit. The bank debits Notes Receivable $5,000,000, and credits Demand Deposits $5,000,000. The firm then withdraws $5,000,000 in currency, reducing its deposit by this much. To meet this withdrawal, the bank obtains $5,000,000 in Federal Reserve notes from the central bank. As a result, its legal reserves drop from $6,000,000 to $1,000,000. Meanwhile its deposits, which momentarily had hit a peak of $6,000,000 plus $5,000,000, or $11,000,000, fall back to $6,000,000 again. Its reserve ratio, however, is now down to $16\frac{2}{3}\%$, because most of its original reserves have been converted into currency and paid out to Firm A. Yet the whole procedure is most welcome to the commercial bank, which now holds $5,000,000 of earning assets (plus $1,000,000 of legal reserves) instead of $6,000,000 of nonearning assets, as in the beginning. The bank can now make a profit on its operations.

During the two months while the first loan is outstanding, Firm A hires labor, makes goods, sells them, and gets a new dollar for an old. At the end of the period the firm deposits $5,000,000 in cash in the bank, and pays off its loan of this amount.

In order for the whole process to go without a hitch, the other five firms must sit still, and must not reduce their own deposits at the bank. They must keep their own compensating balances up to size. But if they fail to play the game according to the rules, they will get the bank into trouble. Its reserve ratio will drop below the legal limit of $16\frac{2}{3}\%$. The bank will be forced to rediscount some of its eligible paper, and borrow against the notes receivable it bought when it loaned $5,000,000 to Firm A. It will be obliged to pay interest to the Federal Reserve Bank at the present rediscount rate, which is close to the prime rate at which it made the loan to the depositor. This will take most of the profit out of the deal. To prevent such an outcome, the bank will insist that firms B, C, D, etc., leave their compensating balances intact.

Furthermore, Firm A must repay on time, or else no loan can be made to Firm B when its turn comes. And Firm A must then keep its own compensating balance of $1,000,000 idle for ten months until its own turn to borrow comes again. Everyone must observe the rules.

In the model described above, the bank's ratio of loans to deposits is $5,000,000/\$6,000,000 = 83\frac{1}{3}\%$. This particular ratio, of course, is tied to all the other specific assumptions, namely the figure of 20% as the required compensating balance, $16\frac{2}{3}\%$ as the required reserve ratio, two months as the length of each loan, and 100% as the amount of a loan paid out in currency. (These last two assumptions are extreme, and were chosen merely to make the arithmetic easy.)

If part of the loan had been paid out other than in currency, with a check being written and used to transfer funds to some other bank, then the first bank would still have suffered a drop in reserves. Currency or transfer, the result is the same.

When a large number of banks are doing business with a multitude of firms, is the result altered? In this case, Firm A may be paying money out in the morning to one person, and receiving money in the afternoon from another. If so, its balance on deposit stays the same, and it does not need to borrow after all. It can then make do with a mere working balance on deposit. It needs no line of credit.

Likewise, when a bank has a large group of salaried persons as depositors, these customers enjoy no formal line of credit, and seldom borrow. The funds that they deposit, however, can be loaned to Firms A, B, C, etc. If on occasion these firms do not need the money, it can be invested in Treasury bills for the time being. Such bills serve as a so-called secondary reserve. It is complications like these that make a bank's balance sheet differ from the imaginary one described at first

When Firm A pays 6% to borrow $5,000,000 for two months, the interest charge comes to $50,000. And when it lets $1,000,000 lie idle for ten months rather than invest it at 4.2%, let us say, the interest lost is \$175,000. The total cost of the \$5,000,000 loan therefore, is \$225,000 for two months, or 13.5% annually.

Why do firms pay such a high rate? They do so because they can make a profit of much more than 13½% on the money. If they could borrow it elsewhere for less, they would do so. Their creditworthiness, however, is not well known. Other lenders dare not deal with them. Hence they go to their own bank for accommodation. Meanwhile the bank will often give them a loan at only 6%, even though rates elsewhere are somewhat higher, because the bank wants the use of their compensating balance at other times of the year.

The so-called "demand for money" is tied up with the need for compensating balances. These balances are usually much larger than required for mere convenience. The excess does not circulate. Its presence holds down the average velocity of circulation for bank deposits as a whole. When velocity is held down like this, money does less work, and the general price level stays lower than it otherwise would do. All of this is in accordance with the Quantity Theory of Money. Clearly, banking rules about compensating balances should be considered a major factor in monetary theory as a whole.

## 8. Self-Liquidating Loans

Loans made to finance work in process or stock-in-trade are self-liquidating. Money borrowed for this purpose does not need to be paid back in small instalments stretching over many years. Instead, borrowers can discharge a debt of this sort with one single payment made on the due date.

If a mill borrows money to buy wool tops, and then spins this wool into yarn and weaves it into cloth and sells it for cash, the mill receives money at the end of the process that can be used to pay the debt incurred at the start. A mill that borrows \$1,000,000 for this purpose will be required, however, to back up its loan with another \$1,000,000 of its own capital. This second million will then be used for fixed expenses and the payment of wages to mill hands. When the product, whose full cost is now \$2,000,000, is sold to the clothing manufacturers, the mill receives money wherewith to pay off its bank loan. If the cloth is sold for \$2,500,000, let us say, the mill is entitled to keep the profit of \$500,000. But if the cloth is sold for only \$1,800,000, the mill must nevertheless shoulder the loss of \$200,000.

Yet the mill is always able to repay the loan of only $1,000,000 regardless of whether it makes a profit or a loss on this particular transaction. Hence in either event the loan is self-liquidating.

Manufacturers, wholesalers, and retailers are the main users of self-liquidating loans. Since it takes only a few months, or a year at most, for the manufacture and sale of the merchandise to take place, self-liquidating loans usually run for three, six, nine, or twelve months, depending on the kind of business that is using the money. In any event, their term is short.

A self-liquidating loan differs from a loan made on producers durable goods. A loan on durable goods can only be paid out of profits. If losses are sustained, it can never be paid at all. Unlike a self-liquidating loan, a loan on durable goods is not well protected against loss.

Self-liquidating loans are usually repaid all at once, whereas loans on plant and equipment are usually repaid in many instalments. Moreover, self-liquidating loans, being short-term loans, are usually made by commercial banks, whereas loans on plant and equipment, being long-term loans, are usually made by insurance companies, pension funds, and other investors whose liabilities are also long-term in character. Each kind of loan suits a particular kind of lender.

Short-term borrowing, like long-term borrowing, is held in check by arbitrary rules that completely disregard the profit the borrower hopes to make. A short-term borrower must maintain a two-to-one quick asset ratio, and must display a good record of past earnings. Much of the time he would like to borrow more than the lender is willing to lend. The lender sets the limit. In fact, as a first approximation, we might draw up our model in such a way as to let self-liquidating loans, like all other loans but Treasury loans, be pushed to the limit set by the equity capital and the past earnings of the borrowers. Such a model would come close to the truth.

## 9. Commercial Paper

Commercial paper is much like customer loans. This paper is usually bought by commercial banks, and the proceeds usually go into self-liquidating loans, just as is the case with ordinary loans made by a bank to its own customers. The paper is issued by large corporations whose borrowings are so great that they want to be able to secure money from a long list of different banks. They sell their IOUs to dealers like Goldman, Sachs and Company, who buy the paper at one price, and resell it to banks and other investors at a slightly higher price. Meanwhile the borrowing companies maintain large balances on deposit with their home banks, from whom they also borrow directly and with whom they have a large unused line of credit. These home banks furnish credit information concerning the borrower to any other bank that wishes to buy its paper.[3]

Commercial paper makes it easy for banks in various parts of the country to smooth out the seasonal demand for loans from their local borrowers. In the dull season these banks buy commercial paper from outsiders; in the busy season they use all their funds to make loans to their own customers. Sometimes they even urge their customers to sell commercial paper to other banks too.[4]

The volume of commercial paper outstanding has recently undergone a sharp increase. At the end of July, 1972, it amounted to $33.9 billion compared with $158.6 billion in total loans. At that time nonbank investors were important lenders. Ordinarily, however, commercial banks are the main lenders, and so the volume of such paper is ordinarily limited by the volume of legal reserves held by these banks. Therefore it is usually possible to lump commercial paper and customer loans together under a single heading in any analysis of the forces that determine interest rates in general.

The space labeled Commercial Paper on Diagram I represents in part money loaned by some nonfinancial corporations to other nonfinancial corporations. If one firm has idle cash in the summer, it can loan this money to another firm that needs it, and in the winter the lending can be reversed, all by means of the commercial paper market. Sometimes the lending goes through the hands of a commercial bank, which accepts the money from the lender as a time deposit, represented by a negotiable certificate of deposit, or CD, and uses the money to buy commercial paper for itself.

It is cheaper for a large corporation to avoid bank borrowing if it can do so. Suppose that such a company needs an extra $100,000,000

---

[3] The creditworthiness of each borrower is appraised by Dun and Bradstreet, an independent agency that has performed this task for the banking community for many years.
[4] Cf. Leon B. Gould, "Banks and the Commercial Paper Market" in *The Financial Analysts Journal*, November-December 1969.

to use for three months in the busy season. The money can be raised by the sale of long-term bonds at 6%, let us say, if the would-be borrower can show the required interest coverage. In the quiet season the extra money can be invested in commercial paper at 5%, let us say. While this procedure involves a loss of 1% for nine months, it is better than keeping a compensating balance of $20,000,000 idle for twelve months. The loss of interest on the compensating balance at 5% would amount to $1,000,000 for twelve months, whereas the loss of interest on the $100,000,000 reloaned for nine months would be only $750,000. Long-term financing of short-term needs thus affords a saving of $250,000 when the spread in interest rates is 1%. If there were no spread at all, the saving would come to $1,000,000.

Long-term borrowing, moreover, is safer than short-term. It does not require repeated renewals, some of which may come due at bad times in the company's history. Calculations of this sort have led many firms to sell bonds and participate in the commercial paper market. In recent years this market has grown so large that it is sometimes called the "independent banking system".

In order to deter large corporations from selling bonds to provide temporary working capital for themselves, the banks try to keep the prime rate lower than the bond rate. In this way they can encroach on the long-term market, as explained by my Encroachment Theory in Chapter IX. Competition by the banks against the bond market thus brings it about that short-term rates are usually lower than long-term.

## 10. Collateral Loans

Although most collateral loans are used to finance speculation in the stock market, some are used for other purposes. Thus when banks lend money to small businessmen to buy plant and equipment, they often ask them to hypothecate stocks or bonds as security even though they consider the loans sound enough to stand on their own feet anyway. The collateral is just frosting on the cake.

Collateral loans of this sort (often called "nonpurpose loans") are made on a much thinner margin than loans to stock speculators require. On a blue-chip stock like American Telephone, for instance, a bank might lend a businessman 70% of its market value. If this stock then declined 15%, the bank would ask him for more margin even though the proceeds of his loan had gone into a venture that was fundamentally sound in its own right. Failure to put up more margin would provoke the bank into selling the stock at the current low price, causing a bad loss to its owner. How much better off is the firm that is large enough to borrow just on its financial statement, getting its loan merely on the strength of its balance sheet and income account! Such a firm can weather a bear market in stocks unharmed.

When banks call these collateral loans, and sell out the stocks behind them, they do a lot to make a bear market worse.

In contrast to business loans, other collateral loans are made in large volume for purposes purely speculative. Such loans are usually granted to stockbrokers, who relend the money to their own customers at a higher rate. These loans go by the name of "brokers' loans", "call loans", or "loans to dealers". The Federal Reserve Board specifies the margin required on them. Recently this margin was very high. Speculators were required to put up $80 to buy a stock costing $100, with the result that their loan was only $20. The stock could then fall to $30 or so before the brokers would demand more margin for their own protection. The wide gap between purchase margins and maintenance margins nowadays keeps the stock market as a whole from being so frightfully unstable as it was in 1929, when both margins were nearly the same.

The proceeds of collateral loans made by banks to business firms, so-called "nonpurpose loans", are often put to long-term use. These loans are seldom self-liquidating. Yet they are demand loans, and so they should be classified as short-term rather than long-term paper. The interest rate on these loans, therefore, is the short-term rate, and the main lenders are commercial banks rather than savings banks and insurance companies.

Incidentally, loans secured by real estate, as contrasted with loans secured by common stocks, are less dangerous for the borrowers. These loans are usually held by insurance companies. They are long-term loans, not demand loans. And the collateral behind them is not subject to frequent reappraisal, inasmuch as no market price for it appears in the newspaper every day. If a real estate speculator buys when prices are very high, just before a smash in the market, he can still hold on, waiting for a recovery. So long as he continues to service his mortgage promptly, he will not be told that his loan is suddenly under water, and his collateral is going to be sold tomorrow morning. Yet this is just what often happens to the man who borrows on his common stocks.

## 11. Construction Loans

Construction loans granted to a building contractor to let him pay the cost of erecting a new house are self-liquidating loans.

The builder functions as a manufacturer of houses, and the finished houses are the merchandise he offers for sale. The builder may spend $5,000 to buy the land, borrow $15,000 from a commercial bank, sell the house for $25,000, repay the bank its $15,000, and come out with $10,000 in cash, half of which is profit that he uses to cover his own living expenses meanwhile.

A construction loan of this sort is self-liquidating because it is paid out of the proceeds of the sale. Payment does not hinge on the earning power of the house. The loan is thus unlike a loan to an airline, secured by a lien on an airplane, where repayment depends on the earning power of the plane, and where the plane itself is not sold to the passenger for cash. This latter kind of loan, in contrast to a construction loan, is not self-liquidating.

When the builder sells his house, and the homeowner borrows money from a savings bank to pay for it, the new mortgage loan, unlike the old construction loan, is not self-liquidating. Instead this new loan depends on the earning power of the borrower. Hence it must be a long-term loan, not a short-term loan like the original construction loan. While both loans may be secured by mortgage deeds, one after the other, they are unlike in other respects.

## 12. Capital Formation

Construction loans are usually made by commercial banks, who buy the builder's note and credit his checking account. The money the builder gets is thus created by a stroke of the pen. When this money is spent on the construction of a house, capital formation occurs. No saving goes on meantime. The capital formation occurs without any need for saving. If the loan had not been made, and if the house had not been built, the carpenters and plumbers would have sat home in idleness, wasting their time. This waste was prevented by the bank when it created new money out of thin air.

Yet saving as such takes place in the end. When the homeowner buys the completed house, and makes periodic payments to a savings bank to reduce his mortgage loan, he engages in contractual saving. Capital formation thus comes first, and saving afterwards. They are not simultaneous.

Once the savings bank has made this particular loan to the homeowner, and in the absence of any new mortgage lending by the bank, it will use the cash from the repayments on this loan to buy bonds from a dealer. The dealer himself will sell the bonds out of his inventory. The savings bank will pay the dealer with money on deposit in some commercial bank, and the dealer himself will use this money to reduce his collateral loan with his own bank. The assets and liabilities of this latter bank will then shrink side by side. The bank will undergo liquidation. The whole process is deflationary, just as the original credit creation was inflationary. In the end the commercial banking system as a whole will revert to the same condition it was in before the construction loan was made to begin with.

Meanwhile the house will remain in existence. It will have been paid for with contractual savings, with savings made long after the original capital formation took place. In the end, no trace of the process will remain on the books of any bank. But the homeowner himself will be richer by the amount of the debt he has discharged (provided the house does not depreciate meanwhile). Postponed saving explains this result.

The foregoing analysis assumes, to be sure, that the economy is not already working at full capacity when the commercial bank makes its original construction loan to the builder. The analysis assumes that some slack exists, so that new money can put idle hands to work. Of course, if this assumption does not hold good, then new money put into circulation cannot increase output still further. Instead, new money will only force wages and prices up. It will only fan the fires of inflation.

## 13. Term Loans

Term loans often run for two, three, four, or even five years. Usually they are not self-liquidating. Seldom is the money spent for merchandise or work in process that is itself resold afterwards. Instead the money goes into motor trucks, airplanes, machinery, and other pieces of equipment that are put to work to earn a profit. Part of this profit is needed to cover depreciation. The rest is divided between interest, income taxes, and net income. If the equipment fails to earn a profit, no money will be forthcoming to pay interest and amortization. This explains why term loans cannot be called self-liquidating.

Because banks possess much more lending power than they can use for strictly self-liquidating loans, they are eager to make term loans too. In so doing, they encroach on the long-term market. This distorts the term structure of interest rates in the way described by my Encroachment Theory.

In granting term loans, commercial banks take great pains to make sure that the money will be put to good use. They loan only to companies who are making a profit on their present plant and equipment already. The banks hope that the earnings on present assets will suffice to pay interest and amortization on the new equipment too even if its purchase should prove ill-advised in the end.

Sometimes term loans are secured by chattel mortgages. Thus a term loan made for the purchase of jet planes by an airline might be so secured. If the airline fails to meet its interest and amortization, the planes can be taken over by the lending bank and sold to another airline.

A variation of this procedure lets the bank retain ownership of the airplanes from start to finish, merely leasing them to the airline year after year. The bank then depreciates the airplanes itself, and considers any rental in excess of depreciation to be a form of interest on its investment. Leases are thus in effect merely term loans under another name. Banks sometimes prefer them because accelerated depreciation on the airplanes saves income taxes for the bank.

The interest rate on term loans often changes with that on short loans month by month. Thus, if the prime rate on short loans is 5% in the beginning, the rate on term loans may be 5½% to start with. If the prime rate then rises to 5½% and later to 6%, the other rate will rise too, going to 6%, and then to 6½%. Afterwards, if the prime rate drops, the term loan rate will drop too. Here is a case where the long-term rate is obviously a function of the intervening short-term rates, the differential of ½% being a premium for the extra risk taken by the bank on a term loan as contrasted with a self-liquidating loan. The resulting rate for term loans is the same as if borrowers and lenders could both make perfect forecasts, and then act according to the Expectations Theory of long and short-term interest rates.

Some long-term bonds are long-term in name only. If they are issued when interest rates are very high, and are callable in five years, they are really nothing but five-year term loans. In fact, they are not even as good as outright term loans, because the borrowers retain the right to postpone payment if they see fit when the time comes. A notable issue of this sort was the Pacific Telephone and Telegraph Co. 9⅛% debentures offered on December 3, 1969 to yield 9.10%. These bonds carried an AAA rating, but were callable in five years—though at a high premium. Short-term lenders did not like them, because their date of redemption was indefinite. Long-term lenders did not like them either, because these bonds would surely be called under the very circumstances when the lenders would not want to let them go. The bonds as a result were neither flesh nor fowl nor good red herring. No wonder they needed such a high coupon!

Home mortgages, like most bonds, are subject to call when interest rates decline. If a homeowner secures a mortgage when rates are high, and agrees to pay 8½%, let us say, for 25 years, he can refinance his house later, if rates fall, and perhaps obtain his new loan at 5½%. When this happens on a great scale, savings banks are forced to cut their dividends to their own depositors.

## 14. Loans to Finance Companies

Loans to finance companies like the General Motors Acceptance Corporation, for instance, are term loans rather than self-liquidating loans. The money goes from the bank through the finance company to a person who uses it for the purchase of an automobile. The buyer of the car is not like a retail merchant. He does not put his car in inventory, and does not resell it at a profit within a few months. Instead he buys the car for his own use, just as an airline buys a jet plane. Unlike the airline, however, the car buyer does not make his purchase earn a profit for him, and he does not plan to make this profit cover the interest and amortization on his loan. Instead he pays the interest and amortization, or the instalments as they are called, out of his monthly wages.

Lenders, to protect themselves against loss, require borrowers to contribute part of the purchase price of their cars. The loans therefore come to only a fraction (such as two-thirds or three-quarters) of the price of the car. Although the lender retains a chattel mortgage on the car, this car has resale value only to the extent that some other buyer could afford to meet the instalments on it if he bought it as a used car.

Finance companies sell most of their paper to large corporations who have cash lying idle at certain seasons of the year. This paper is very liquid, because the finance companies make a practice of buying it back before maturity if the lender needs his money sooner than expected. Finance paper thus competes with Treasury bills as regards liquidity. It yields slightly more, however, because its interest is not exempt from state income taxes, while Treasury bills enjoy this advantage. Both kinds of paper, however, are subject to the federal income tax.

## 15. Instalment Loans

Instalment loans to consumers for the purchase of automobiles, household appliances, furniture, and other durable goods amounted to $128 billion in 1972.[5] The increase, however, was only $10 billion. Most of the money for new instalment loans comes from repayments on old loans. Only the *growth* in instalment debt affects the interest rate.

Unlike mortgage loans, instalment loans are not held in check by the rate charged on them. These loans are short-term loans, and so the demand for them is very inelastic. The rate is limited to 6% by the usury laws. Yet the effective rate is much higher than 6%, as we shall now see.

When a man buys a new automobile costing $4,000, let us say, and is allowed a credit of $1,000 for his old car accepted as a trade-in, he signs an instalment note for $3,000 payable over 30 months. The payments on principal thus come to $100 a month. Interest at 6% of the entire $3,000 is always charged throughout the entire life of the note, even after the unpaid balance has become very small. The interest itself thus amounts to $180 a year or $15 a month, and so each monthly instalment comes to $115 in all. The average rate over the whole life of the loan is thus about 12%, since the average unpaid balance is only $1500.

At the end of 30 months, or two and one half years, the buyer owns his car free and clear. By then, however, its trade-in value has fallen a great deal, and may amount to only $1500. Nevertheless the owner's equity in his car is now larger than it was to start with, this equity now

---

[5] See the Bankers Trust Co. Table 14, estimate for 1972.

being $1500 instead of $1,000. Evidently the owner has engaged in a process of contractual saving without being aware of it.

For the nation as a whole, a tremendous amount of saving takes place in this way. Such saving is one of the things that has made the country rich, the wealth in this case consisting of a huge inventory of usable motor vehicles.

If the owner of the car that is only two and one half years old now chooses to run it until it wears out completely, he can get another ten years of service out of it. While he is doing so he is consuming his wealth. He is dissaving. In the end he must save a new sum of $1,000 as a down payment on a new car to replace his old car. But if he trades his car in while it is still worth $1,000, he can borrow $3,000 again without any cash payment. Once more he will go into debt, and will pay off his debt by resorting to contractual saving. All told, however, he will achieve no net saving.

Net saving goes on only when the country's inventory of motor vehicles is increasing. The increase is financed with bank loans in the beginning, and with contractual saving in the end. This saving, however, is not performed in response to any payment of interest received by the saver as wages of abstinence. Instead, the saving is incidental to the purchase of transportation.

Interest is involved in the process, of course, but the interest is received by the lenders, not the savers. The lenders, moreover, let some of the interest accumulate, unspent by themselves as owners. It is credited to Surplus. In this way the revolving fund used to finance the nation's inventory of cars grows at compound interest.

If the loan fund held by the finance companies ever fails to grow fast enough in any given year, the shortage can be made up by recourse to bank borrowing. It is not necessary to hold demand in check by a rise in the interest rate. In fact, such a rise would be illegal.

## 16. Tax Anticipation Notes

A great many cities and towns borrow from commercial banks by selling tax anticipation notes to them. If real estate taxes come due on October 31, for instance, the municipality may borrow in April or May against these future receipts. You and I might consider it improvident to anticipate our salary checks in this way, but the practice is very common among cities and towns. Although a huge volume of municipal short-term debt originates in this way, the increase from year to year is not very large. Commercial banks are eager to buy these notes because they are tax-exempt, and carry little risk.

Like all short-term loans, tax anticipation notes involve an extremely inelastic demand. The volume of such borrowing is determined by outside factors, and does not shrink when the interest rate rises. If a city or town needs more money, it simply borrows earlier in the year. Its demand curve then shifts to the right, crowding all other curves to the right also, and making composite demand for funds a bit larger than before.

## 17. Restricted Growth of Total Assets

Commercial banks differ from savings banks, insurance companies, and pension funds in that their total assets cannot grow at compound interest year after year without any outside restraint. On the contrary, commercial banks are always held in check by the Federal Reserve Board, which always puts some limit on the total reserves of the banking system as a whole.

Yet if this limit is always rising, because the Board keeps adding to bank reserves, then growth can go on after all. Federal Reserve policy thus determines the rate of growth. Commercial banks suffer from this special constraint. Other lenders do not. Banks as a group can grow only as fast as the Federal Reserve Board will let them grow. Therein lies one peculiarity of commercial banks.

In another way, however, commercial banks are just like savings banks. They obtain the money wherewith to make new loans from their receipts on old loans. When John Doe discharges his loan at a commercial bank, excess reserves come into being, and permit the bank to make a new loan to Richard Roe. But so long as total reserves stay constant, total loans and investments stay constant too

## 18. The Contrast Between Time and Demand Deposits

Time deposits, unlike demand deposits, are not created by a mere stroke of the pen. Instead time deposits are secondhand money. They consist of money that was created elsewhere as a demand deposit, money that has now come into the hands of a saver who deposits this money in his savings account, or uses it to buy a certificate of deposit at a commercial bank.

A bank cannot create a time deposit by purchasing a piece of negotiable paper and simply giving the seller credit on his time deposit account. This procedure, resembling that for a demand deposit, won't work. A seller of an IOU will not let such a time deposit remain a time deposit. He will treat it just like a demand deposit, because he borrowed the money from the bank in the first place for the sole purpose of getting cash to spend.

When a borrower spends his cash, it reappears elsewhere in the banking system as a demand deposit, not a time deposit. Only if the money had remained unspent would it still be a time deposit. A time deposit cannot jump back and forth from bank to bank in the way a demand deposit can. It must stay put.

## 19. Certificates of Deposit

When a customer of a bank makes a large deposit with the understanding that he will not withdraw the money during the next 90 days, or the next 180 days, or the like, he receives a certificate of deposit if the amount is very large. Such certificates are often issued in denominations of $1,000,000. They bear interest at a specified rate, and are negotiable. If the depositor should need his money before the due date, he can sell his certificate to someone else at a price that includes the interest accrued in the meantime. A certificate of deposit, therefore, is almost as liquid as a demand deposit.

The money that the customer puts into the bank as a time deposit is money that he received from someone else who had borrowed it from the bank in the beginning. This money started out as a demand deposit, and comes into his hands as a demand deposit too. When the new owner of the money uses it to buy a certificate of deposit, his bank debits its own demand deposits and credits its time deposits. If demand deposits need a legal reserve of 16%, let us say, and time deposits only 4%, then reserves of 12% are released. Using these free reserves, the bank can now go ahead and make new loans to other customers, issuing demand deposits against these loans. For every $1,000,000 of idle money converted into time deposits, $750,000 of new demand deposits can be created. (The recent change from 4% to 5% in the required reserve will reduce the figure of $750,000 somewhat.)

If the banks are all loaned up, with no free reserves, and if the owner of a certificate of deposit (or CD as it is often called) needs his money ahead of time, he must find someone outside the banking system to sell his certificate to. This buyer must use idle money of his own to make his purchase. Evidently the issuance and resale of CDs helps to put a lot of idle money to work.

The rate of interest that banks pay on CDs is determined by competition between CDs and commercial paper in particular, and between CDs, Treasury bills, and other short-term issues in general.

Because CDs give banks new lending power, and make it easier for many firms to obtain bank loans, these firms do not need to sell bonds instead. Consequently firms whose balance sheets let them borrow either short or long crowd into the long-term market less insistently, and so interest rates there are held down. The effect of CDs, and of time deposits in general, is thus to lower interest rates everywhere somewhat.

## 20. Eurodollars

Eurodollars are American dollars kept on deposit in a European bank.

Eurodollars often originate from imports into the United States. If a dealer in London sells a thousand bales of wool to a dealer in Boston, and gets paid in dollars, and if he then deposits this check in a London bank, the money becomes Eurodollars.

In the ordinary course of events the owner of these Eurodollars would exchange them for pounds sterling, and the buyer of these dollars would then use them to purchase cotton or some other commodity for importation into England. All of this will be prevented, however, if no exchange takes place. When interest rates in the United States are high, holders of Eurodollars will lend them on demand to American banks. Holders will draw interest on this demand loan, inasmuch as the law forbidding interest on domestic demand deposits does not apply to foreign deposits too.

If the London bank leaves its deposit with the American bank intact, the latter bank will benefit. Since the law requires no reserves to be held against foreign deposits—or did not until recently—the reserves that were formerly tied up against these deposits when owned by an American are released. They can now be used to support new lending to other borrowers within the United States. This makes it easier for American borrowers-either-way to secure short-term loans from banks, and avoid issuing long-term bonds to insurance companies. The net effect of Eurodollars, therefore, is to hold American interest rates down a little.

Since British owners of Eurodollars enjoy the option of exchanging these dollars for pounds, and investing the money in British securities, a strong force is always at work to keep interest rates in England equal to those in the United States. Eurodollars provide the link. This link is not strong enough, however, to make interest rates exactly the same all over the world. Investors lack the knowledge needed to shift their funds from place to place without any hesitation at all.

## 21. Disintermediation

Banks that accept time deposits from nonfinancial corporations and other large lenders often issue negotiable certificates of deposit, or CDs, to these lenders. The banks then invest the proceeds in customer loans or commercial paper. These CDs run for 90 or 180 days.

This process can be undone by a procedure called "disintermediation". When the Federal Reserve Board, acting under Regulation Q, set a limit of 6¼% on certificates of deposit in denominations of $1,000,000 or more, as the Board did in 1966, it made the rate on these certificates less than that on commercial paper. Holders of certificates then let them run off at maturity, and used the money to buy commercial paper directly. The banks consequently had less money to lend to their own customers, and so these borrowers were forced to sell their paper elsewhere. In this case they sold to the former holders of CDs. The net result of Regulation Q, therefore, was to make borrowers deal directly with lenders. A corresponding shrinkage in bank loans and time deposits took place meanwhile. Disintermediation in and of itself, however, did nothing to make the money market tighter. Nor did it raise interest rates in general.

Disintermediation at commercial banks need cause them no loss. The runoff of CDs is matched by the runoff of short-term paper held. The banks do not need to sell such paper at a loss before maturity. It is not like the long-term bonds held by savings banks, whose bonds have fallen far below cost since their purchase years ago. At savings banks, disintermediation can do a lot of damage, but not at commercial banks.

Although savings banks in 1969 were paying dividends to their depositors at the highest rate in many years, nevertheless some of these depositors were afraid these rates would not last for long. Meanwhile noncallable Treasury bonds gave a yield much better than the banks were paying. People could take their money out of the banks and reinvest it elsewhere to advantage. When they withdrew their money, the banks were often forced to sell some of their own bonds to raise the money. The banks, in fact, sometimes found themselves selling their bonds to their own depositors without knowing it.

Yet disintermediation at savings banks, like that at commercial banks, is neutral in its ultimate effect on interest rates as such. When depositors withdraw their money, and force savings banks to sell bonds to raise this money, the depositors buy the bonds themselves, directly or indirectly. The extra supply of bonds forced onto the market by disintermediation is thus met by an extra demand for bonds as a result of this very disintermediation. The two forces cancel.

Bond prices may be disturbed temporarily, to be sure, but in the end no lasting change in the rate of interest need occur.

At life insurance companies disintermediation occurs when policy loans are written. If a businessman holds a policy for $200,000, let us say, on which he has paid large premiums for many years, and against which the insurance company has accumulated a reserve of $120,000, the man can borrow $100,000 or more if he wishes. On such a loan the interest rate is 5%, as prescribed by law. Yet recently the rate on customer loans at commercial banks has been 9%. Moreover, these loans have often been hard to get. Many small businessmen, therefore, have taken out policy loans. These loans have used up money that the insurance companies could otherwise have spent for bonds with a coupon of 8% or more. The net result has been to withdraw money from the long-term market and put it into the short-term, but with no change in the total supply for the two together.

# CHAPTER XVI
# MONETARY POLICY

## 1. Controlling the Price Level

Can the Federal Reserve Board hold prices down? Does it possess the right tools to do the job?

Let us begin with an imaginary case, a very extreme one, and see how the process works. Assume that a new President and Congress have just been elected, and are pledged to do three things, as follows:

1) raise wages
2) hold prices down
3) keep full employment

Their first step is to pass a law raising the legal minimum wage 15%, and their next is to raise all other money wages 8%, without waiting for any gains in the productivity of labor. Meantime they order the Federal Reserve Board to do its best to prevent the cost of living from rising. In response the Board refuses to allow any increase in member bank reserves, even though the member hanks are already fully loaned up.

Businessmen, now faced with higher hourly wages to pay, try to borrow extra money from the commercial banks, but are told they must make do with their present cash holdings. This forces them to shorten the work week about 8%, but most workers keep their jobs. While hourly wage rates are now 8% higher, daily take-home pay is unchanged. Total spending by consumers then remains the same as before. Yet the cut of 8% in the number of hours worked causes a cut of 8% in units of output. The scarcity of goods then sends prices up 8%.

In this case, the wage level makes the price level, not vice versa. Clearly the endeavors of the Federal Reserve Board prove useless. Prices go up, and a little unemployment may appear too.

Let us next consider another imaginary case, one less extreme. In this second case, Congress goes no further than to raise the legal minimum wage. As for other wages, labor unions are given free rein to put them up if they can. Let us assume that the unions succeed in lifting the hourly wages of their own members 8%. Firms then raise the wages of their nonunion workers the same amount, in order to dissuade these other workers from forming unions of their own. The government also raises the wages of its own employees. In short order, all wages rates rise 8%. Meanwhile the Federal Reserve Board permits no increase in bank reserves and in the volume of demand deposits. Firms can borrow no extra money, and so they are forced to shorten the work week 8%, just as before. As a result, output drops 8% and prices rise 8%. Again it is the wage level that makes the price level.

Let us now consider a third imaginary case. This case is just like the previous one except that the Federal Reserve Board, loath to hurt business activity, defies the command to fight inflation. Instead, it makes bank reserves rise 8% when hourly wages rise 8%. Firms then borrow extra money, and pay rates 8% higher, but they make no cut in hours or output. As a result, the money income of labor as a whole rises 8%, and prices rise 8% too, because the volume of goods offered for sale is no greater than to start with. This process combines cost-push with demand-pull inflation. Here too, the wage level makes the price level.

Cost-push and demand-pull inflation are two sides of the same process, like debit and credit. When wage rates go up, costs rise, but so do incomes. With extra money in their pockets, consumers bid prices up enough to cover the extra costs.

Let us finally consider a fourth imaginary case, just as extreme in its own way as the first. This time Congress passes no wage laws, but it severely curtails the power of unions to strike. No wage increases, therefore, are forced upon employers, and no extra borrowing is required. Since the member banks have enough legal reserves already, the Federal Reserve Board feels no obligation to add to these reserves. Consequently no rise in workers income takes place, and no rise in prices occurs. Again, wages make prices, but this time prices stay down because wage rates stay down.

In none of these four cases does the government succeed in fulfilling all three of its pre-election promises. Its failure is caused by the fact that the promises conflict with each other. If one is granted, another must be denied.

In none of these cases, moreover, is the Federal Reserve Board responsible for the rise in prices or the absence of them. Yet the Board is likely to get the blame for whatever happens. This is very unfair, because the Board is asked to do the impossible.

## 2. Controlling Interest Rates

It is quite possible for the Federal Reserve Banks to lower the short-term interest rate intentionally. To do so they can increase the legal reserves of the member banks. When these reserves increase, the member banks go out and buy finance paper and other short-term obligations. 'The short-term rate then declines. Borrowers-either-way, seeing this, decide to borrow short instead of long, if they think the Federal Reserve Board will persist in its easy money policy for quite a while. An easy money policy expected to last for many years shifts a lot of borrowing from long to short, and curtails new bond issues a good deal, with lower yields as the result.

Meantime the total supply of money to lend increases. Consequently long-term rates fall at first. With extra money now going into circulation, however, the earnings of firms and households both rise in due course. Would-be home buyers can then show higher take-home pay, and can afford to make larger monthly interest payments on mortgage loans. But the savings banks themselves, with their cash flow still limited by old contracts signed with earlier borrowers, have no more money to lend than before. The increased demand for these funds now puts mortgage rates back up, not down as desired by the Federal Reserve Board. The Board's attempt to rig the long-term market, therefore, proves a failure in the end.

If long-term rates now seem too high, the government can order commercial banks to lower their prime rate on short loans. However, when the prime rate goes down, borrowers-either-way rush to borrow short. Then the banks cannot honor all their lines of credit without the help of more legal reserves. A credit crisis will result, and the government will be forced to let the prime rate stay up after all.

Quite a different procedure, however, would make rates fall, and stay down. A new rule might be adopted forbidding savings banks to lend more than 60% of appraised value on conventional mortgages, rather than 70% as now. This rule would push many applicants out of the market, for lack of adequate down payments. Mortgage rates would decline, to be sure, but many people would get no loans at all. In fact the very people whom the government was trying to help would be the ones to be hurt most. Again it would turn out that government intervention would prove a failure.

Credit rationing would seem to be the only course likely to succeed. The government could restrict the sale of bonds by corporations, and thus make room for extra mortgage lending by savings banks. Meanwhile the issue price of new bonds would rise, and old bonds would at once be bid up to the same price. In due course, however, restrictions on corporate borrowing would impair capital formation and reduce employment—just what the government wanted to avoid. Clearly government attempts to control long-term interest rates are most unwise.

### 3. Controlling the Volume of Trade

The Federal Reserve Board is quite able to control the volume of trade. If we look at Fisher's formula for the quantity theory of money, we can see why this is so. The formula reads as follows:

$$MV = PT$$

where $M$ is the quantity of money, $V$ the velocity of circulation, $P$ the price level, and $T$ the volume of trade. As we have already seen, the wage level, and thus the price level $P$, is beyond the control of the Board. The same is true of $V$, the velocity of circulation of money; this velocity depends on the frequency of pay days, rent days, and due days on charge accounts, as well as on the size of compensating balances kept at commercial banks. As a result the only two variables in the formula are $M$ and $T$. If $M$ rises, then $T$ rises—provided that slack exists in the economy, so that it is physically possible for $T$ to rise.

To get more money into circulation, the Federal Reserve Banks buy Treasury bills, and thus make member bank reserves increase. The member banks then cut their prime rate. Borrowers-either-way shift to short-term loans, and move out of the long-term market. Mortgage borrowers, however, quickly increase their loans when long-term rates ease. Total borrowing, both short and long, becomes larger than before. Extra money thus gets into circulation, and increases employment and output. In short, the purchase of Treasury bills to start with makes the volume of trade increase in the end.

Sometimes the growth of the money supply can get out of hand because the member banks resort to rediscounting on a huge scale in order to honor their lines of credit. Net borrowed reserves at the Federal Reserve Banks then show a huge increase, as in the spring of 1973, and again in 1974. If the boom outruns both plant capacity and labor supply, shortages will appear, and all prices will rise. The result will be demand-pull inflation.

So long as surplus labor is available, however, and so long as employees are willing to work longer hours in return for more pay per week, an expansionary monetary policy will remain noninflationary. Eventually, to be sure, workers will want to work fewer hours per week, and will make a trade-off between income and leisure that will tend to send the wage rate up. By then, however, productivity may have gained enough to let labor cost per unit stay down.

Meantime corporate profits rise. When output rises, dollar sales rise too, and so does the balance left after the payment of wages. All three dollar figures rise in proportion. But overhead remains constant. When this fixed overhead is subtracted from rising gross profit, net profit rises even faster than gross. Net always changes more than gross, rising faster in a boom, and falling faster in a slump. There is nothing sinister about all this. It all goes back to the fixity of interest charges, property taxes, and other such expenses in good times and bad.

# CHAPTER XVII
# THE ELASTICITY OF DEMAND AND SUPPLY

## 1. Meaning of "Demand and Supply"

Standard theory talks about the demand for savings and the supply thereof. This terminology must not be confused with the demand for notes, bonds, and mortgages, on the one hand, and the supply thereof, on the other hand. These two ways of talking about the same problem are really the opposites of each other. Yet both are correct.

A demand for savings is a demand from a borrower for money to be lent to him. The borrower signs an IOU, and sells this legal document, this piece of paper, to a lender. In this way the borrower who shows a *demand* for loans also creates a *supply* of paper. The investment banker then talks about the *demand* for savings in one breath, and the *supply* of new issues in the next. The reader can find this talk confusing unless he is alert to the dual terminology.

Likewise, when dealers speak of a low price for bonds, they mean a high rate of interest. When they say bonds are weak, they mean interest rates are strong. And when they say offerings of new securities are heavy, they mean the demand for money to borrow is large

Standard theory often uses Figure 1 in Diagram XIII to show the demand and supply of new savings, while I will sometimes use Figure 2 to show the demand and supply of new issues. Whenever the interest rate $i$ goes up in one figure, the cost $c$ of bonds goes down in the other.

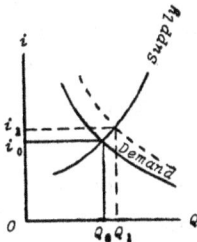

Fig. 1  Demand Increasing
for Savings

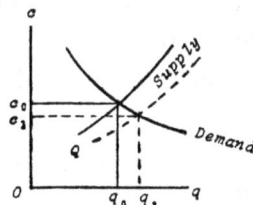

Fig. 2  Supply Increasing
for Bonds

Diagram XIII: Demand for Savings, or Supply of Bonds

In Figure 1 the horizontal distance $Q$ represents the *amount of money* borrowed and loaned, measured in dollars. When the demand from borrowers for loans increases, the demand curve moves to the right along a stationary supply curve for funds to lend. The amount of money $Q$ borrowed and lent increases, and the interest rate $i$ goes up, as shown by the dotted lines, according to standard theory.

In Figure 2, on the other hand, the horizontal distance $q$ represents the *number of bonds* bought and sold, measured in units of $1,000 face value. Thus $q$ means the quantity of paper going into the portfolios of investors, the cost of each piece being $c$. As a result, the amount of money loaned is represented by the area $Q = cq$. If the supply curve in this figure were to move to the right along a stationary demand curve, the number of bonds $q$ would increase, and their unit cost $c$ would go down, as shown by the dotted lines.

Standard theory always draws the supply curve for money to lend as shown on the left above, where the curve has an upward slope. It assumes that a rise in the rate of interest $i$ will call forth a larger supply of lendable cash $Q$. I make no such assumption. I say that almost all saving is contractual, and does not respond to changes in the rate of interest within a single year. Regardless of whether the interest rate is high or low, the volume of saving remains the same. Hence I treat $Q$ as a constant. This would make the supply curve for money to lend a vertical line in the left-hand figure. It also makes the demand curve $c = Q/q$ a rectangular hyperbola in the right-hand figure. Such a curve has an elasticity of unity. The evidence in support of this premise has been given in earlier chapters.[1]

## 2. Composite Demand and Supply

When demand comes from two or more sources, total demand can be found by adding individual demands together. Total demand is also known as composite demand. Composite supply is like composite demand in that it represents the total supply from two or more separate sources.

In the money market, the demand from borrowers may be classified into three varieties, namely the demand for short-term loans, the demand for long-term loans, and the demand for loans either way. The sum of these three demands is the composite demand. Likewise, the supply from lenders may be classified into two varieties, namely the supply of short-term funds, and the supply of long-term funds. On the supply side of the market there exists very little money willing to be loaned either way; most lenders have good reason for preferring one

---

[1] See Chapter IV, §10, in particular.

way to the other. The sum of short-term lending and long-term lending is the composite supply of money to lend.

What matters most is the shape of the individual demand and supply curves. The shape of these curves then gives the shape of the composite curves. Each separate curve shows the relation between the rate of interest and the quantity supplied or demanded. I claim that all of the curves but one are vertical lines (or nearly so). The one curve that slants downward, and displays any elasticity at all, is the demand curve for long-term loans. This curve makes the composite demand curve slant downward too. Meanwhile the two component supply curves remain vertical lines, because the volume of money available for lending short or long is not responsive to the current rate of interest during a period of a few years only, as I have shown. Hence the composite supply curve for lendable funds turns out to be a vertical line too.

If a short-term loan is made early in the year, and paid off during the year, or if a long-term loan is refunded, this loan does not count in the figures for the demand and supply curves. Only new and additional loans made during the year, whether they be short or long, are loans that count. An *increase* in total loans must occur. Then the curves can be made to show demand *per year* and supply *per year*.

In drawing composite demand and supply curves, do we run afoul of a problem in dimensions? Can short-term and long-term demands be added together? Or are we guilty of adding apples and oranges?

Fortunately this difficulty does not arise. Either kind of demand for money to borrow gives rise to a loan, an IOU, a piece of paper. When a lender makes a loan, he buys a piece of paper. If he has $100,000 to invest, he can buy paper due in one year, two years, or twenty years. His outlay is the same for each kind. But if he buys one kind, he will lack the money to buy another kind. Thus it becomes possible to add the various kinds of paper together, because each kind is measured in the same way, namely by its cost in dollars.

Diagram XIV shows how the individual demand and supply curves fit together to give composite curves. These composite curves then determine the rate of interest that will emerge when the market is in equilibrium.

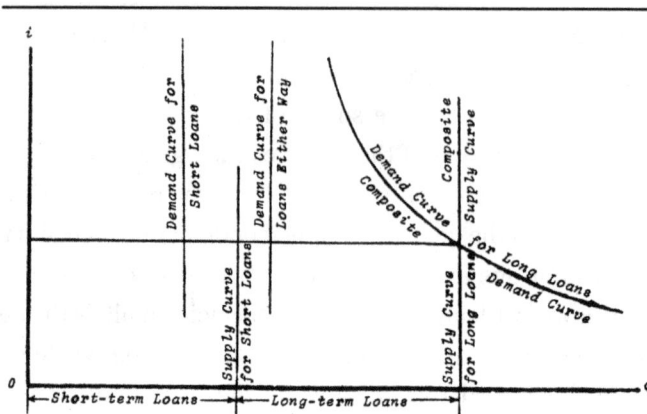

Diagram XIV: Composite Demand and Supply

There are two kinds of borrowing: Industrial and nonindus-
trial. The latter, many times the larger, is outside the scope
of the Cobb-Douglas formula.

## 3. The Elasticity of the Composite Demand for Loans

Most people who borrow short have a very inelastic demand for
loans. A merchant, for instance, who is stocking inventory to sell in the
Christmas season, and who buys wholesale at a discount of 35% or 40%
from retail, is not responsive to changes in the rate of interest he has
to pay. His loan runs for too short a time. A rate of 4% a year means
only 1% for three months, and a rate of 6% a year only 1½%. Rentals
on his store and wages for his salesclerks worry him much more than
interest does.

A penny saved is a penny earned, of course, and so the merchant
will strike the best bargain he can, comparing one bank with another,
but he will not refuse to borrow at all just because the rate is too high
to please him. Only a rate of 30% or 40% a year would make him think
twice; a mere 5% or 6% is too low to fuss about. Hence it can be said
that his demand for loans is highly inelastic, and the demand curve for
borrowers like him is a vertical straight line.

For loans of somewhat greater length the same rule holds true. A
man borrowing to buy an automobile, with payments due each month
for thirty months, still finds that the interest rate as such is only a minor
matter. If his loan is for $3,000 to start with, and if the interest charge
is 6% per annum, or 1/2% per month on the full amount continually,
then his monthly interest is only $15. His monthly amortization,
however, is much larger, coming to the sum of $100. Total payments
then amount to $115 in all. However, if the interest rate were to be only

5% per annum, his monthly interest charge would decline to $12.50, and he would save $2.50 a month. But this saving is trifling. His total payment for interest and amortization would fall very little, only from $115.00 to $112.50. Consequently he would remain unresponsive to the lower rate of interest. A change in the rate would have almost no effect on his decision to borrow or not to borrow. His demand would be highly inelastic, and his demand curve would be a vertical straight line in the region where the interest rate lies around 5% or 6%.

For very long loans, however, the answer is quite otherwise. For loans of thirty years rather than thirty months, the rate of interest becomes very important. Moreover, thirty-year bonds seldom have a sinking fund large enough to pay the whole issue off at maturity. The final balance then is expected to be refunded at maturity.[2] Often there is no sinking fund at all. Amortization is then absent altogether. If so, a rise of 1% in the coupon will be quite enough to impair the interest coverage on a new issue somewhat, and lower the rating given by Moody. To avoid this, a competitive firm—but not a public utility or the federal government itself—may be forced to reduce the size of the issue. Likewise, when a family is planning to buy a house, a rise of 1% in the rate of interest is quite enough to make them buy a house that is a somewhat smaller than they had chosen at first. Consequently it is true that many long-term borrowers are indeed responsive to the interest rate. They show an elastic demand for loans. Their demand curve is sloping, not vertical.

When the elastic demand from some long-term borrowers is added to the inelastic demand from all short-term borrowers, the total demand—in other words, the composite demand—turns out to be somewhat elastic, or at least not wholly inelastic. The resulting demand curve displays a pronounced slope; it is not a vertical straight line.

As always, price and quantity are determined by demand and supply together. If either curve shifts, the interest rate changes. And it changes because composite *demand* is elastic, even though composite *supply* is not, as we shall now see.

### 4. Fixed Composite Supply of Money to Lend

The supply of money to lend, in contrast to the demand therefor, is extremely inelastic.

[2] The formula connecting the elasticity of demand with the true length of the loan is worked out in the mathematical Appendix at the end of the book.

The lending power of commercial banks is fixed by their capital-loan ratio and by the size of their legal reserves. This ratio and these reserves do not wax and wane with each rise and fall in the rate of interest. Instead the supply of money that the commercial banks can lend is quite inelastic. No rise in the rate will increase this supply.

For savings banks, the supply of money to lend comes mostly from interest and amortization on loans already outstanding. High interest rates, moreover, do not lure depositors to save faster, because the rates never get high enough to make much difference. People who are accumulating the down payment on a house or car just go ahead at the same speed whether the rate is high or low. Changes in the rate have little effect on them.

For insurance companies, the supply of money to lend likewise comes from interest and sinking fund on present investments, and from premiums on insurance in force. Both payments are fixed by contracts already written, and do not change when the interest rate goes up or down. Hence the supply of money from insurance companies to lend is quite inelastic too.

Pension funds likewise depend on contractual receipts. These receipts come from current savings, but their size does not respond to a change in the rate paid on them. Here again the supply is inelastic.

Corporate saving also is inelastic. Dividends are seldom cut in order to let a company lend its current earnings at a high rate of interest. As for the reinvestment of net income in plant and equipment, that goes its own way quite in defiance of the ups and down of interest rates. In particular, low rates during a depression do not stimulate investment in new plant. Carrying charges on such plant are much too high to let it be built ahead of time.

And so it goes, from one lender or investor to another. Neither contractual savers nor optional savers take much notice of the interest rate. Only the hope of gains of 50% or 100% a year, such as the stock market pays at times, will make most families revise their budgets. Usually their hopes are unfulfilled. Meanwhile they continue to save on contract just as before. They pay off the loan on their house and their car. And they pay for their life insurance and their pension plan. As far as the rate of interest goes, when this rate hovers between 3% and 8%, the response of most families to a change in rate is imperceptible.

Therefore, when the supply curves of the various individual lenders are all added up, the composite supply curve turns out to be extremely inelastic too. In fact, the curve can best be represented by a vertical line. In the short run, composite supply is fixed.

In the long run, to be sure, composite supply increases steadily. The assets of insurance companies, pension funds, and savings banks all grow at compound interest year after year, and so does their lending power. The loans and investments of commercial banks grow likewise, because the Federal Reserve Board sees to it that their legal reserves increase about five or six percent annually. As a result, all supply curves shift slowly to the right. Their shape, however, stays the same. In any given year, the composite supply curve remains a vertical straight line.

The curve for composite demand, like that for supply, shifts to the right every year too. As the country grows and the money supply increases, all borrowers become better able to bid for loanable funds. The shape of each individual demand curve, however, stays much the same even though its position may change.

## 5. The Overflow of Short-Term Money

Money available for short-term loans, most of it coming from commercial banks, is in excess supply. Meanwhile the demand from strictly short-term borrowers is not large enough to absorb the entire supply at any price, not even at a zero rate of interest. Consequently lenders must look elsewhere. They find takers among borrowers-either-way, including manufacturers, oil companies, real estate operators, state and local governments, and even the U.S. Treasury on occasion. But these borrowers-either-way, as I call them, always need more money than they can get from strictly short-term lenders. Hence they do business with long-term lenders too, and sell long-term bonds to insurance companies, pension funds and savings banks. In this way the short-term market is linked to the long-term market.

As far as the short-term market alone is concerned, we find a strange situation existing. In this market the demand curve and the supply curve never cross. Unlike the curves in an ordinary demand and supply diagram, these curves are vertical lines, at least in the region where interest rates lie around 3%, 4%, and 5%, or even 10% and 12%. With no crossing of the curves, no price emerges in the usual way. Standing alone, the short-term interest rate would fall to zero. In order to get a solution to the problem, we have to resort to composite demand and composite supply curves. This lets us take notice of the liaison between long and short-term interest rates. The problem can then be solved. It turns out that the short-term rate is copied from the long-term rate, with adjustment for risk and for growth.

## 6. Balance of Demand and Supply

In each year the demand for loans impinges on a supply of money to lend whose size is fixed and unalterable for the year in question—provided that Federal Reserve policy remains neutral. Consequently the diagram of demand and supply looks as follows for any given year:

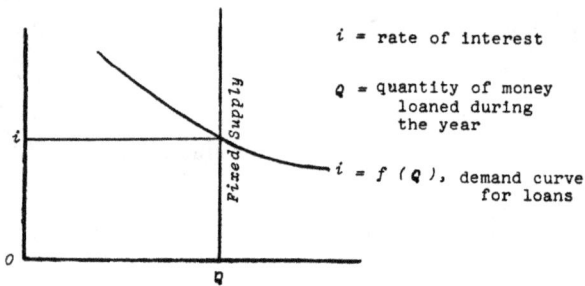

$i$ = rate of interest

$Q$ = quantity of money loaned during the year

$i = f(Q)$, demand curve for loans

*Diagram XV: Fixed Supply, According to the New Theory*

The supply curve is a vertical line for each year, since the size of the loan fund in any given year is fixed by events in the past, not the present, as I have already shown. The supply of money $Q$ to lend in the year $n$ does *not* respond to the rate of interest $i$ reached in that year, standard theory to the contrary notwithstanding. Hence the supply curve in this diagram does not slope upwards to the right, as it is usually drawn.(See Diagram XVI below.)

Although the supply is fixed, the demand is flexible. As shown in Diagram XV, the composite demand curve for loans both short and long slopes downwards to the right. From year to year, it also shifts sidewise as the country grows. Its elasticity may likewise change a little.

## 7. Contrast Between the New Theory and the Old

The diagram below shows how the rate of interest was said to be determined in the era of Böhm-Bawerk, Alfred Marshall, and Irving Fisher:

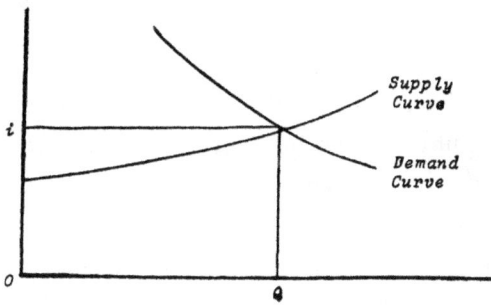

*Diagram XVI:   Equilibrium According to the Old Theory*

In this diagram the supply curve for savings slopes upwards, whereas in mine it is a vertical line rising from a fixed point Q.

The old theory said the volume of saving today depends on the rate of interest right now, but the new theory says the volume today depends on the average rate in years gone by. Today's rate hardly matters.

A revised version of standard theory finds fault with Diagram XVI, to be sure, saying that a diagram like this should be used only for cases of partial equilibrium, whereas interest is a case of general equilibrium. Since interest and wages are determined simultaneously, according to these critics, some other diagram is needed. With this criticism I do not agree. I maintain that wages are negotiated against a background of fixed overhead reflecting old debt already outstanding, not additional new debt about to be contracted. Old debt being much larger than new debt, the fixed rate on the old debt rules the outcome. The rate about to be negotiated on the new debt is a minor matter.[3]

The critics of Diagram XVI offer the Cobb-Douglas formula instead.[4] To my mind, however, this formula of theirs has faults of its own. It assumes that saving is done mainly by persons preparing to lend afresh, rather than by borrowers repaying loans made long ago. Furthermore, the Cobb-Douglas formula assumes that demand comes mainly from industry rather than homeowners. Neither of these premises is correct, as I have shown in earlier chapters.

---

[3] Many years ago I was a firm believer in traditional theory myself. I even wrote a paper entitled *Wages and Hours*, in which I used indifference curves and opportunity cost curves to show how interest and wages, labor and leisure were all determined by a set of simultaneous equations in the spirit of Walras and Pareto. I now believe, however, that firms, when they bargain about interest and wares, are prisoners of history.

[4] Cf. Paul H. Douglas, *The Theory of Wages*, (New York: The Macmillan Company., 1934), See especially p. 217, Chart 29, devised by S.W. Wilcox.

In Diagram XVI standard theory says that the demand curve for savings is determined solely by the productivity of capital goods, whereas mine says it is shifted far to the left by legal restraints. The law imposes a closer limit on borrowing than profit maximization does. Borrowers cannot reach the maximum they seek.

Bank examiners, as we have seen, forbid savings banks to buy bonds of doubtful quality. Insurance examiners do likewise for their companies. As a result the supply of bonds coming onto the market each year is held tightly in check. This holds the price of bonds up and keeps the interest rate down. Diagram XVII below shows these legal constraints at work:

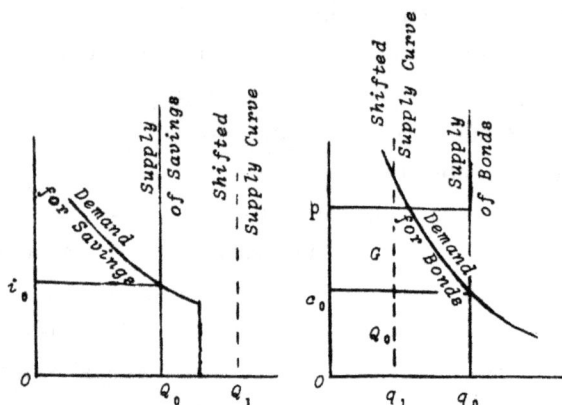

Fig.1 Limited Demand      Fig.2 Limited Supply
     for Savings               of Bonds

Diagram XVII: Legal Restraints on Lending

In Figure 1 the demand curve for savings reaches a cutoff point at its right end. Beyond this point the curve stops entirely, because any bonds issued beyond this limit would lack proper interest coverage. If the vertical supply curve for money to lend were now to shift so far to the right that it went past this limit, and rose upwards from $Q_1$ instead of $Q_0$, then the rate of interest would drop suddenly to zero. The amount of money seeking investment would exceed the amount that firms could borrow and still stay within the rules and regulations regarding interest coverage and the debt-equity ratio. Competition to lend the excess supply of savings would then send the interest rate down to zero.

Short of the cutoff point, the rules and regulations have a different effect on the outcome. These rules now serve to determine the position and the shape of the demand curve itself. The more stringent the rules,

218

the lower the demand curve lies. The harder it is for borrowers to offer good security, the less they are able to borrow. Whenever the rules are stiffened,the demand for savings drops. Were the debt-equity ratio to be suddenly changed from 1 for 1 to 1 for 2, the curve might fall so far, and its cutoff point might move to the left so much, that this point would lie inside the present supply curve for savings. Should this happen, the interest rate would drop to zero, as said before. Such an outcome would demonstrate, for all to see, how much, how very much, the actions of the bank examiners affect the rate of interest.

In Figure 2 of Diagram XVII the same facts are shown. If a change in the rules were to curtail severely the supply of bonds legal for savings banks and insurance companies to buy, while the demand for bonds stayed the same, the cost $c$ paid by purchasers of IOUs might rise until it nearly reached the price $p$ at which these pieces of paper would be paid off when borrowers redeemed them.

Short of this point, the effect of rules regarding safety is to push the vertical supply curve for new issues far to the left of where it might otherwise lie. Yet were the wishes of would-be borrowers all that mattered, the supply curve would shift to the right, and more bonds would be sold, and their price would be lower, much lower, than now. Such an outcome would conform to the Marginal Productivity Theory of Interest, whereas the present closely regulated market does not. As things now stand, the law won't let borrowers reach all the way out to the theoretical margin. The bank examiners, it seems, have pulled the rug out from under the whole orthodox theory of interest.

In still another way my theory differs from the old theory. My theory is financial, not psychological. It asks borrowers and lenders merely to feel their way along, to probe the market, to find the right price simply by experiment. They are not asked to compute the marginal productivity of capital compared with labor, nor to choose between present and future satisfactions. Nor are they asked to forecast the rate of inflation in the years ahead. The old theory, however, expects borrowers and lenders to indulge in all these mental gymnastics. My own theory avoids this. All I ask people to do is to haggle, just haggle, until supply and demand come out even in the end.

The process is seen very clearly in the new issue market, where investment bankers act as go-betweens for borrowers and lenders. The borrowers can use the money very profitably, but they have only a fixed amount of income to show as interest coverage on their new bonds. The higher the coupon rate, the smaller their new issues must be. The lenders likewise have a fixed amount of money to invest. The smaller the new issues, the easier the lenders can absorb them. In order to find out just how many new bonds can be floated successfully, the bankers spend a lot of time on the telephone, talking with both borrowers and lenders. They ask the insurance companies and the pension funds in particular how many bonds they would buy at various hypothetical prices. In the end, the bankers hit upon a price that will float the new issue successfully. This is how the *Cash Flow Theory of Interest* works.

# CHAPTER XVIII
# INTEREST AND GROWTH

## 1. Credit Expansion

Credit expansion is the technical term for the process of making demand deposits increase when the lending power of commercial banks is increasing too.

The simplest way to increase this lending power is for the Federal Reserve Board to reduce the legal reserve ratio. Another way is to increase legal reserves themselves. To do this, the Federal Reserve Banks can buy Treasury bills from the commercial banks, or can purchase promissory notes from them. The former process is usually called "open market operations" and the latter "rediscounting".

When legal reserves are increased, the banks can grant new customer loans, buy more municipal bonds, or otherwise add to their investments, making payment with credits to demand deposits. These credits are what give the name "credit expansion" to the process. The name is not a good one, though, because the credits to demand deposits are exactly matched by debits to invested assets, and so the process as a whole is no more a credit expansion than a debit expansion.

"Credit expansion" by the commercial banks adds just that much to the total volume of money flowing to the money market and seeking an outlet with borrowers of all kinds, whether these borrowers be firms, municipalities, home buyers, or what not. The effect is to push the composite supply curve of lendable funds to the right. (See Diagram XIV.)

The extra money can all be loaned to someone eventually, provided his credit standing is good enough. Often it is hard to find a short-term borrower, however. But borrowers-either-way are easy to find. When these borrowers accept short-term loans, they ease the demand for long-term loans. This reduces the rate of interest levied on homeowners. Although these latter borrowers are limited to repayments of 25% of their aftertax income, nevertheless their fixed repayments will service a larger loan when the interest rate is low than when it is high. Therefore a cut in the rate will get newly created money out on loan in due course. The outcome is purely mechanical.

This does not end the matter, however. The extra money put into circulation by credit expansion soon affects the demand for goods in general. When home buyers borrow more money than before, and spend it for larger houses, the builders pay the extra money to carpenters, plumbers, and other, who in turn buy more food, clothing, and other goods, or pay higher prices for these same goods. In the end, all consumer demand curves shift to the right. Employment increases and hours of labor lengthen, at least to start with. The aftertax earning of other prospective home buyers rise, and their borrowing power rises too. This still further increases the effective demand for mortgage loans. As a result, interest rates on mortgages finally turn up again. While the first effect of credit expansion is to put long-term rates down, as argued earlier, the second effect is to push them back up, as argued now.[1]

In any given situation the initial change in rates will be restrained and postponed by speculation on the expected course of future rates. If prospective borrowers think a rise in rates is only temporary, they will delay their borrowing, but if they think a rise will hold and even get worse, they will hasten their borrowing. As a result, the actual rate on any particular day will reflect hopes and fears for the future quite as much as true supply and demand in the present.

## 2. Borrowing and Business Activity

When someone borrows from a bank, the nation's money supply is thereby enlarged. And when the money is now spent for labor and materials, the output of goods and services increases. What happens, however, if the borrower does not deal with a commercial bank, but secures his money by selling new bonds to a savings bank, an insurance company, or a private person? Does output still rise? Yes, it does so rise. All borrowing, in fact, is "inflationary" in the sense that it increases the quantity of money being offered for goods and services.

Had no new bonds been sold to someone, then the erstwhile buyer of these bonds would have been obliged to let his savings lie unspent, as idle cash. To avoid this, the saver would have purchased old bonds when new issues were not for sale. When he bought old bonds, someone else would have had to sell them to him. To meet this demand, dealers would have sold their own inventories off. With the proceeds, the dealers would have repaid their own bank loans. When these loans were

---

[1] Cf. Milton Friedman's comments at the Symposium on Money, Interest Rates, and Economic Activity, sponsored by the American Bankers Assoc., on April 6, 1967: "Growth of the stock of money...will...raise income, and this in turn will raise the demand for loanable funds." (p. 101).

canceled, demand deposits would likewise have been extinguished. The nation's money supply would then have declined. Thus savings that might have been used to buy new bonds and give employment to willing workers would finally have been used to buy old bonds and extinguish existing demand deposits. The whole process is deflationary. It reduces output and employment. While commodity prices and wage rates may not decline, production is sure to shrink. Saving of this sort is called abortive saving.

Abortive saving will not occur if savers lend all the money they save, and let borrowers spend it for them. Borrowing thus offsets saving. Consequently we may say that all borrowing is inflationary, and all saving deflationary, whenever the member banks have free reserves (but not otherwise).

It makes no difference how the borrower borrows. He can sell his notes or bonds to commercial banks, or he can sell them to private persons. So long as he sells at all, someone must buy. If he sells to a bank, the bank pays with newly created money. If he sells to a private person, the buyer pays with money that would otherwise have found its way back to the bond dealers and then to the banks. The sale of new bonds prevents all this.

Furthermore, it makes no difrerence what borrower borrows. Anyone can sell new bonds or notes, and go into debt thereby. Whoever runs a deficit achieves the same result. The Federal government can run a deficit and sell bonds, or the Telephone company can sell bonds, or my brother can sign a mortgage note to buy a house. The process is still the same. To say that a balanced budget achieved by the U.S. Treasury will all by itself put a stop to inflation is to miss the point entirely. In order for Treasury borrowing to be any more inflationary than other borrowing, it is necessary for the Federal Reserve Banks themselves to buy some of the new Treasury bills, and increase bank reserves in the process. Otherwise it does not matter who the borrowers are. They all make demand deposits increase just dollar for dollar with debt.

An increase in the labor force, and in the capital equipment used by it, is the one sure way to offset the rise in prices that heavy borrowing tends to cause. New workers can then produce extra goods, and the sale of these extra goods will absorb the extra money put in circulation by the new borrowing.

If borrowing goes on no faster than output rises, the price level will hold steady. It is the task of the Federal Reserve Board to see that this occurs. Yet the best efforts of the Board may sometimes fail, because it often lacks the tools to do its job successfully.

A mild recession may cause a rise in saving by consumers. When people see a few of their friends out of work, they become cautious, and refuse to take on new debt for the purchase of a house or a car. Meantime they continue to pay off their old debt month after month. They thus engage in contractual saving. Although interest rates are often high at this time, the high rate of interest is not the cause of the high rate of saving, as is sometimes said. Instead, the two phenomena are a mere coincidence with no chain of cause and effect running between them. Each has a cause of its own.

### 3. The Repayment of Mortgage and Instalment Debt

If saving goes on faster than borrowing occurs, deflation results, as noted earlier. Contractual saving can easily produce this result. In the United States today, where almost every household is burdened with a heavy load of mortgage and instalment debt, the volume of such contractual saving is immense. This saving is always a menace to prosperity.

During a mild business depression, when the demand for new loans is somewhat reduced, savers are nevertheless obliged to pay off their old debts as fast as ever. Saving may then become larger than borrowing. Bank deposits are extinguished. The deflation that results makes the depression worse. Consumers, laden with debt, are forced to economize on food and clothing. Goods then pile up unsold in retail stores. Merchants refuse to reorder, and factories run on short time. Some people are thrown out of work. Others fear the same fate, and start to economize too. Were it not for the heavy burden of contractual saving to which so many people are committed, things would not thus go from bad to worse so easily. But as it is, the depression feeds on itself.

In due course, interest rates fall very low, because contractual saving is so large and borrowing is so small. Yet the low interest rates fail to discourage saving. So long as most saving is contractual rather than optional, it does not respond to a change in the rate of interest.

## 4. Interest Paid on Bank Loans

Is all money borrowed money? Is somebody somewhere paying interest on all the demand deposits and all the currency now in circulation? Is the money in your pocket and mine, in your checking account and mine, money that first came into existence when some person unknown to us secured a loan from his own bank, and had the proceeds credited to his account?

Yes, all this is true in the United States today, where no gold coins circulate, and where silver certificates, national bank notes, and greenbacks have all been retired and replaced with Federal Reserve notes. Some subsidiary coins, to be sure, are in common use for making change, having been issued by the Treasury as fiat money, but otherwise all our money comes from commercial banks, who create it when they grant a loan or buy a bond. As this borrowed money goes into circulation, it reaches the pockets of many people, who then deposit it in their own banks. In this way a bank in Boston may come to hold a demand deposit that was created in the beginning by a bank in Albany or Augusta. Nevertheless this money is still borrowed money, and someone, somewhere, must pay it back someday to the original lending bank.

When this money was created in the beginning, the borrower needed to use it right away, and spent it promptly for some good purpose. If he was a manufacturer, he bought materials and hired workmen, who then produced goods for sale. The borrowing and spending of this money thus led to a rise in the output of useful goods for the nation as a whole. When the goods were sold to retailers and then consumers, the manufacturer got his money back, and repaid his bank loan. Meantime he paid interest to the bank while the money was in circulation and held by the general public. But the public did not stop to think that its pocket money and its bank deposits were all borrowed at first by someone else, by someone somewhere who was paying interest to his own bank on all this money.

If the money, while it was out in circulation, came into the hands of a homeowner who used it to meet the monthly payment on his mortgage loan, then his savings bank, when it received the money, promptly lent it out again. This same money thus gave rise to a second loan, and this second loan came into existence before the first loan was ever paid off. One sum of money, with two loans involved, was the result. Moreover, after the money finally got back to the original borrower—the manufacturer in this case—and after this borrower repaid his bank loan and saw the money destroyed by this act, long after all this happened, the second loan remained in existence. The savings bank still held the new mortgage note it bought with the money received from the homeowner. Although the money came and went, the new debt stayed in force.

The new debt is outside the commercial banking system. It is debt against which no demand deposit now exists. The debt is owed to someone, to be sure. It is someone's asset, and it is matched by someone else's liability. In this case the asset is a promissory note held by a savings bank. It is matched by an equal liability on a homeowner's books. If the debt were owed to a life insurance company, it might be represented by a bond or debenture held as an asset by the insurance company. It too would be matched by an equal liability on some corporation's books.

A huge volume of notes, bonds, mortgage loans, and other evidences of indebtedness has come into existence in this way. All of these securities have a total value far in excess of the quantity of demand deposits and currency now in circulation. And all of them bear interest. Consequently the interest paid on these securities far exceeds the interest paid to the commercial banks who created the money in the first place.

## 5. The Money Needed to Pay Interest

Borrowers are under contract to repay both interest and principal on their bank loans when these come due. Where can the extra money come from that is needed to pay this interest? Since borrowers can spend only as much as they borrow, and no more, their outlays for wages, expenses, and dividends are thereby limited. How then can consumers acquire any extra money? How can they pay a price high enough for the output of industry to yield producers a profit? And if producers fail to make a profit, how can they pay the interest they owe their banks? Will not a shortfall[2] occur somewhere?

In order for the sales receipts of firms in general to become large enough for borrowers to pay both interest and principal when due, it

---

[2] A similar problem was propounded by Foster and Catchings in their book *Profits*. They left the question unanswered.

is necessary for the amount of money in circulation, and the volume of buying by the public, to increase just enough to cover this interest charge. Extra money is needed. This extra money must be created somehow by the commercial banks themselves. Do banks usually do their part as they should?

To answer these questions, we must study the behavior of banks. As soon as a bank makes a loan, it can look forward to the receipt of interest thereon in due course. If the bank now goes ahead and pays wages to its clerks and dividends to its stockholders even before the interest due it is actually received, then it will put extra money into circulation at once. This extra money will reach the general public, and will enable the borrower to sell his output at a slight profit. He can thus get his hands on enough money to pay the interest as well as the principal on his loan when the time comes to settle with his bank.

But where will the bank itself get the money to spend on wages and dividends? Since all money is created by debiting bank assets and crediting demand deposits, what entry is to be made on the bank's books in this case? For loans on which the interest or discount is paid in advance, a bank can simply debit Notes Receivable for the full value of the note, credit Demand Deposits for its discounted value, and then credit Interest Prepaid for the discount itself. Thereafter the bank, as it pays out money for wages and supplies each week, can debit Expenses and credit Cashiers Checks or the like. When these checks are deposited by the recipients, they become demand deposits. Afterwards the Expenses are charged against Income, and Interest Prepaid is credited thereto.

But what really matters is not the bookkeeping entries; instead, it is the date of disbursement for the interest earned that counts. The bank must spend the money it has earned soon enough to get it into circulation promptly; the bank must make this money reach the army of borrowers in time for them to use it to pay their own debts when due. If the bank hangs onto its earnings and hoards its prepaid interest, then it will arrest the even flow of money, and will hurt business for the country as a whole, just as any other hoarder would do. Trade cannot go on day after day unless money keeps passing from hand to hand all the while. To keep their customers solvent, the banks must spend their earnings before their loans come due, not afterwards.

## 6. Inflation and Interest Rates

When inflation begins, interest rates *ought* to rise at once to compensate the lender for the loss in purchasing power he will suffer when his loan is repaid.[3] But what interest rates *ought* to do, and what they *will* do, are not one and the same thing. Even if rates are very slow to rise as far as they should, most people will still save for their old age as best they can. They will accept a loss on their money meantime, rather than go hungry later.

In any event, it is only private persons, not insurance companies and savings banks, who will worry about a shrinking dollar. Private persons, however, are but minor factors in the whole market, as the Bankers Trust Co. figures show. This may explain why interest rates stayed so low in the 1930s, when President Roosevelt was doing his level best to induce inflation, even trying to scare people into making it occur.

Borrowers, in their response to inflation, are far more important than lenders. Borrowers, if they possess unused borrowing power because they have not yet mortgaged their plants to the hilt, can always dream up a huge list of additions and betterments. They may undertake these outlays at once if they fear that inflation will make them cost more in the future. The demand for loans can thus increase very sharply within a couple of years. It is the increase in demand from eager borrowers, rather than a decrease in supply from frightened lenders, that makes the fear of inflation raise the rate of interest.

Forecasting alone, however, is not the main explanation of why inflation puts interest rates up. Instead the process is more mechanical than psychological. A sudden rise in wages will enable home buyers to bid higher for whatever mortgage money is available, and this will lift interest rates on home loans. Inflation will also raise the cost of labor

---

[3] See Irving Fisher, "Appreciation and Interest," *Publications of the American Economic Association*, Third Series, Vol. XI, No. 4 (August 1896), pp. 331-442. See also his *Theory of Interest* (New York: Macmillan, 1930), ch. II, "Money Interest and Real Interest", and ch. XIX. "The Relation of Interest to Money and Prices"; also his *Rate of Interest* (New York: Macmillan, 1907), Appendix to ch. V, 1 "History of Theory of Appreciation and Interest".

See also Alfred Marshall, *Money, Credit, and Commerce* (New York: Macmillan, 1923), p. 74, and his *Principals of Economics* (New York: Macmillan, 1922), 8th edition, p. 594.

See also my *Investment Value*, Chapters VIII, IX, and XIX, where I show what degree of depreciation in bond prices would be consistent with a specified degree of forthcoming inflation in consumer prices. I now believe, however, that private investors are not so influential as I thought when I first wrote this book.

and material in manufacturing, and will require firms to borrow extra money from their banks for working capital. To meet this enlarged demand for loans, banks will be forced to sell their bonds, and bond prices will fall. When insurance companies buy these bonds, they will have less money to invest in mortgages, and mortgage rates will rise as a result.

Inflation will also increase the cost of new plant and equipment. Some industrial firms, however, may not be able to borrow the extra money they will need. Their present debt-equity ratio may not be good enough to support enlarged borrowing. Moreover, if their profits fail to rise step by step with the rise in the cost of buildings and machinery, these firms will not show the proper interest coverage to support new bond issues. Rising prices, therefore, do not always produce a corresponding increase in the effective demand for loan money.

All of these effects are mechanical, not psychological. Consequently their timing may not agree with borrowers' and lenders' careful forecasts of the price level. A lag may occur.[4]

## 7. Effects of Inflation

The ratio between (1) the annuity of repayments that borrowers can pledge and (2) the amount of cash that lenders can lend, this ratio, to repeat, depends on the rate of growth in the national income. If population is growing 1½% a year and labor productivity 2½%, and if the price level is rising at the rate of 1% a year; then the aftertax income of the population as a whole will be rising 5% a year. Consequently the demand for mortgage loans will likewise be rising 5% a year, and the interest rate itself will be 5% a year, other things being equal.

If trade unions should now become strong enough to force money wages up rapidly, and if the central bank lets the money supply increase equally fast, then aftertax incomes might rise 10% a year, for instance, instead of only 5%. In the first year of this inflation the borrowing power of home buyers would be 5% larger than it would otherwise have been, and the ratio $\pi/Q$ in Table II in the Appendix would change from 7.095% to 7.450%. Whereas the old ratio made the interest rate come out to 5%, the new ratio would make it come out to 5½%. In the second year of rapid inflation the borrowing power of home buyers would be some 10% larger than otherwise, and the interest rate would exceed

[4] Cf. Thomas J. Sargent, "Anticipated Inflation and the Nominal Rate of Interest" in *The Quarterly Journal of Economics*, Vol. LXXXVI, pp. 212-24, May 1972.

6%. In the third year it would rise still higher. And in the end a 10% yearly growth in borrowers' take-home pay would produce a 10% rate of interest, according to the Growth and Discount Theorem. Evidently part of the rise in the rate of interest on mortgage loans in recent years has been caused simply by the rapid rise in hourly wages throughout the whole economy for several years in a row.

It is the duration, the persistence, the cumulative effect of inflation, even more than the speed thereof, that raises the rate of interest.

The other part of the rise in the home loan rate must have been caused by a shrinkage in loanable cash $Q$ held by mortgage lenders. If corporations, faced with higher costs already, and fearful of still higher costs to come, sell huge volumes of new bonds, and keep insurance companies from buying apartment house mortgages, then the ratio $\pi/Q$ will rise for this reason too.

To a large extent, the heavy sales of new bonds by borrowers have been involuntary. Public utility companies, whose demand for loans is inelastic anyway, have been caught with their expansion programs already under way. The Treasury has had to finance the war in Vietnam. Short-term borrowers, whose demand is also inelastic, have been forced to finance work in process and stock-in trade at higher prices. Their demand for bank credit has crowded borrowers-either-way into the long-term market. Bonds sold by these latter borrowers have then drawn funds out of the mortgage market, forcing rates up there. All told, the rise in mortgage rates can be largely explained by the effect of inflation on borrowers, on borrowers of all kinds. On lenders, inflation has had much less effect.

## 8. Interest Rates and Business Depressions

A sudden rise in interest rates can cause a fall in business volumes.

When interest rates go up, firms whose bonds come due at that time, and who must refund old issues with new, find they cannot show good interest coverage on these refunding issues. Let us assume that their debt-equity ratio stays at one-to-one and their tax rate is 50%. At 4% these firms might have shown their present interest covered eight times before taxes, but at 8% they can show it covered only four times. Meantime their aftertax coverage would fall from 3½ times to 1½ times, as shown in the accounts below.

*Comparative Interest Coverage*

|  | Before Refunding | After Refunding |
|---|---|---|
| Bonded debt | $100,000,000 | $100,000,000 |
| Capital and surplus | 100,000,000 | 100,000,000 |
| Operating profit | $ 32,000,000 | $ 32,000,000 |
| Interest @ 4%, and 8% | - 4,000,000 | - 8,000,000 |
| Pretax income | 28,000,000 | 24,000,000 |
| Income taxes | -14,000,000 | -12,000,000 |
| Net income | 14,000,000 | 12,000,000 |
| Interest coverage: |  |  |
| before taxes | 8 times | 4 times |
| after taxes | 3½ times | 1½ times |

When a rise in rates makes it hard for a company to refund its old debt, this company certainly cannot assume any new debt. Then it stops growing. New construction is not undertaken with borrowed money as heretofore. Since net income and reinvested earnings shrink when interest charges rise, new construction must be curtailed still more. Everywhere men are thrown out of work in the capital goods industries, and the depression soon spreads to the whole economy.

The rise in interest rates hurts other borrowers too. Savings banks, who in effect borrow money on demand from their own depositors, see the quoted value of their bonds decline. They also know full well that their long-term mortgages could never be resold at par to another bank in case of a run on their own bank. Meanwhile they face the threat of disintermediation, a process that occurs when depositors withdraw their money and buy bonds at low prices in the open market. Wholesale disintermediation can quickly convert the "technical insolvency" of a bank into genuine insolvency. To guard against this risk whenever interest rates go up quite suddenly, savings banks reduce their mortgage lending, and invest their cash flow in bonds that enjoy a ready market. As a result, home buyers cannot get mortgage money, and home building stops. A depression then results.

Life insurance companies are in the same fix as savings banks. When bond prices fall badly, these companies become technically insolvent, even though they usually manage to keep their insolvency a secret from their creditors, who in this case are their own policyholders. Since the policy contract gives the holder the right to get a policy loan at the low rate of 5%, some of these holders withdraw their money in this way, and use it to buy good bonds yielding 8%. Disintermediation of this sort, which can go on for several years, keeps the insurance companies from making mortgage loans on commercial properties in the usual volume. Here too the initial rise in interest rates hurts the building industry.

When interest rates are high, poor credit risks cannot borrow at all. If their bonds come due at this time, they are thrown into receivership. Their creditors sustain losses, and these losses may cause further bankruptcies. The mere fear of such losses makes other firms hold onto their cash, and become "slow pay" themselves. Meanwhile other firms liquidate their inventories and use the proceeds to pay off their bank loans. Demand deposits that might have been used to hire workers and produce goods are thus extinguished. High interest rates are indeed deflationary in many ways.

The whole process is mechanical. It is not psychological, at least to start with. But it can easily set off a panic, and make the depression far worse in the end.

## 9. Fiscal Policy

Fiscal policy has two equal sides; spending is one, and taxing plus borrowing is the other. If taxing exceeds spending, however, so that the government shows a surplus in its budget, then borrowing becomes negative and the Treasury reduces its debt.

When the Treasury retires some of its outstanding bonds, notes, and bills or fails to replace them at maturity, banks and other holders who sell to the Treasury receive money which they must reinvest elsewhere, and so the demand for loans and discounts, bonds and mortgages increases by exactly the amount of the government debt retired. The effect is to push the supply curve of lendable funds to the right. This curve then intersects the demand curve at a lower point, and interest rates decline. (See Diagram XIV.) Briefly, a budgetary surplus of $10 billion amounts to an increase of $10 billion in the supply of money to lend.

The money the government takes away from consumers in taxes is not destroyed. On the contrary it goes back into the income stream at once when the Treasury reduces its debt, and the sellers of Treasury bills, notes, and bonds turn around and relend their principal elsewhere. A government surplus, therefore, is not deflationary, provided that the commercial banks keep loaned up. Instead it is neutral, except in one respect.

By putting more funds into the capital market, the surplus causes more capital formation to take place. Workers shift into the production of capital goods and out of the production of consumers goods. But total outlays on wages remain as high as ever, and so the reduced supply of consumers goods now raises their price.

The new capital goods, meanwhile, do not come onto the market. They are not sold to consumers for cash during the year while they are being made. Instead they are sold afterwards, and sold on the instalment plan even then. Payments are spread over many years, until all the bonds and mortgages issued against them are finally paid off.

A government deficit, like a surplus, is neutral except for the shift between producers' and consumers' goods that it entails. If the government fails to collect enough taxes to pay all its bills, and is forced to borrow money, it thereby adds to the total demand for lendable funds, and shifts the composite demand curve to the right. Meantime the composite supply curve holds still. It now crosses the demand curve higher up, and interest rates rise. The sale of Treasury bills, notes, and bonds crowds some other issues out of the market, and obliges firms and home buyers to borrow less. Capital formation shrinks. Workers leave the construction industry, and start making consumers goods instead. The increased supply of these goods then depresses their price.

No extra money is created by a government deficit, even if it is financed by Treasury bills sold to commercial banks. These bills merely crowd other short-term paper out of bank portfolios. If the banks have no excess reserves, borrowers-either-way are then forced into the long-term market. This reduces the supply left for loans on capital goods. The total supply of lendable funds, however, remains constant, being fixed by the contractual cash flow of savings banks, insurance companies, and pension funds. So long as the Federal Reserve Board makes no move to augment member bank reserves, the lending power of these banks, and the quantity of money in circulation, shows no increase. Consequently a government deficit, in and of itself, is not inflationary.

Once the economy has swallowed the deficit for any given year, and once the government budget has returned to balance, with no further sales of bills, then interest rates return to normal.

Financing the deficit to begin with, however, sends interest rates up for the time being, and so the Federal Reserve Board usually tries to put rates down again. In order to shift the composite supply curve of lendable funds to the right, the Board increases member bank reserves. This lets commercial banks buy new Treasury bills, and pay for them by crediting demand deposits. The whole process is then inflationary. Yet it need not occur if the Board refuses to interfere.

When the new money is spent, it gradually increases the incomes of would-be borrowers, who then bid higher for long-term money, and send these rates up. Long after the original Treasury financing has been completed and forgotten, interest rates and the price level both remain higher than they would have been.

Evidently it is *monetary policy*, in the form of changes in member bank reserves, and not *fiscal policy*, in the form of taxation or a government deficit, that controls inflation and the price level.

## 10. Growth of the National Dividend

In order for the phenomenon of interest to persist, the national dividend, measured in dollars, must continue to grow.

Growth often starts with the retailer. He appraises the demand for the coming season, and makes a guess, based on past experience, that his sales to the public will increase 5%, let us say, this year. Accordingly he places orders with the manufacturers 5% larger this year than last. This is step No. 1. But if retailers lack confidence in the business outlook, the growth of the national dividend can be halted right here, before the process ever gets under way.

When the retailers place their orders with the manufacturers, the manufacturers then place orders of their own with the suppliers of raw materials like steel, paper, textiles, and so forth. All of these orders are 5% larger than last year, and so all producers need 5% more money to finance their output. To get this extra money, they ask their banks for loans 5% larger than last year. This is step No. 2.

Many things must go just right with this second step in particular. For one thing, the would-be borrowers must be creditworthy. Their balance sheets must show an increase in equity capital during the previous year. Otherwise they must show a surplus left over from earlier years.

Then the banks themselves must have lending power to spare. They must show an increase in their legal reserves on deposit with the Federal Reserve Banks. To acquire these reserves, the commercial banks can sell Treasury bills to the Reserve Banks (or they can rediscount other paper, which is only a temporary expedient). Otherwise the Treasury itself must sell bills to the Reserve Banks. When the Treasury spends the proceeds, the money is deposited in commercial banks by the recipients of the spending, and bank reserves rise by the same amount. To provide the banks with additional secondary reserves too, the Treasury will need to sell bills directly to them also. Such sales of bills by the Treasury may result from a government deficit, or from the refunding of long-term Treasury bonds with short-term bills and notes.

Besides showing an increase in legal reserves, the commercial banks must also report an increase in equity capital. Prudence requires them to maintain an adequate ratio of capital to risk assets. Unless the banks make a profit year after year, and reinvest part of it in their business, they cannot safely add to their loans again and again.

The next step in the process is for manufacturers, miners, farmers, and other producers to spend the money they have just borrowed, and use it to hire workers. These workers must accept employment, and not go on strike. They must also perform their tasks faithfully, so that the economic engine will produce enough goods to feed, clothe, and shelter the population well. This is step No. 3.

Workers, having been paid wages 5% larger than last year, must now spend all the money they receive. They must use it to buy the enlarged inventories on the merchants shelves. Young couples must show the courage to get married, and other families must be willing to make down payments on houses and cars. Or they must deposit their savings in a bank where it will be loaned to someone else to use. There must be no abortive saving. The money must not be hidden under the mattress. Nor must it be taxed away by a government operating with a surplus and using its extra receipts to reduce its own bank debt. Likewise the money must not be used to answer margin calls from stockbrokers during a bear market. Money so used reduces collateral loans and destroys demand deposits. Moreover corporations in general, when they sell their inventories in the busy season, must not use the proceeds to make permanent reductions in their bank loans. Instead, all of the extra money paid as income to consumers must be put back into circulation. This is step No. 4. Many things, as we have just seen, can go wrong with it.

However, if nothing goes wrong with any step, then all participants will show a gain for the year. Merchants will have 5% more working capital, and commercial banks will have 5% more lending power. Households will be able to bid 5% more for mortgage money next year than this. Municipalities, public utilities, farmers, and competitive industrial firms will all enjoy an increase in borrowing power, and so the demand for long-term loans will increase 5%. In this way a 5% growth in the national dividend will support a 5% rate of interest (if we assume that people let their savings deposits grow at that rate too). The Growth and Discount Theorem shows why this happens.

## 11. Growth Past, Present, and Future

Growth in the past is what makes interest appear in the present. Time must elapse. The demand for loans must increase. Cause and effect are spread over many years.

As a result, my theory is not a theory of stationary equilibrium. Therein it differs from standard doctrine, which makes no reference to years past and gone. My theory, in contrast, considers the historical setting to be all-important.

According to the Growth and Discount Theorem, the faster the rate of growth in the past has been, the higher the rate of interest in the present will be. Furthermore, if growth were to end today, and if lenders were to reloan all their interest received, then interest would finally vanish in the distant future. But again, time would have to elapse. It would take a generation or so for the rate to reach zero. Only if the volume of lending were the same now as it was long years ago would interest as such come to an end.

If the central bank suddenly slows the growth of the money supply, as the Federal Reserve Board did in 1969, the immediate effect will depend on the particular circumstances. In this actual case, rapid inflation was under way. Companies needed to add to their current assets. When they tried to borrow from the commercial banks on their lines of credit, they forced these banks to sell municipals and other bonds at a loss. To make these sales worth while, the banks needed a high return on customer loans, and so they put the prime rate up, all the way up to 8½%. In response to this, many borrowers turned to the bond market instead. The flood of new issues then pulled money out of the mortgage market, and sent home building into a slump. In all these ways the sudden cessation of growth in the money supply sent a shock throughout the whole economy.

The immediate effect of less growth in the money supply was quite unlike what the long-run effect would have been. After a while the Federal Reserve Board reversed itself. Consequently we never had a chance to see what twenty-five years without growth would have done to the rate of interest.

# CHAPTER XIX
# SUMMARY

Every new idea needs a name, a handle, a trademark. Accordingly I have chosen the following phrases, three for the premises, and three for the conclusions, thus:

## 1. Premises

1. *The search for safety* makes banks and insurance companies steer clear of risky bonds and mortgages. These lenders insist on high interest coverage. But the higher the coverage, the smaller a new issue must be. Because new issues are thus restricted in size, borrowers can seldom raise money enough to reach all the way out to the limit set by marginal productivity as such. The Legal List won't let them.

2. *Contractual saving* describes the periodic payments made to life insurance companies and pension funds by policyholders and contributors, and to savings banks by mortgagors. Systematic saving of this sort vastly exceeds hit-or-miss saving. Moreover its volume remains unaffected by changes in the rate of interest in any given year.

When population grows and productivity increases, the national income, measured in dollars, grows too, if bank reserves are allowed to grow at the same rate. Then borrowers enjoy a rise in earnings; and are able to service larger loans year after year.

3. *Borrowers-either-way* connect short-term and long-term interest rates. These borrowers deem it more risky to contract short-term debts than long-term, and so they require lower rates on their bank loans than on their new bonds—unless they believe the short rate will drop below the long quite soon.

## 2. Conclusions

1. *The Cash Flow Theory of Interest* states that lending institutions must keep their intake and outgo of cash in balance.

When a savings bank makes a typical 25-year mortgage loan, it buys an *annuity certain*. This annuity consists of the payments of interest and amortization the bank will receive year after year. Each payment is limited to 25% of the borrower's take-home pay. The *present value* of this fixed annuity is set by the rate of interest at which these prospective payments are discounted today. The higher the discount rate, the lower the present value of the payments, and the less the cash outgo of the bank will be. At some rate of interest, then, income and outgo will balance for the bank. The same rule holds for insurance companies and pension funds when they buy bonds and mortgages, where the volume of new issues is held in check by rules about interest coverage.

All of these lenders enjoy a cash flow whose size is fixed by contracts made long ago with borrowers, policyholders, and contributors. In order to make outgo equal income for lenders, they move the interest rate up or down from time to time. Cash flow thus controls the interest rate.

Although the demand for money to borrow on short-term is always inelastic, on long-term it is quite otherwise, except for public utilities and the U.S. Treasury. For the home loan and municipal sector the demand shows an elasticity of unity. Residential volume, in fact, is so large that the whole theory might well be called the *Home Loan Theory of Interest*.

2. *The Growth and Discount Theorem* states that growth in the demand for long-term loans over a stretch of twenty or thirty years in the past is a major factor in fixing the supply of funds to lend in the present and the rate of interest today. Often the past rate of growth and the present rate of interest become nearly the same. Thus growth at 5% leads to interest at 5%. Growth and interest go hand in hand. History rules the outcome.

3. *The Encroachment Theory* explains the term structure of interest rates. It says that short-term rates are lower than long-term whenever commercial banks have lending power to spare, and can encroach on the bond and mortgage market. Then the banks quote short rates low enough to attract business from firms who can borrow either short or long. The process of encroachment depresses short rates, increases demand deposits, expands the money supply, stimulates employment, enlarges consumer incomes, improves borrowing power, and often raises long-term rates eventually. As a result, the term structure usually displays higher rates at the long end.

# APPENDIX
# THE MATHEMATICS OF INTEREST RATES

## 1. The Present Worth of an Annuity

When a savings bank makes a home loan, it buys an annuity certain. Each instalment in this annuity is discounted at compound interest to find its present value. The individual values are then added up. Their sum should be just equal to the size of the loan itself, thus:

Let $Q$ = sum loaned by bank and borrowed by its customer, a known constant

$V$ = present value of the annuity, to be determined

$\pi$ = size of each periodic payment = $1,000 year, for instance

$n$ = number of payments = 25 years, for instance

$i$ = interest rate, unknown

(1) $v$ = discount factor = $\dfrac{1}{1+i}$ , by definition

Then

(2) $V = \dfrac{\pi}{(1+i)} + \dfrac{\pi}{(1+i)^2} + ... + \dfrac{\pi}{(1+i)^n}$ , by definition

Insert (1) into (2) and get

(3.1) $V = \pi(v + v^2 + ... + v^n) = \pi \sum\limits_{n=1}^{n=n} v^n$

(3.2) $V = \pi v\left(1 + v + ... + v^{n-1}\right)$

Multiply by

(4) $1 = \dfrac{1-v}{1-v}$

and get

(5) $V = \pi v\dfrac{(1-v^n)}{(1-v)} = \pi\dfrac{(1-v^n)}{\dfrac{1}{v}-1}$

Insert (1) into (5) and get

(6.1) $V = \pi\dfrac{(1-v^n)}{(1+i-1)}$

and

(6.2) $V = \pi \dfrac{(1-v^n)}{i}$

(6.3) $\dfrac{\pi}{V} = \dfrac{i}{1-v^n}$

and

(7) $\dfrac{\pi}{V} = \dfrac{i}{1 - \dfrac{1}{(1+i)^n}}$

When $\pi = 1$, equation (6.2) becomes

(8) $V = (1-v^n)/i = a_{\overline{n}|i}$

where $a_{\overline{n}|i}$ is a special symbol used by the actuarial profession to designate the present value, at the rate $i$, of an annuity of one dollar per year for $n$ years, with each payment due at the end of the year.

When a bank buys an annuity at a given price, the bank enters this annuity on its books of account at cost, cost in this case being the cash $Q$ spent for the annuity Hence we can set

(9) $V = Q$

and then solve equation (7) for $i$ and $v$ by referring to the proper tables in a book on the Mathematics of Finance.

# APPENDIX

## 2. The Implied Interest Rate

In equation (6.2) for the present value $V$ of an annuity, the total amount of money $Q = V$ that the bank will lend to all its borrowers together is a known constant, since $Q$ is simply the cash receipts of the bank in the current year. The number of years $n$ is also a known constant, because a typical borrower seeks the longest loan he can get, and bankers deem it too risky to make loans running for more than a certain number of years (such as twenty-five). Therefore the only two variables in equations (6.2) and (7) are the size of the cash payments $\pi$ and the rate of interest $i$, thus:

(10)
$$\frac{i}{1 - \dfrac{1}{(1+i)^n}} = \frac{\pi}{Q}$$

In this equation, $\pi$ is the independent variable, and $i$ the dependent variable. The equation shows that the larger the ratio $\pi/Q$ is, the larger $i$ will be, so long as $n$ remains constant.

For example, if a group of savings banks has $25,000,000 to loan each year on 25-year mortgages, and if $1,000,000 a year is all that applicants can pledge for the right to borrow this sum, then the implied rate of interest will be zero. In this case the annual payments $\pi$ will just suffice to amortize the debt $Q$; they will leave nothing for interest.

However, if applicants can pledge a much larger annual payment, such as $1,760,000 a year for 25 years, then the rate of interest will have to rise to 5% to bring demand and supply into balance, and keep $V = Q$ in equation (9).

Likewise, if applicants can pledge $1,940,000, the rate will be 6%. In this last case, the applicants, who borrow $25,000,000, will repay (25) x ($1,940,000) or $48,800,000 in all. In other words, for every dollar they borrow today they will repay nearly two dollars in the end. Yet they are willing to pay so much in all because they are permitted to spread their repayments over so long a period, namely 25 years all told.

If a larger group of applicants had twice as much money to pledge, and a larger group of banks had twice as much to lend, the interest rate would still come out the same. Evidently it is the *ratio* of yearly payments $\pi$ to lendable funds $Q$ that determines the interest rate $i$ for any given number of years $n$.

The table below gives various values for $i$, as determined by the ratio $\pi/Q$ in equation (10), thus: If annual instalments are only 4% of a 25-year loan, then the interest rate must be 0%. However, if these instalments are larger, and come to 4.541% of the loan, the rate is 1%. Likewise, if instalments come to 5.122%, the rate is 2%. But if instalments are much larger, and come to 7.095% of the loan, the rate is 5%, while if the instalments come to 7.823%, the rate is 6%, and so forth, all as shown in the table below:

*Table I. The Ratio of Pledges to Loans*

| If | $\pi/Q$ | | | and $n = 25$, | then $v$ | | and $i =$ | |
|----|------|---|---|----------|-----|---|------|---|
| If | $\pi/Q$ | = | 4.00% | and $n = 25$, | then $v$ | = 1.000 | and $i =$ | 0% |
| " | $\pi/Q$ | = | 4.541% " | " " " | " $v$ | = 0.990 | " $i =$ | 1% |
| " | $\pi/Q$ | = | 5.122% " | " " " | " $v$ | = 0.980 | " $i =$ | 2% |
| " | $\pi/Q$ | = | 5.743% " | " " " | " $v$ | = 0.971 | " $i =$ | 3% |
| " | $\pi/Q$ | = | 6.401% " | " " " | " $v$ | = 0.962 | " $i =$ | 4% |
| " | $\pi/Q$ | = | 7.095% " | " " " | " $v$ | = 0.952 | " $i =$ | 5% |
| " | $\pi/Q$ | = | 7.823% " | " " " | " $v$ | = 0.943 | " $i =$ | 6% |
| " | $\pi/Q$ | = | 8.581% " | " " " | " $v$ | = 0.935 | " $i =$ | 7% |
| " | $\pi/Q$ | = | 9.368% " | " " " | " $v$ | = 0.926 | " $i =$ | 8% |
| " | $\pi/Q$ | = | 10.181% " | " " " | " $v$ | = 0.917 | " $i =$ | 9% |
| " | $\pi/Q$ | = | 11.017% " | " " " | " $v$ | = 0.909 | " $i =$ | 10% |

## 3. The Banks' Demand for Mortgage Notes

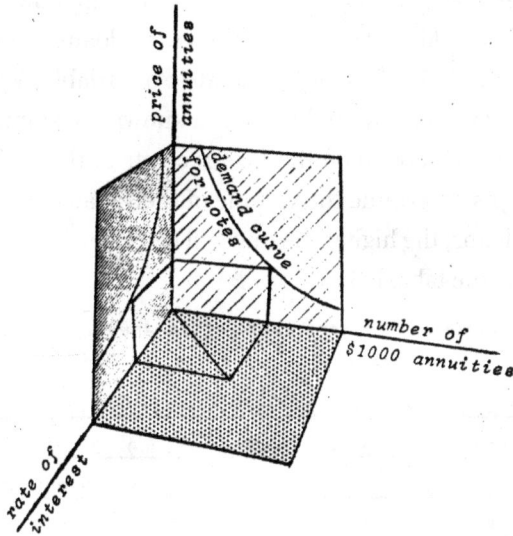

*Diagram XVIII: Rate of Interest as shown by Price of Annuities*

The demand curve for the mortgage notes, or 25-year annuities, bought by savings banks is a rectangular hyperbola with unit elasticity, because the banks have only a fixed sum of money to spend for these annuities. The banks, in other words, have just so much money to lend and no more. The larger the number of $1000 25-year annuities they buy, the less they can spend for each, as shown on the back wall of the cube above.

The price paid for an annuity implies a corresponding rate of interest at which its future payments are discounted. This interest rate, in other words, is merely another way of expressing the price of the annuity, as shown on the side wall of the cube

The interest rate is thus a function of the number of annuities bought by the banks, as shown on the floor of the cube.

## 4. Demand Curves for Loans of Various Lengths

By taking the proper choice of knowns and unknowns, we can make equation (10) yield a set of demand curves for loans. Let us assume that the volume $Q = V$ of money to lend is a variable, while the yearly repayment $\pi$ offered by applicants is a known constant. Then the rate of interest $i$ will depend on the cash receipts of the savings banks, for these receipts determine the volume of their loans $Q = V$. The less the volume of loans, the higher the rate will be, according to equation (10), as shown in the table below:

Table II. Present Worth of an Annuity of $1,000
a Year at Various Rates and Durations

|  | $n=1$ | $n=2$ | $n=5$ | $n=10$ | $n=15$ | $n=20$ | $n=25$ | $n=50$ |
|---|---|---|---|---|---|---|---|---|
| $i = 0\%$ | 1,000 | 2,000 | 5,000 | 10,000 | 15,000 | 20,000 | 25,000 | 50,000 |
| $i = 1\%$ | 990 | 1,970 | 4,853 | 9,471 | 13,865 | 18,046 | 22,023 | 39,196 |
| $i = 2\%$ | 980 | 1,942 | 4,713 | 8,983 | 12,849 | 16,351 | 19,523 | 31,424 |
| $i = 3\%$ | 971 | 1,913 | 4,580 | 8,530 | 11,938 | 14,877 | 17,413 | 25,730 |
| $i = 4\%$ | 962 | 1,886 | 4,452 | 8,111 | 11,118 | 13,590 | 15,622 | 21,484 |
| $i = 5\%$ | 952 | 1,859 | 4,329 | 7,722 | 10,380 | 12,462 | 14,094 | 18,256 |
| $i = 6\%$ | 943 | 1,833 | 4,212 | 7,360 | 9,712 | 11,470 | 12,783 | 15,762 |
| $i = 7\%$ | 935 | 1,808 | 4,100 | 7,023 | 9,108 | 10,594 | 11,654 | 13,801 |
| $i = 8\%$ | 926 | 1,783 | 3,993 | 6,710 | 8,559 | 9,808 | 10,675 | 12,233 |
| $i = 9\%$ | 917 | 1,759 | 3,890 | 6,418 | 8,061 | 9,129 | 9,823 | 10,962 |
| $i = 10\%$ | 909 | 1,736 | 3,792 | 6,144 | 7,606 | 8,513 | 9,077 | 9,992 |
| $i = 15\%$ | 870 | 1,626 | | | | | | |
| $i = 20\%$ | 833 | 1,527 | | | | | | |

The values of $V$ in the column labeled $n = 25$, when paired with the interest rates $i$ in the very first column, give the data for the 25-year demand curve (when $\pi$ is constant), thus:

Table III. Present Worth of Annuity of
$1,000 for 25 Years at Various Rates

| $Q$ | $i$ | |
|---|---|---|
| 25,000 | 0% | |
| 22,023 | 1% | |
| 19,523 | 2% | |
| 17,413 | 3% | |
| 15,622 | 4% | $\pi = 1,000$ |
| 14,094 | 5% | |
| 12,783 | 6% | $n = 25$ |
| 11,654 | 7% | |
| 10,675 | 8% | |
| 9,823 | 9% | |
| 9,077 | 10% | |

If $i$ is plotted as a function of $Q$, the resulting curve is the banks' 25-year demand curve for mortgage paper, as shown below:

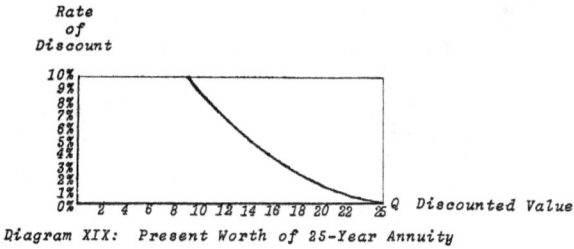

Diagram XIX:  Present Worth of 25-Year Annuity

If we now take an altogether different set of values for $Q$, namely the figures in the column labeled $n = 1$ of Table II, and pair these new values with those in the very first column, we get the data for quite a different demand curve for IOUs, namely a one-year demand curve, as shown in the left-hand double column below:

Table IV.  Present Worth of $1,000 and $25,000 Due in One Year

| | $\pi = \$1,000$ | | | $\pi = \$25,000$ | |
| | $n = 1$ | | | $n = 1$ | |
| $Q$ | | $i$ | $25\,Q$ | | $i$ |
|---|---|---|---|---|---|
| 1,000 | | 0% | 25,000 | | 0% |
| 990 | | 1% | 24,750 | | 1% |
| 980 | | 2% | 24,500 | | 2% |
| 971 | | 3% | 24,275 | | 3% |
| 962 | | 4% | 24,050 | | 4% |
| 952 | | 5% | 23,800 | | 4% |
| 943 | | 6% | 23,575 | | 6% |
| 935 | | 7% | 23,375 | | 7% |
| 926 | | 8% | 23,150 | | 8% |
| 917 | | 9% | 22,925 | | 9% |
| 909 | | 10% | 22,725 | | 10% |
| 870 | | 15% | 21,750 | | 15% |
| 833 | | 20% | 20,825 | | 20% |

In order to make it easy to compare this new one-year demand curve with the preceding 25-year demand curve, a second double column is shown above, in which the repayment pledged is $25,000 instead of only $1,000. This new double column shows how the interest rate will rise as the size of the loan shrinks from $25,000 to $24,700, $24,500, and so forth. When $i$ is plotted as a function for $25Q$, with $i$ the dependent variable, the resulting curve is the demand curve for one-year loans, discounted by the lending bank, as shown below:

Obviously the one-year curve, unlike the 25-year curve, is highly inelastic. In other words, borrowers at short-term cannot easily be driven away by a rise in the rate of interest. Instead they pay whatever they must. Many borrowers at long term, in contrast, are quick to retire from the market if the rate goes up. As a result, it is long-term borrowers, particularly homeowners and municipalities, who set the interest rate for everybody else in the whole economy. Short-term borrowers need pay no more, because they can resort to successive renewals.

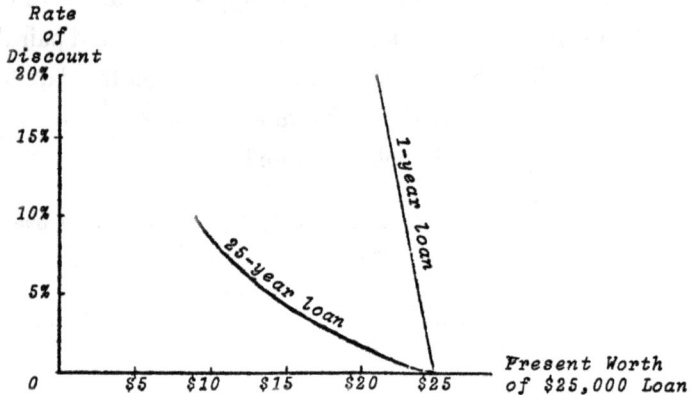

Diagram XX: Demand Curves for One-Year vs. 25-Year Loans

## 5. The Total of Payments to Bank Each Year

Assume that a bank has 25 groups of borrowers, labeled A to Y. Group A is the oldest, Group Y the youngest. Members of Group A took out their mortgage loans 25 years ago, and will make their last payment this year. Group Y took out their loans at the start of this year, and will make their first payment at the end of this year. Other groups took out their loans at intervening times, but each group will make one of its payments at the end of this year. All told there will be 25 payments received by the bank this year.

Let Group A's payments year after year be designated $a_1=a_2=a_3=...=a_{25}=a$, and let Group B's be designated $b_1$, $b_2$, etc. In the year when Group A made its second payment $a_2$, Group B made its first payment $b_1$. Now, when Group A is making its last payment $a_{25}$, Group B is making its next to last payment $b_{24}$, and Group Y is making its first payment $y_1$. Let $Q$ be the sum of all 25 payments to the bank this year. Then

(11)　$Q = a_{25}+b_{24}+c_{23}+ ...+x_2+y_1$

Assume that the population served by the bank is growing steadily. Then Group A will have the smallest number of members, and Group Y the largest. If labor productivity and hourly wages are rising steadily too, then Group Y will enjoy a much larger income today than Group A did 25 years ago when it took out its own loans. Hence Group Y can afford to sign up for much larger loans today than Group A could years ago. Payments $y_1$, etc., therefore will be much larger than payments $a_1$, etc., are.

If the bank makes it a rule to limit payments for interest, amortization, and taxes to 25% of take-home pay, as is now customary, and if borrowers are eager to secure the largest loan they can get, as usually happens, then payments pledged each year by one group after another will grow as fast as incomes grow. Call this growth rate $g$. If incomes are growing 5% a year, for instance, then $g = 5\%$.

When growth is steady, then the payments to the bank from Groups A, B, etc., are related as follows:

(12)　$b = 1(1+g)$

(13)　$c = b(1+g) = a(1+g)^2$
　　　etc.

Each of these payments is a contractual payment whose amount, once agreed upon, cannot be altered in later years. Let $y_1$, be the contractual payment made in year 25 by Group Y, then

$$(14) \quad x_2 = \frac{y_1}{1+g}$$

$$(15) \quad a_n = \frac{y_1}{(1+g)^{n-1}}$$

The sum $Q$ of all contractual payments on loans already outstanding, as we have seen, is

$$(11) \quad Q = y_1 + x_2 + w_3 + \ldots + b_{24} + a_{25}$$

whence

$$(16) \quad Q = y + \frac{y}{1+g} + \frac{y}{(1+g)^2} + \ldots + \frac{y}{(1+g)^{n-1}}$$

We have called $g$ the growth rate, looking forwards from A to Y. Now let us call $s$ the shrinkage rate, looking backwards from Y to A. Then

$$(17) \quad s = \frac{1}{1+g}$$

We can now express the total $Q$ of contractual payments on old loans as follows:

$$(18) \quad Q = y + ys + ys^2 + ys^{n-1} = y(1 + s + s^2 + \ldots + s^{n-1})$$

Multiply by

$$(19) \quad 1 = \frac{1-s}{1-s}$$

and get

$$(20) \quad Q = y \frac{(1-s^n)}{(1-s)}$$

This is the formula for the sum of the payments received this year from all the *old* loans already outstanding. This sum is also the total amount of cash that can be loaned to *new* borrowers in the coming year. No matter how eager the demand from new borrowers may turn out to be, new loans cannot exceed this sum $Q$. The sum $Q$ is fixed by contracts already in force, and cannot be altered.

## 6. Value of New Loans Now Being Made

In the coming year new loans will be made to a new group of borrowers, called Group Z, who will make payments

(21) $\qquad z_1 = z_2 = ... = z_{25} = z = \pi$

Assume that growth continues at the former rate $g$. Then payments $z_1 = z_2 = ... = z_{25}$ will be correspondingly larger than payments $y_1 = y_2 = ... = y_{25}$. In each case, of course, every payment in the same annuity will be the same in size as every other payment therein.

If growth continues in the future at the same rate $g$, then

(22.1) $\quad z = y(1+g)$

The bank will make the new loans to Group Z at the start of the 26th year, but will not receive its first repayment until the end of this year. Consequently, even this first repayment

(23) $\qquad z_1 = \pi$

must be discounted at some interest rate in order to find its present value. All subsequent payments $z_2$, $z_3$, etc., must likewise be discounted backwards at this same rate of compound interest.

What uniform rate of interest $i$ should be used to discount all these future payments?

The proper rate to use is the rate that will make income and outgo just balance for the lending bank.

These future payments as a whole make up an annuity certain whose present value $V$ is given by the usual formula

(2) $\qquad V = \dfrac{\pi}{1+i} + \dfrac{\pi}{(1+i)^2} + ... + \dfrac{\pi}{(1+i)^n}$

Here

(1) $\qquad v = \dfrac{1}{1+i}$ , by definition

and so, as shown before,

(3.2) $\quad V = \pi v + \pi v^2 + ... + \pi v^n$

(3.3) $\qquad = \pi v \left(1 + v + ... + v^{n-1}\right)\left(\dfrac{1-v}{1-v}\right)$

(5) $\qquad = \pi v \left( \dfrac{1 - v^n}{1 - v} \right)$

This formula shows the present value $V$ of the annuity certain that the bank will buy with its cash intake $Q$. This annuity purchased, otherwise known as the total of all loans made in the given year, will he entered on the books of account at its cost to the bank. In other words, as said before,

(9) $\qquad Q = V$

### 7. Special Case Where Growth and Discount Rates Are Equal

Using equations (20) and (9) and (5) for $Q$ and $V$ found in the preceding sections, we may now write

(24) $$y\frac{\left(1-s^n\right)}{\left(1-s\right)} = Q = V = \pi v\frac{\left(1-v^n\right)}{\left(1-v\right)}$$

In preceding sections we saw that

(22.2) $$y = \frac{z}{1+g}$$

and

(23) $$\pi = z$$

and

(17) $$s = \frac{1}{1+g}$$

and so

(25) $$y = \pi s$$

Substituting (25) in (24) we get

(26) $$\pi s\frac{\left(1-s^n\right)}{\left(1-s\right)} = \pi v\frac{\left(1-v^n\right)}{\left(1-v\right)}$$

or

(27) $$s\frac{\left(1-s^n\right)}{\left(1-s\right)} = v\frac{\left(1-v^n\right)}{\left(1-v\right)}$$

This last equation holds good only when

(28) $$s = v$$

Therefore, by (17) and (1), we get

(29) $$\frac{1}{1+g} = \frac{1}{1+i}$$

and

(30) $$g = i \qquad \text{q.e.d.}$$

In other words, the rate of interest $i$ is equal to the rate of growth $g$ under the assumptions that

1) the bank relends all its cash receipts $Q$, and
2) withdrawals and deposits offset each other, and
3) expenses and losses are nil, and
4) growth continues in the new year at the same rate as in the past.

The foregoing result is a special case of the Growth and Discount Theorem.

If we were to find it helpful later to depart from the foregoing assumptions that define an ideal savings bank, we might then need to consider some of the following complications:

1) the cost of running the bank.
2) the credit losses sustained.
3) the amount of dividends that depositors withdraw in cash, and do not leave behind to grow at compound interest.
4) the excess (if any) of new deposits made over old deposits withdrawn.

In another special case, namely one where no growth whatsoever in the demand for loans is seen, and where no growth in deposits occurs either, because depositors take all their dividends out in cash, in this special case, to repeat, a steady rate of interest will emerge nevertheless, year after year. The ratio of (1) payments $\pi$ pledged by applicants to (2) the cash inflow $Q$ of the bank will give the equilibrium rate of interest, according to equation (10) above, just the same as in the case of a bank that enjoys persistent growth.

## 8. Generalized Growth and Discount Theorem

We have already shown that the total cash $Q$ which a bank can lend is

$$(20) \qquad Q = y\frac{(1-s^n)}{(1-s)}$$

If $z$ is the annual repayment $\pi$ pledged in the 26th year by homeowners who borrow the cash $Q$, and if growth in this year proceeds at some new rate $h$, then equation (22.1) changes to

$$(31) \qquad z = y(1+h)$$

We have already shown that the present worth of these future repayments is

$$(5.1) \qquad V = zv\frac{\left(1-v^n\right)}{\left(1-v\right)}$$

Substituting (31) in (5) we get

$$(32) \qquad V = y(1+h) \times v\frac{\left(1-v^n\right)}{\left(1-v\right)}$$

Using both (20) and

$$(9) \qquad V = Q$$

and eliminating $y$, we get

$$(33.1) \qquad v\frac{1-v^n}{1-v} = \frac{1}{1+h} \times \frac{1-s^n}{1-s}$$

or

$$(33.2) \qquad \frac{1-v^n}{\dfrac{1}{v}-1} = \frac{1}{(1+h)} \times \frac{1}{s} \times \frac{1-s^n}{\dfrac{1}{s}-1}$$

Using (1) and (17), we get

$$(29.2) \qquad \frac{1-v^n}{i} = \frac{1+g}{1+h} \times \frac{1-s^n}{g}$$

Let

$$(8) \qquad \frac{1-v^n}{i} = a_{\overline{n}|i} \text{ , by definition}$$

and

$$(34) \qquad \frac{1-s^n}{g} = k_{\overline{n}|g} \text{ , by definition}$$

Then

(35) $\qquad a_{\overline{n}|i} = \dfrac{1+g}{1+h} \times k_{\overline{n}|g}$

Since the parameters $n$ and $g$ are known, the annuity $k_{\overline{n}|g}$ can be found in the tables of a book on the Mathematics of Finance. This information lets us use the parameter $h$ to find $a_{\overline{n}|i}$, and infer the unknown variable $i$ therefrom.

In the special case already discussed, where growth continues at the same rate in the coming year as in the past, $h = g$ and so

(36) $\qquad a_{\overline{n}|i} = k_{\overline{n}|g}$

As a result $i = g$. In this special case, therefore, the rate of interest today is equal to the rate of growth in the past, as shown before.

In quite another case, one where new deposits are not large enough to offset expenses and withdrawals, then total cash receipts $Q$, net of expenses etc., will fall short of the sum estimated in (18) and (20) above. One way to express this shortfall is to reduce $y$, $ys$, $ys^2$, etc., each alike by using a leakage factor $l$, where $l$ is the percentage of receipts needed for expenses, etc. A bank whose expense ratio was 1% of deposits might thus show a leakage factor $l = 10\%$, figured thus

```
Amortization      4% of loan, for instance
Interest          6%  "      "    "     "
   Total Received 10% "      "    "     "
Less Expenses    -1%  "      "    "     "
   Balance        9%  "      "    "     "
```

We have already seen that

(20) $\qquad Q = y\dfrac{(1-s^n)}{(1-s)}$ when there is no leakage,

but when leakage $l$ is present, the lendable cash of the bank will be

(37.1) $\qquad Q' = y(1-l)\dfrac{(1-s^n)}{(1-s)}$

(37.2) $\qquad = y(1-l)\dfrac{(1/s)(1-s^n)}{(1/s)(1-s)}$

(37.3) $\qquad = y(1-l) \times \dfrac{1}{s} \times \dfrac{(1-s^n)}{\left(\dfrac{1}{s}-1\right)}$

Inserting the value for $s$ given in (17) we get

$$(38) \quad Q' = y(1-l)(1+g)\frac{(1-s^n)}{g}$$

Using (34) we get

$$(39) \quad Q' = y(1-l)(1+g)k_{\overline{n}|g}$$

We have also seen that

$$(32) \quad V = y(1+h) \times v\frac{(1-v^n)}{(1-v)}$$

$$(40) \quad \phantom{V} = y(1+h)\frac{(1-v^n)}{i}$$

Using (8), we get

$$(41) \quad V = y(1+h)a_{\overline{n}|i}$$

Set

$$(9) \quad Q' = V$$

and eliminate $y$, to get

$$(42) \quad (1-l)(1+g)k_{\overline{n}|g} = (1+h)a_{\overline{n}|i}$$

whence

$$(43) \quad a_{\overline{n}|i} = (1-l)\frac{(1+g)}{(1+h)} \times k_{\overline{n}|g}$$

With $l$, $g$, $h$, and $n$ given, the resulting value for can be located in the tables for annuities, and then the corresponding $a_{\overline{n}|i}$ value for $i$ can be read off. The figure thus found is the interest rate at which new loans will be made when leakage is present and the growth rate changes.

## 9. Housing Shortages

What is a "housing shortage"?

A housing shortage need not be severe in order to raise the interest rate. Millions of people need not be sleeping on the sidewalks, as in India today. The shortage can be mild, as in the United States. Yet it can still give rise to a demand for more shelter, even though every family already has a roof over its head.

In the argument to follow, a housing shortage is said to exist whenever a large number of families would like to live in more space than they now enjoy.

A bad housing shortage will produce a high interest rate, as the following simplified model of the economy reveals:

Imagine a city of 100,000 families all of whom live in large apartment houses. These buildings are fitted with movable partitions that permit the size and number of rooms to be changed. If new buildings are constructed in a certain year, and some families move out of the old buildings into the new, then the tenants who remain behind can enjoy larger quarters. In this way the housing shortage will be relieved somewhat. And if the process is repeated again and again, the shortage will be relieved more and more.

In order to generalize the argument, let us drop all restrictions on mortgage loans, and say that banks are willing to lend families more than 25% of their aftertax income if requested to do so.

Rents will now be determined by the consumer's choice between food, clothing, and shelter. A surface of indifference describes the options open to consumers. The quantity of shelter is a known constant to start with. If this quantity is increased, its price will decline relative to the prices of food and clothing. For simplicity, let us assume that the quantity of money and its velocity of circulation remain constant. Just how much the price of shelter will then decline depends on what offsetting changes occur in the consumption of food and clothing. Once an indifference surface for all these goods has been specified, a demand curve[1] for housing can be drawn like that below:

---

[1] Demand curves can be derived from indifference curves or indifference surfaces by the method described in Chapter V of my *International Trade Under Flexible Exchange Rates* (Amsterdam: North Holland Publishing Co., 1954).

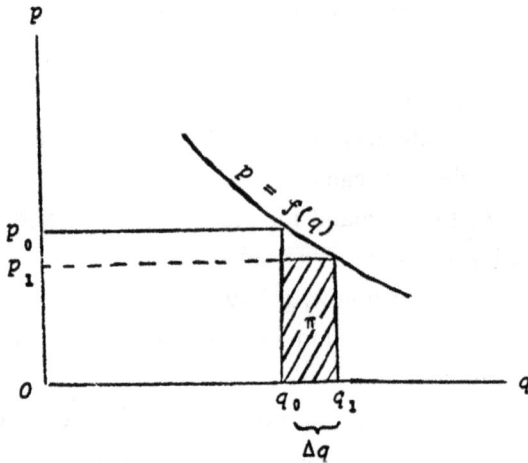

*Diagram XXI:* Demand for Housing

This diagram shows the demand curve for housing to be

(1)     $p = f(q)$

where     $p_0$ = price of housing per sq. ft. per year, at start

    $p_1$ =  "  "  "   " "  "   "  " end

    $q_0$ = quantity " "   in sq. ft.   "  " start

    $q_1$ =   "  ' "   " "  "   "  " end

(2)  $\Delta q = q_1 - q_0$ = increase in housing during the year.

    $p_0 q_0$ = total yearly rent paid on old housing at start

    $p_1 q_0$ =   "   "  "   "  "  "   "   " end

    $p_1 \Delta q$ =   "   "  "   "  " new "    " end

It is assumed that families who move into the newly built housing occupy space of the same quality as they left behind. They now enjoy larger quarters, however, and so do the families who do not move.

The families who move pay rent $p_1 \Delta q$. Call this amount $\pi$ so that

(3)   $\pi = p_1 \Delta q$

This rent is used to pay the instalments of amortization and interest on the cost of constructing the new apartment houses.

Call this cost per sq. ft. $c$. The total cost of the construction undertaken in any given year will then be $c\Delta q$.

If the cost $c$ varies with the volume of new construction $\Delta q$, then the supply curve for new housing is

(4)   $c = \Phi(\Delta q)$

Payment for this new housing is spread over $n$ years, with $n$ being equal to 25 in this case.

Savings banks furnish the money for the construction of the new buildings. These banks lend all their net cash receipts. These net receipts are equal to the total of interest and amortization on all their old mortgage loans outstanding at the start. Call these known receipts $Q$. Since these receipts are all used to pay for the new construction, we have

(5) $\quad c\Delta q = Q$

For simplicity, assume that the mortgage loans on the new buildings come to 100% of the cost of construction, and no equity capital is used. All of the rentals are devoted to interest and amortization on the new loans. No real estate taxes or outlays for operating expenses complicate the problem.

When the banks make their mortgage loans, they are buying an *annuity certain* consisting of annual instalments of the amount $\pi$ payable at the end of each year for 25 years. Call the present value of these instalments $V$ thus:

(6) $\quad V = \pi \sum_{n=1}^{n=25} v^n = \pi a_{\overline{n}|i}$

The right-hand side of this equation is the formula for an annuity.

Since the value $Q$ of what the banks pay out is equal to the value $V$ of what they buy in exchange, we have

(7) $\quad Q = V$

The interest rate $i$ implied by equation (6) is then an unknown quantity that remains to be determined. This interest rate may be expressed as a discount factor, thus:

(8) $\quad v = \dfrac{1}{1+i}$

We now have a system of eight equations in eight unknowns which may be summarized as follows:

Knowns: $\quad p_0, q_0, n, Q$

Unknowns: $\quad p_1, q_1, \Delta q, \pi, c, V, v, i$

One way to solve this sytem for i is to proceed as follows:

| | | | | | |
|---|---|---|---|---|---|
| I | Use (5) | $c\Delta q = Q$ | to find | $c$ | and |
| II | and (4) | $c = \phi(\Delta q)$ | to find | $\Delta q$ | |
| III | Use (2) | $q_1 = q_0 + \Delta q$ | to find | $q_1$ | |
| IV | Use (1) | $p_1 = f(q_1)$ | to find | $p_1$ | |
| V | Use (3) | $\pi = p_1 \Delta q$ | to find | $\pi$ | |
| VI | Use (7) | $V = Q$ | to find | $V$ | |
| VII | Use (6) | $V = \pi \sum_{n=1}^{n=n} v^n = \pi a_{\overline{n}|i}$ | to find | $v$ | |
| VIII | Use (8) | $v = \dfrac{1}{1+i}$ | to find | $i$ | $q.e.f.$ |

A bad housing shortage cannot be cured in a single year. Instead, new housing must be built year after year. Rents will then fall step by step, and so will the rate of interest. Gradually this rate will approach zero in the case of an ideal savings bank in an imaginary economy where housing is the only outlet for savings.

If the foregoing equations ever yield a negative rate of interest as their solution, the cause will be found in the cost of construction c. When this cost is too high, the housing shortage cannot be relieved at any rate of interest feasible for the banks. In this case the banks will refuse to lend the yearly inflow of interest and amortization they receive from their old loans. They will simply let this money pile up as idle cash.

Although many complications could be added to this simplified model, they would not change the thrust of the argument. It would still remain true that the demand for housing gave rise to the phenomenon of interest.

One very important thing that Diagram XXI reveals is this:
*A sudden rise in the demand curve p = f(q)*
*will cause an abrupt rise in the rate of interest i.*

During the years 1966-69 such a rise in demand did indeed occur, because wage rates rose sharply then. This rise let would-be home buyers bid higher for mortgage loans. As a result, interest rates charged by savings banks rose from 5¾% or so in 1965 to 8% or more in 1969. Rising money wages were an important cause of this advance.

Demand alone, however, does not settle the matter. Supply too, in the guise of cost of production, is also important here as always. The diagram shows what effect the cost of construction c has on the rate of interest i. This cost c determines the quantity of new housing $\Delta q = Q/c$

that will be built, and thus the yearly rental $\pi = p\Delta q$ that will be paid by families who move into new housing. If the demand curve $p = f(q)$ is elastic, this rental $p\Delta q$ will increase as $\Delta q$ increases. And when $\pi$ increases, $i$ increases too, according to equation (6). But if the demand is inelastic, $\pi$ will shrink as $\Delta q$ increases. In this case, unlike the other one, a fall in construction costs $c$ will cause a fall in the interest rate $i$.

## 10. Complicating Factors in the Interest Formula

When a country suffers from a housing shortage, even a mild one, many families buy new homes, and borrow from savings banks to finance their purchase. As they move out of their old quarters, they leave more space for those families who remain behind.

While my model fits a free market where home buyers may bid as high as they want for new houses, it does not quite fit a market where mortgage loans are held down in some arbitrary way. The discrepancy, however, need not be bad. If lenders, when they set a limit of 25% of aftertax income for interest, amortization, and real estate taxes combined, happen to name a figure that is close to what the free market demand would be anyway, then the discrepancy will be small. But if 25% is much too low, the discrepancy will be large at first. In due course, however, as more and more new houses are built, the housing shortage will gradually abate, if population is not increasing. Then the free market will fall until it reaches the arbitrary figure of 25% set by the banks themselves. Once this happens, the banks can then accommodate all applicants who are willing to pay a sufficiently high rate of interest without overextending themselves creditwise.

The next step will be for the interest rate itself to decline. And as housing becomes still more plentiful, people may decide to spend less than 25% of their aftertax income on shelter. This decision will make it harder than ever for the banks to find an outlet for their entire cash flow. The interest rate will then decline still more. This very fall in the rate on new loans, however, will gradually reduce the cash flow of the banks in future years, thereby shrinking the supply of funds to lend, and bringing it into balance with the demand for loans.

In the end, of course, if population fails to grow and if money income fails to rise, and if no improvement in the quality of housing occurs, and all wear and tear is made good, and if housing ceases to be a status symbol, then the supply of housing will finally become adequate for all needs. When this millenium arrives—if it ever does— the demand for housing loans will end, and the rate of interest will decline toward zero.[2]

---

[2] The possibility of an interest rate as low as zero was first suggested to me by Schumpeter, who mentioned it in class one day in 1933.

Meantime it will remain necessary to consider various complications when applying Diagram XXI to the market for new houses. These complications include the following items:

1) the particular limit, like 25%, set by banks as their arbitrary ratio of instalments to aftertax income.

2) the particular limit, like 70%, set by banks as their arbitrary ratio of money lent to market value for a mortgaged house.

3) the loss of interest suffered by the home buyer when he sinks his own funds into a new house.

4) the income tax deduction that the homeowner enjoys as an offset to the mortgage interest and real estate tax he pays.

5) the failure of the homeowner to make an exact mental evaluation of the contractual saving involved in each instalment on his loan.

www.ingramcontent.com/pod-product-compliance
Lightning Source LLC
Chambersburg PA
CBHW060333200326
41519CB00011BA/1926